Going Global with
GOD

Going Global with

GOD

Reconciling Mission
in a World of Difference

TITUS LEONARD PRESLER

Morehouse Publishing
NEW YORK · HARRISBURG · DENVER

Unless otherwise noted, the Scripture quotations contained herein are from the New Revised Standard Version Bible, copyright © 1989 by the Division of Christian Education of the National Council of Churches of Christ in the U.S.A. Used by permission. All rights reserved.

Morehouse Publishing, 4775 Linglestown Road, Harrisburg, PA 17112
Morehouse Publishing, 445 Fifth Avenue, New York, NY 10016
Morehouse Publishing is an imprint of Church Publishing Incorporated.
www.churchpublishing.org

Cover art courtesy of Thinkstock
Cover design by Laurie Klein Westhafer

Library of Congress Cataloging-in-Publication Data

Presler, Titus Leonard.
      Going global with God : reconciling mission in a world of difference / Titus Presler.
          p.   cm.
      Includes bibliographical references (p.   ) and index.
      ISBN 978-0-8192-2410-1 (pbk.)
      ISBN 978-0-8192-2734-8 (E-book)
1. Missions. 2. Globalization—Religious aspects—Christianity. I. Title.
BV2061.3.P74   2010
266—dc22
                                                                          2010024756

Printed in the United States of America

CONTENTS

ACKNOWLEDGMENTS

The broad scope of this book prompts a wide-ranging gratitude. The reflections I offer in *Going Global with God* are informed by conversations and relationships with the many people around the world with whom I have gone global with God, especially in southern Africa and south Asia. Whether in village churches or scholarly conferences, they have formed my spirit and stimulated my thinking.

The eager enthusiasm and hard questioning that students have brought to mission classes I have taught in seminaries have invariably led me to think about old questions in new ways. Their vision for mission has confirmed that ancient quandaries, stubborn problems and new possibilities continue to need pondering.

I am thankful for ongoing patterns of consultation with mission colleagues, especially those from the diverse organizations that make up the Episcopal Partnership for Global Mission. The Global Anglican Project and, more recently, the Anglican Indaba Project have offered intensely interesting times of creative conversation.

For this book, I am grateful to the missionaries and mission leaders who offered their time and focus to conversation and correspondence with me about their experience and work. It has been enriching to learn more about the work and thinking of mission activists in the Evangelical Lutheran Church in America, the Presbyterian Church (U.S.A.) and the United Methodist Church.

I thank the staff of Church Publishing for their enthusiasm for this project. It has been good to collaborate with editor Stephanie Spellers, who was especially helpful in discerning patterns in the writing as it emerged.

Jane, my wife, is a perennial colleague in mission who makes startling connections and offers inspiring insights. As always, I am grateful for her companionship in difference.

INTRODUCTION

"We got the questionnaire from downtown asking what our congregation is doing in mission, and I wasn't sure how to fill it out," Susan said over breakfast before the mission conference organized by the Episcopal Diocese of Western New York. "So I asked our pastor about it because I wasn't sure what to include, and we ended up listing ten things our congregation is doing."

Susan's congregation is based in rural farmland, and the average Sunday attendance is only twelve people. And yet they rally to reach out both locally and globally. They provide food for poor families, tutor challenged children, send money to help a school in Africa, and one member was going on a short-term mission trip to Honduras. The passion of this small band of Christians was not unique, for about fifty out of over sixty congregations sent in responses to the questionnaire, many with similar lists. About a hundred people turned out for the first ever mission conference of the diocese.

Congregations of the historic mainline churches are engaged in mission in the twenty-first century as they have rarely been before. Drawn into direct global engagement, people have found their horizons stretched and their lives changed. They have started asking big questions: "What are we doing? What is God up to? How have we done mission before, and how should we think about it today? Why is mission such a powerful experience? How can we do it thoughtfully and faithfully?" That pattern of reflection following action is an important model of learning, and it is similar to how theology itself is a reflection on our experience of God.

Going Global with God highlights individuals and communities who have been called and sent into mission with God, and it reflects on their discoveries on the road. Throughout this book, we will listen closely to their impressions of their own mission work, as related in conversations, correspondence, blogs and other writing. What people say and write about what they are doing in mission is revelatory. It is often through them that we discern the contours of how the Holy Spirit is moving God's people into mission.

Chapter One, "A Movement Underway: Global Ferment in Local Churches," features a sampling of stories of mission engagement by individuals, congregations and mid-level groupings of the churches. It opens a window on the diverse landscape of mission today.

Today's mission enterprise differs significantly from the mission movement represented at the World Missionary Conference of 1910 in Edinburgh, Scotland, an important event being commemorated a hundred years later. As we compare today's developments, we see that mission activists are not necessarily guided or sent by the top-down structures that were shaping mission work one hundred years ago and earlier in North America and Europe. They are simply on fire for God's mission, and they are enacting the democratizing impulses that are shifting so much of life today. We explore this movement and its biblical warrant in Chapter Two, "From the Ground Up: Mission Democratized."

The next two sections take us deeper as we ask, What are these mission participants discovering out there, on the road, now that they have gone global with God? What challenges have they faced? What light does today's mission flourishing shed for people in congregations, mid-level church units and churchwide agencies, and those who study and analyze Christian mission—as we all reflect and refine our participation in God's mission?

First, today's movement calls us to understand mission more clearly: its nature, its terrain, its direction and its mode. This is the theme of Part II. Chapter Three, "Sent by God: The Nature of Mission," acknowledges the difficulty of discerning how to move in mission when the word can mean quite different things to different people. I offer a comprehensive definition of the nature of mission, one that is flexible enough to encompass all that God sends us to do but specific enough to be useful to practitioners who ask for clarity to guide their work.

In Chapter Four, "Ministry in the Dimension of Difference: Mission's Terrain," we consider a functional understanding of mission as ministry in the dimension of difference. Biblical, theological and historical considerations show that difference is a premise of virtually all mission. Naming this reality explicitly—including naming its historic downsides—helps us reflect and mobilize for mission. It also connects us with postmodern reflection on difference.

If difference is the terrain of mission—that is, the ground on which mission happens—then reconciliation is its purpose. This is the theme of Chapter Five, "Reconciliation: The Direction of God's Mission." Virtually all the spiritual and social conditions addressed by mission derive from estrangement in difference or from systems of oppression built on the exploitation of human difference. This chapter highlights the scriptural accounts of God's desire to heal relationships marked by alienation, and God's call to the church to engage the urgent ministry of restoration.

Chapter Six, "The Mode of Mission Today: Accompaniment and Companionship," explores the churches' movement beyond the partnership model of the late twentieth century. Missionaries, church leaders and church statements together attest to the growing desire to "be with" instead of "do for," to develop mutually transformative relationships between diverse people groups rather than parachute in to fix problems. This is a shift that scripture and theology solidly reinforce.

In Part III we address the challenges inherent in these emerging understandings of mission and explore possible resolutions. Each challenge pairs with a theme from a chapter in the first two sections of the book. In Chapter Seven, "Networking for Mission: A Challenge in Democratization," we discuss the strategic difficulties arising in the movement toward democratization in mission. Then we highlight models of mission networks and communities of practice that link individuals, congregations, mid-level church groupings and wider church bodies around their shared passion.

Chapter Eight, "Missionary Calling and Identity: A Challenge in Being Sent," addresses the difficulty of claiming our calling as participants in God's mission, given the history of insensitivity and imposition that sometimes accompanied Western mission activity. In a world so beset by difference, Christians sometimes feel it is not only easier but wiser not to witness to Christ across boundaries of difference. This chapter identifies ways to reconcile the idea of mission with faithful life in a world of difference.

While it is crucial for mission activists and the churches to engage difference as the unique terrain of mission, there is a danger that we may objectify those who are different or focus so much on addressing difference that we do not move toward the reconciliation and wholistic transformation the gospel demands. Chapter Nine, "Poverty and Wholistic Mission: A Challenge in Difference," explores this issue in light of the phenomenon of poverty, the major dimension of difference addressed by contemporary mission efforts in the churches.

Increasingly, the vision of reconciliation seems unattainable in the face of the controversy and division that mark global Christian relations today. In Chapter Ten, "Churches in Turmoil: A Challenge in Reconciliation," we see how differences in approaches to human sexuality have affected mission work, and we review efforts churches and mission activists have taken to heal relationships within and beyond their church families.

The proliferation of short-term mission trips raises the question of how mission activists can steward resources and build relationships in a way that enhances companionship. Chapter Eleven, "Meeting as Pilgrims: A Challenge in Accompaniment," suggests pilgrimage as a different starting place for envisioning and planning the initial encounters between church communities in different parts of the world.

Part IV sums up the themes of the book in Chapter Twelve, "Seven Marks of the Mission Companion," which envisions the major elements of what it means to be faithful in global mission today.

Before we set off on this journey, some comments about terms and perspectives are in order:

While cross-cultural global mission is the principal concern of this study, mission is discussed as a category of ministry in which difference, not geography, is the key distinctive. Forms of local mission are cited in various parts of the discussion, but the term "local initiative" generally refers to mobilization for world mission that has its source in congregations and middle levels of the churches rather than in their churchwide offices. Appearing alone, "mission" is used generically to include both local work and global work.

Several important aspects of mission are touched on at various points but do not receive major reflection on their own. One is the interreligious encounter that is intrinsic to Christian mission, and another is a more detailed analysis of mission's intercultural encounter. I focused on both in an earlier book, *Horizons of Mission*, and here they appear principally in fresh reflection on the centrality of difference in a functional understanding of mission. A third major concern that does not receive focused attention is the environmental concern of mission in the integrity of creation.

Broad ecumenical developments are in view throughout. Canvassing all church traditions would require a compendium beyond the scope of this book, so four churches of the historic Protestant mainline in the United States and their related communions are the main reference points: the Episcopal Church U.S.A., the Evangelical Lutheran Church in America, the Presbyterian Church (U.S.A.) and the United Methodist Church. They are not representative of all churches, but the trends they highlight are significant for the world Christian movement.

This book takes a global view of mission and seeks to offer a vision relevant for mission activists on all continents. The specific contemporary developments it analyzes, however, are mainly those arising in the Global North and especially the U.S.A., simply because those happen to be my concern in this study. Yet I believe these developments may resonate with the experience of others elsewhere, and certainly the biblical and theological reflection on the nature, terrain, direction and mode of mission is intended for the broadest possible audience.

Settling on a generic term for the level of churches between congregations and churchwide headquarters is not easy. The word "judicatory" is commonly used, but its connotation is primarily that of governance, whereas my concern is with the supporting and mobilizing role of a diocese, synod, presbytery or conference as a community within the church. So I use such terms as "middle level of the churches" or "mid-level groupings" or "regional church bodies" in referring generically to the Episcopal diocese, Lutheran synod, Presbyterian presbytery and Methodist conference.

In referring to churches as a whole, I generally prefer the word "church" in order to highlight their ecclesial nature. I use the term "denomination" less often because it connotes bureaucracy and is associated with division in the Christian movement. In view of the increasingly sacramental under-standing of their own life that mainline churches are developing, I take the liberty of using the term "communion" generically in connection with the worldwide expression of particular church traditions such as the Lutheran World Federation, the World Alliance of Reformed Churches, the World Methodist Council and the Anglican Communion.

Speaking of liberties, I refer to the Anglican Communion's body in the United States as "the Episcopal Church U.S.A." or as "the Episcopal Church" where the geography is clear from the context. In ecumenical and interna-tional discourse, the more recently authorized name, "The Episcopal Church," is not sensitive to other "Episcopal" churches in the Anglican Com-munion, such as those in Scotland, Sudan, Spain, Rwanda and Jerusalem and the Middle East. The older usage and its abbreviation, ECUSA, is not sensitive to the church's own jurisdictions outside the United States, which include Anglican expressions in Taiwan, Honduras, Colombia, Ecuador, Haiti, the Dominican Republic, Venezuela, the British Virgin Islands and parts of Europe. However, "the Episcopal Church U.S.A." has the advantage of being a longstanding terminological anomaly rather than a newly intro-duced fresh one.

Terms for entire parts of the world are notoriously problematic, and there is no ideal solution. Historically in the modern period, much mission initia-tive moved from Europe and North America to Africa, Asia, Latin America and Oceania. I prefer the term "Two-Thirds World" for the latter sector, because it highlights how these parts of the world include two-thirds of the world's people and two-thirds of its land mass. "Global South" is another con-venient term, although not as accurate since much of Asia is north of the equator. "Global North" as a term for the historically originating areas in modern mission has similar problems, but I frequently use it as well. "North Atlantic" is an alternative for the countries of western Europe and North America. "Third World" is not used because of its association with now out-moded Cold War alignments. The terms "developed" and "developing" are avoided because they normatize the cultural and economic trajectories of Europe and North America. For the same reason I avoid unmodified use of the term "development" in referring to educational, medical and socioeco-nomic initiatives in mission. Sometimes I mention "infrastructure develop-ment" but more often specify the types of initiative involved.

A term more peculiar to my writing is "USAmerican" as an adjective for the United States and its people. Geographers recognize the plural Americas as comprised of North America, Central America and South America, and people in those areas routinely use these regional terms in religious, cultural, economic and political discussion. In this light, it is hegemonic for the unmodified term "American" to be used with reference to the life and people of one country within the Americas, namely, the United States, a superpower with quite enough associations of hegemony already.

As even this discussion of terms indicates, mission reflection contends with dense conceptual thickets made up of complex issues, cherished stereotypes, inevitable misunderstandings, historical grievances, shifting configurations and fresh hopes. It will always be so, precisely because mission by its very nature takes us to edges—the edges of our comfort and confidence, the edges of our assumptions and worldview, the edges of our spirituality and faith. In mission we meet the different. As we cross over that border, we engage immediately with all the great contentions of our time and any time—religious and philosophical, cultural and economic, political and ecological.

As with any other enterprise in difference, there is no guarantee that we will get it right. Indeed, we are sure that we will sometimes get it wrong. Yet unlike cross-cultural ventures in other spheres—economic, political, military—Christian mission is committed to persons and communities as intrinsically precious to God and intrinsically precious to all other persons and communities. This incarnational solidarity with the human story has continued through two thousand years, so it is known for its endurance. Moreover, its practitioners have been reflecting and writing over that entire period—telling stories, pondering mysteries, asking questions.

This book is one more contribution to that stream of reflection.

PART I

What's Happening Today in Global Mission?

"You know how to interpret the appearance of the sky, but you cannot interpret the signs of the times," Jesus said to religious leaders who asked him to show them a sign from heaven (Matthew 16:3).

In the second decade of the twenty-first century, there are many signs of the times that affect global mission. Christianity's center of gravity has shifted decisively from its modern heartlands in Europe and North America to Africa, Asia and Latin America, yet Global North Christians retain many levers of power. Conflict between religious communities, especially between Muslims and Christians, is on the rise even as vast numbers of religious people believe that different faiths have many meeting points. Electronic communication connects people instantly, but wide gaps in perspective persist. The gulf between rich and poor deepens, even as multitudes become more affluent in the world's largest countries, India and China. Ecological threats to planet Earth are intensifying amid the rising living standards that help people flourish in the image of God. And these are just a few of the signs.

There are also signs within the churches, and two of these are the focus of Part I: the flourishing of global mission and its increasing democratization. More people than ever are engaged in global mission, and they are propelled and supported by local mobilization, rather than wider church structures. These movements are signs we should watch and, as Jesus suggests, interpret. They have developed over time and are very much with us. And they say important things about how God may be calling us to go global in the future.

CHAPTER ONE

A Movement Underway:
Global Ferment in Local Churches

Christian congregations and their members are mobilizing for mission and engaging the world far beyond themselves. This local initiative is a major fact in the life of historic churches in North America in the twenty-first century.

The concept of "the global village" took hold in the twentieth century, but well into the 1980s many USAmerican church members continued to be quite parochial Christians at the same time that they were global citizens. They had a world perspective on everything but their faith life. They attended international conferences and participated in world projects in education, art or finance, but they were unaware of Christianity's flourishing in the Two-Thirds World—its numerical growth, the new indigenous churches and new theologies. USAmerican church members might go on safari in Kenya but never think to ask what church nearby might be especially interesting to visit on Sunday. They might attend a conference in Manila or Mexico City but never consider engaging local Christian communities.

Many congregations were similarly insular. They were concerned about world poverty, violence and oppression, but they were reluctant to get involved as churches beyond sending money for disaster relief. Their impressions of how European and North American missionaries had misunderstood peoples in other parts of the world made them hesitant about taking initiative as Christians elsewhere. "Better leave that to the development agencies," they reasoned, "because we'll just mess it up if we get into it with our religious stuff." Beyond that, initiative was left to denominational mission offices, which had managed their churches' mission work for well over a century and continued to send missionaries, nurture interchurch relationships and fund work in education, healthcare and economic vitality. Yet the churchwide lack of interest resulted in centralized mission offices having to cut budgets, staff and missionaries. Calls by mission activists for local communities to engage with the wider world were greeted with skepticism.

Now much of that has changed. Today it is unusual to find an Episcopal, Lutheran, Presbyterian or Methodist congregation that does *not* have some direct link with a Christian community far away, most often in the Two-Thirds World—Africa, Asia, Latin America or Oceania. Many congregations have two or three such links. Typically, at least several members have been to the companion community, correspondence is being exchanged, and people are collaborating on a project, often with money being raised on the North American side. Sometimes members of the companion community visit the USAmerican congregation.

In the historic mainline churches, the international engagement of congregations often receives strong support from the regional level of church organization that stands between the congregation and churchwide headquarters—the Episcopal diocese, the Lutheran synod, the Presbyterian presbytery, the Methodist conference. These groupings now have a startling array of global connections. Sometimes congregations' international work is keyed to programs at the regional level, but just as often it is quite particular to the congregation. Similarly, the regional bodies' work often has little to do with the work of churchwide mission offices, which continue to struggle with reduced budgets as denominations spread declining income over multiple urgencies.

The God-talk in the grassroots mission movement is strong and vivid. People speak about "discerning how God is leading" and "seeing what God is doing." As they trace how very personal connections have led to congregational and regional links, they declare that the Holy Spirit has been active in making it happen. Above all, they celebrate the personal relationships they now have with people they call "sisters and brothers in Christ" in other parts of the world. They talk about discovering the fullness of the Body of Christ as they come to know other communities and how these relationships have enriched their own spiritual lives. They marvel at the new perspectives they now have as a result of interacting with people who are very different in multiple ways—language, culture, ethnicity, income and lifestyle. In both public and private they pray faithfully for their new companions in Christ.

The bottom line? World mission is becoming a local affair. It is local to the regional level of the church, but it is even more local to the congregation. There, people are building on connections that come their way to form relationships abroad that involve lots of people on both sides, often over a considerable period of time, even decades.

Stories of communities going global with God and engaging in reconciling mission are exciting. Here is a sampling:

Young Adults Abroad: Symbiotic Catalysts for Mission

Edward Johnson

"Am I my brother's keeper?" asked Edward Johnson as he explained why he went to minister in South Africa as part of the Young Adults in Global Mission Program of the Evangelical Lutheran Church in America. "I have constantly been challenged to answer the question, 'Why South Africa? Why not stay here in the U.S., where we have our own problems that require our dedication and strength?'" For inspiration, Edward pointed to Proverbs 3:27–28 in the Contemporary English Version: "Do all you can for everyone who deserves your help. Don't tell your neighbor to come back tomorrow, if you can help today."

While Edward was in college, participating in a mission trip from the Southern Ohio Synod to its counterpart in Tanzania, the East of Lake Victoria Diocese, was what moved him toward mission. "I gained a new definition and perspective on what the meaning of the word 'neighbor' is," he explained. "Our neighbors are each and every one of God's children placed on this planet, not just those who live in our immediate vicinity, look like us or talk like us." His reflection expresses how, when people encounter human difference, the mission impulse within them responds with a desire to bridge, know and relate.

Edward spent a year participating in a Lutheran community outreach in the Hillbrow section of Johannesburg, an area devastated by poverty and the HIV/AIDS crisis. Why South Africa? "The issues of sub-Saharan Africa are absolute and extreme problems," he said, "while the issues of the U.S. are of a relative nature. The problems of Africa are so extreme that basic life needs cannot be consistently met."

Edward's African American heritage facilitated solidarity with those he was serving. "A huge part of my experience was that I looked like the people I was with for the first time," he said. "I also think that it meant a lot to people to see that the person fighting for them and with them was one of them. It served as inspiration to say that they are capable as children of God—God did not only bless his fair-skinned children, but the brown and black ones, too."

The home congregation, St. Philip's Lutheran Church in Columbus, Ohio, mobilized to support Edward and helped make the venture possible. "They were quite excited to see one of their favorite sons engaging in international mission work and did support me," he said. "As part of an extremely small group that labels ourselves 'black Lutherans,' St. Philip's was motivated to show the ELCA that we are here and we are strong."[1]

Edward is part of a growing movement of one-year missionaries in denominational programs designed over the last two decades especially for young adults, typically defined between the ages of twenty-one and thirty. He was one of thirty-nine outgoing young missioners at the two-week Lutheran orientation he attended before going to South Africa.

Melanie Jianakoplos

"How amazing it is to look back and realize how recently I was in your shoes. Mission trips, overnights, the Italian dinner." So wrote Melanie Jianakoplos from the Philippines to the youth group at Grace Episcopal Church in Kirkwood, Missouri, where she grew up. "Those moments made a huge impact on my life and spiritual formation. Grace Church gave me the foundation on which I built myself as I went off to college. My greatest joy, strength and refuge through those four years was Episcopal Campus Ministry at the University of Missouri. When I graduated I decided to take some time, and my young unbound energy, and do some service work in the Philippines. I'm excited to hear that you all have been reading some of the blog posts and looking at the pictures."[2]

Melanie's letter is a striking instance of how local churches and campus ministries today are inspiring mission service. The mission trips she undertook from Grace to Habitat for Humanity projects around the U.S.A. cultivated a habit of looking beyond herself and her own community to the world's needs. Now teens in the youth group of which she was once a part were reading about the cultural transitions and new gospel understandings she was experiencing while working with the Igorot people in the mountains of the northern Philippines. Melanie established a feedback loop of mission experience and inspiration that is likely to result in still more global engagement by Christian young people in Kirkwood. A Millennium Development Goals emphasis at the Episcopal campus ministry helped move her to mission through the Episcopal Church's Young Adult Service Corps, which usually sends about fifteen people a year to various parts of the world.

Church bodies get especially excited about young adult mission programs. The mainline denominations are struggling with declining membership and realize they need to reach the young adults who are missing from their pews. Young missionaries tend to assume iconic status: "Look at these young people who are excited about Jesus and about the church! And they're even going out in mission!"

Representing a religious alternative to secular initiatives like the Peace Corps, young adult mission programs attract not the missing, but those who are spiritually and missionally committed because of what they have experienced in local churches and campus ministries. Many are considering ordained ministry and recognize that exposure to the wider world would be helpful as they undertake seminary studies. They are right, of course, and as newly ordained clergy, they turn around to have powerful ministries with young adults and in congregational mission, and thus the symbiosis of being inspired and inspiring others continues.

Ciona Rouse

An especially dramatic instance of the power of youth in mission is Ciona Rouse of Belmont United Methodist Church in Nashville, Tennessee. "Like breath and water" is how she characterizes the role of prayer in the lives of the South African Christians she experienced during a two-week youth mission there from Belmont in 2005. It was so compelling that she stayed on for a couple of months after the rest of the group returned home. "That's truly what prayer was like for the people I met on the continent," she says. "They needed it like they needed air, and water and breathing and all those essential things."

Coming out of that experience was a documentary film, *Listen: A New African Narrative*, about leaders in several African countries; a book, *Like Breath and Water: Praying with Africa*; and a website she created with others, www.praywithafrica.com, that emphasizes praying *with* Africans, rather than for Africa—all from a congregational mission trip. "Our philosophy is really simple," Ciona says. "It's learn, pray, act. And so we are inviting people to learn each other's stories, pray each other's prayers and then out of those prayers act alongside one another instead of acting out of pity or guilt."[3]

Mission Giants in Congregations

St. John's Episcopal Church, Sonora, Texas

"The people of St. John's are a small parish," says rector Chris Roque, "but in mission they're giants." Located in Sonora in a ranching region of Texas, St. John's Episcopal Church has an average Sunday attendance of about sixty, a size at which many congregations worry about survival and feel they do not have resources for mission. Yet not only does St. John's see horizons beyond itself, but the parish designs its outreach in three tiers: local, regional and international. Locally the youth work ecumenically with other congregations to provide food baskets for needy people at holiday times. Regionally youth and parents team up with another parish to do construction for handicapped and elderly people in communities along the Rio Grande River.

Internationally, St. John's has supported parishioners to go on mission to three continents, in Belarus, Honduras and Uganda. Roque himself went to Honduras twice before he was ordained as part of a five-year project to plant a church, and twice recently with medical and veterinary teams to Mexico. Roque also pastors an even smaller congregation, St. James at Fort McKavett, where the attendance is about fifteen each Sunday. Even there one member is involved in prison ministry and two others have gone on veterinarian and water-well missions in Honduras.

The reflection of Wheless Miller, a rancher, special-needs teacher and member of St. John's, brings together her ten-year spiritual journey, a particular international venture and a new effort to stimulate mission commitment in young people:

> As an Episcopalian, my idea of mission was skewed such that I envisioned heavy evangelism, and this scared me as I viewed my faith walk as something personal and private. I was tricked into my first mission by our interim priest, Bob Burton, who knew that I loved animals and convinced me that the vet mission to Honduras was in need of my "skill" as a ranch girl from West Texas! I told him that I would convert animals but not people. I was a hard case to crack, but because of his gentle guidance and encouragement the true mission was slowly revealed to me. I now know that mission truly blesses all those involved in the act. It is not so much what we say but our actions that matter. In Belarus we had planned for a Vacation Bible School approach with two weeks of fun and God-filled crafts. As soon as we arrived we were told that we could not name God or Jesus or deliver lessons from the Bible. Amazingly, the message was there without saying one word. The orphans hid in the bushes outside our windows as we had devotions each morning. They listened as we sang. They accepted our love and our hugs, which in essence was God's love and his arms taking them in. That is the message of mission. Now we have started Mission in Motion in Sonora, which involves a mission a month available to youth from all the congregations in our town. We want to plant the seeds of mission on a local level so that as the kids mature as Christians their personal walk in mission will be comfortable and one that they are familiar with.

Where does this mission vision come from? "I think it's because they actually understand what Christ has called them to do," says Roque. The congregations' mission engagement is longstanding, but a vestry retreat two years ago sharpened their intentionality. Out of Bible study they developed a mission statement on the basis of Jesus' resurrection appearance to Peter in John 21: "Jesus has given us the example: Feed his sheep and follow him." This articulation highlights the Jesus-centered perspective of much mission initiative today. People tend to make their case not from "Christian principles" or an ethic of humanitarianism but from the teaching and example of

Jesus, a Jesus with whom they feel they have a personal relationship. "Because Jesus told me to," says Jimmy Martin, a rancher at St. James, Fort McKavett, about his eight years of outreach at a maximum-security prison.[4]

First United Methodist Church, Evanston, Illinois

First United Methodist in Evanston is a mid-size congregation that engages mission in what it sees as concentric circles from local to national to international. The church is focusing on poverty alleviation for five years, during which it hopes to engage a growing group of members in various projects that will improve standards of living for those most in need.

Throughout its 156-year history, First United Methodist has supported a strong mission focus, especially through the work of its women's organizations. Reflecting the changing times, there is now growing interest in outreach in the broader membership. "They started out about twelve years ago saying, 'We can make a youth program if we take them on a mission trip,'" said Margaret Ann Crain, a seminary professor connected with the congregation. "Somehow they got the attitude of how to do mission just right, that it's not charity and it's not patronizing other people. They're very much about being in partnership with people. We've worked through denominational structures but have taken to heart our ongoing relationships with these places where we have served."

Through the efforts of Joanna Gwinn, a church member who has a long-standing interest in Africa, the congregation connected with the Methodist Church of Ghana in 2008 through a project listed with the General Board of Global Ministries and sent a ten-member team to Aburi to help renovate a youth retreat center. Learning more about the youth leadership conferences that were held in the renovated space over the following year, First Methodist realized that an ongoing relationship between the Ghana Methodist Youth Division and its own youth program might be possible. Three Ghanaians who worked with the mission team visited First Methodist, further strengthening the developing bonds.

Invited back to Aburi later in 2010, an eighteen-member team helped construct a dormitory at the youth center. The team included the youth pastor and five college students who participated in a leadership conference for Ghanaian youth, adding an international component to their discipleship training. Bringing additional energy to the venture was a First Methodist student who learned about mission through the youth program's Appalachian mission trips and then took what she learned with her on a college semester abroad in Ghana. She inspired other young adults to get involved and has developed a related project to assist a Ghanaian school.

In another outgrowth from the mission trips, the congregation is helping to support the Mo-Dega Agricultural Development project of the

Methodist Church of Ghana, which seeks to address poverty among the Mo and Dega peoples in the semi-arid Brong Ahafo region of Ghana. In a project that has been formally approved by the General Board of Global Ministries, the congregation hopes that by helping farmers buy seeds and fertilizer, improve irrigation and increase storage capacity and marketing, farmers' income will be increased enough so that families can send their children to school and break the cycle of poverty.

"Involvement in mission has opened the eyes of the congregation to the situation of others in the world," says Jim Young, chair of the Mission and Outreach Committee. "People are seeing that there's a higher purpose to the way they live their lives. While benefiting from the vetting process of the General Board of Global Ministries, we've found that it's effective to go with the interests of the people in our congregation."

The finances of such efforts are significant. In one recent year at First Methodist, $42,000 went to outreach work of the Northern Illinois Methodist Conference; $59,000 supported the annual summer youth mission to Appalachia; and $43,000 went to Ghana, including the mission trip expenses contributed by the participants. To catalyze economic empowerment and stimulate the local economy, First Methodist has bought supplies on-site in Ghana. The bottom line? As a high proportion of time and effort is going to the congregation's mission initiatives, the money is following that pattern as well.[5]

St. Thomas Anglican Church, London

Sometimes the mix of congregational initiative and more centralized structures makes for surprising juxtapositions. When William Taylor became vicar of St. Thomas's Anglican Church in the Borough of Hackney in London, England, he embraced a parish located in a poor section of the city, struggling to carry on with an average Sunday attendance of fifty, and working to outgrow its need for financial support from the Diocese of London.

William found that the parish had for years been raising money for Vinjeru, an educational charity in Malawi. How had that come about? Parishioner Walije Gondwe was from Malawi, and she sparked parishioners' interest to the point that the fundraising had become a permanent fixture in St. Thomas's relationship with the world church. Not much more had happened in the relationship, so the link was based on one person's connection rather than various people developing personal stakes in Malawi. Nevertheless parishioners were committed to continuing their support.[6]

Then along came a local Muslim group looking for space to house their literacy program. It turned out that the contact person was a Muslim from Malawi, who expressed interest in the parish's link with Vinjeru. "It was an immediate bond, though I scarcely know where Malawi is on a map of

Africa," said William. "Providing hospitality is part of our mission to our local communities, and it brings about all sorts of unforeseen possibilities of new relationships."

One Sunday Ivy, a parishioner from Montserrat, stood up in church and urged people to support USPG, the United Society for the Propagation of the Gospel, the oldest missionary-sending society in the Anglican Communion, founded in 1701. "You should support USPG because USPG established the church in many places that we came from, so we ourselves are Christians partly because of USPG!" Ivy told the congregation, alluding to fact that St. Thomas's parishioners come mostly from the West Indies and Africa.

"What do you think about USPG?" William asked me. "Is it a good organization?" I responded that USPG is an excellent and venerable organization. Yet the question even being asked indicated how the formerly prominent British Anglican mission societies are no longer central in the mission consciousness of many members of the Church of England. Personal and local links are what generate enthusiasm for world mission today, not commitment to mission organizations, even those with long and distinguished records like USPG's.

Meanwhile William said he was becoming interested in mission because it seemed to him that it was key to the future vitality of St. Thomas's. By mission he said he meant an outward focus rather than an inward focus—the parish being involved with the world beyond itself, both nearby and distant. "Hackney, not Haiti," he said, even as he acknowledged the claim that Haiti's 2010 catastrophic earthquake had on the prayer and generosity of Christians everywhere.

It is a fascinating mission mix—concern with distant Malawi, kept alive by one person's link and with new possibilities arising from a local Muslim group; loyalty to the historic mission bulwark of USPG, but with little knowledge of its current work; and the horizon of Hackney, the parish's own neighborhood, where mission engagement could help St. Thomas grow.[7]

Regional Activism: Support for Congregations' Wider Mission

Presbyterian Mission Celebration

Twenty-five meetings devoted to various parts of the world were held during the second biennial Mission Celebration conference of the Presbyterian Church (U.S.A.) in the fall of 2009 in Cincinnati, Ohio. Some meetings focused on single countries, like Brazil, Cameroon, China, Colombia, Ghana, Honduras, India, Mexico, Pakistan and Vietnam. Others were regional, discussing, for instance, Central Asia, Central America and the grouping of Zambia, Zimbabwe and Mozambique.

Some of the area groups had formal networking names, such as Cuba Partners or El Salvador Mission Network, but all of them functioned as networks. People were sharing information, interests and initiatives and exploring how they could collaborate, typically without any formal organization or structure. Most of the participants were individual mission activists who had catalyzed interest in those parts of the world in their congregations, and some represented organizations. The Haiti group's meeting, for instance, included a missionary couple working with a Haitian farmers' organization; a representative of Fonkozé, a microfinance agency in Haiti; and two representatives of the Haiti Nursing Foundation.

"We want to work across denominational and political lines," said Larry Beckler of the Presbyterian Frontier Fellowship during the meeting of the Kurdish Network, which focuses on Kurds both in their native areas of northern Iraq and Turkey and in expatriate communities in Europe and North America. Congregations represented in the meeting included First Presbyterian in Hollywood, California, where a half dozen people meet regularly for prayer and consultation about ministry with Kurds, and other congregations in Iowa and Ohio.

Present as resources for the group were Greg and Chris Callison, Presbyterian missionaries stationed in Berlin, Germany, where they minister to Kurdish immigrants and, indirectly, to Kurds in the Middle East. The primary purpose of the network's six hours of meetings over three days, however, was not to support the missionaries, but to stimulate and resource the social and evangelistic outreach of the congregations represented.[8]

The Episcopal Diocese of West Texas

"Every human being in the Diocese of West Texas can be involved in mission by going, sending or praying," says World Mission Officer Betty Chumney about the Episcopal diocese that encourages and supports St. John's, Sonora, in its work. For years at the annual council meeting of the diocese's ninety parishes, Betty has concluded her report by asking all who have been on a mission trip to stand up, and typically about a third of the several hundred attendees stand. Then she asks all those who have supported mission trips financially to stand up, and another third do so. After she has called on those who have prayed for a mission team to stand, the entire assembly is standing. She concludes by turning to the bishop: "Right Reverend sir, I present to you the missionary people of the Diocese of West Texas!" a declaration that stresses how integral mission is to the nature of the church.

Evangelism and mission are among the five core values of the diocese, with mission defined as: "We reach beyond ourselves to serve all people in our communities and throughout the world." The World Mission Department's goal to "engage every member and every church of the diocese in the work of evangelism and mission" seems within reach, as each year about seven hundred fifty people go abroad on about sixty short-term mission trips. Twenty-six countries have been touched in some way by the diocese, and they include four in eastern Europe, seven in the Americas and the Caribbean, four in Asia and eight in Africa.

"Very little that we do comes from our office," says Betty. "If I asked someone to consider going to Timbuktu, they'd probably say, 'Why Timbuktu? God's calling me somewhere else.' Every mission initiative we have has been generated by individuals in the diocese who have come to us and said, 'I think God is calling us to do this ministry.'" Threads of Blessing, for instance, which has generated tapestry-making centers in Uganda, Honduras and Mexico, arose out of the friendship one couple struck up with a visiting Ugandan bishop.

Honduras Water Ministry, another initiative in West Texas, arose out of the vision of Episcopal hydrologist Lewis Manz, and it has drilled about twenty wells in Honduras, trained technicians in that country and touched the lives of many short-term team members who have worked on the projects. Recalling a high school trip he took with Water Ministry, Richard Corda, now a college sophomore, says, "Little did I know the experience of drilling a well in two weeks would change my outlook on life forever." Honduras Water Ministry is one of a number of freestanding mission agencies that have grown out of the combination of personal initiative, congregational involvement and the support of the regional level across the denominations.

How is this kind of diocesan coordination funded? In addition to two modest staff salaries, West Texas has a program budget of just $33,000 for world mission. The major funding for the work, close to $1 million, comes from parishes and individuals who support the various teams and their work. About $150,000 comes from specially designated offerings, and the staff raises another $200,000 from events and outside sources.

What about involvement and direction from churchwide headquarters? Staff there offer moral support, but the diocese's work is self-generating. While a few years ago the diocese had a missionary supported by the Episcopal Church's central mission office, churchwide budget cuts have meant that more recent appointees had to be supported locally. On the other hand, within six weeks of the January 2010 earthquake in Haiti, parishes in the diocese had contributed more than $110,000 to be channeled through Episcopal Church Relief and Development, a churchwide agency, thus collaborating with the wider church in a major emergency response. Generally the many projects around the world that West Texas supports—from tree-planting to AIDS work to evangelism and Bible distribution—have been conceived by individuals, who have then tested their discernment with parishes and the diocese. And then people have come on board.[9]

The Episcopal Diocese of New York

Overall, West Texas is a conservative diocese, and in the Anglican Communion's turmoil around sexuality it has come out strongly for a traditionalist stance—and historically world mission has often been championed by the conservative side of the churches. Today, though, liberal sectors of the churches are just as active, and the Episcopal Diocese of New York is a striking example. It has a remarkable array of mission-related groups, many of them reflecting the internal diversity of a diocese where Episcopal services are conducted every Sunday in about fifteen languages.

The Carpenter's Kids is the most broadly based outreach. Initiated jointly by Suffragan Bishop Catherine Roskam of New York and Bishop Mdimi Mhogolo of the Diocese of Central Tanganyika, it links more than eighty New York parishes with the needs of the estimated forty thousand children left vulnerable by the HIV/AIDS crisis in the two hundred congregations of the Tanzanian Anglican diocese. Educational and healthcare needs are the particular focus, and currently close to six thousand children are served, with several hundred thousand dollars contributed annually. Program infrastructure and staffing have been set up under the auspices of Central Tanganyika, and The Carpenter's Kids now draws participation from several other dioceses in the United States, United Kingdom and Australia. Equally important, group pilgrimages take people annually to form relationships with companions in Tanzania, and leaders from there regularly visit New York and the other USAmerican dioceses that are involved.

Pilgrimages to the Diocese of Madras in India, sponsored by the New York diocese's India Network, have nurtured personal companionship with Indian counterparts. Implementing an emphasis on education, the network facilitated a relationship between St. Hilda's and St. Hugh's School in Chennai and its counterpart of the same name in Manhattan. The group is helping the Madras diocese in its project to combat the temple prostitution cult dedicated to the Hindu goddess Mathamma by supporting escaped victims in a productive setting. The group also offers moral support to the Madras diocese's extensive ministry with transgendered persons. Thus this one group's ministry brings together companionship experienced through pilgrimage, traditional infrastructure work in education, interreligious confrontation with the Mathamma cult and social advocacy in a transgender initiative.

The diocese's major connection with churchwide mission work is through helping support missionaries who are appointed by the Episcopal Church but who work in areas of particular interest to the diocese. Elizabeth Boe serves on the Tanzanian staff of Carpenter's Kids, having begun there with the Young Adult Service Corps. Ogé Beauvoir is a Haitian priest serving as dean of the Episcopal seminary in Port-au-Prince, Haiti, having previously served in Manhattan. Sandra Seaborn serves in the Diocese of Madras, and Elyn MacInnis has served for years in China.

"Given what's going on with the Anglican Communion, I feel that we in the Diocese of New York are doing all we can to be a part of the worldwide Anglican family," says commission chair Yvonne O'Neal. "We can all make a difference by talking with each other. Individual clergy and lay people are keeping these relationships alive. At the grassroots there's never going to be a rift, and that's where the church is."

A companion diocese relationship with the Diocese of Matlosane in South Africa has been an international link for Episcopalians in New York for years, with a number of exchanges and projects undertaken, especially during the antiapartheid struggle. Such companion links between regional expressions of the churches have been major mission catalysts in Lutheran synods, Methodist conferences, Presbyterian presbyteries and Episcopal dioceses. It is significant, however, that other kinds of links are now proliferating beyond the formally constructed companionships between judicatories. Thus, in the case of New York, the Tanzanian and Indian connections currently are garnering more energy.

These and additional New York diocesan initiatives—Haiti Network, Global Women's Fund, Global Hospitality Fund, Metropolitan Japanese Ministry and others—are overseen by the Congregational Life for Mission Commission. Its very name emphasizes that the diocese believes that a key criterion for mission engagement is not what the diocesan headquarters may do but whether the 201 parishes are involved. The commission sees its role not so much to initiate international mission as to support the efforts underway and ensure that the many particular initiatives are aware of each other and collaborate as need arises.[10]

These stories are a snapshot of world mission ferment today as churches go global with God. The stories illustrate the stance of many congregations and middle levels of Global North churches. The historic centralized structures for mission are respected and sometimes consulted. Otherwise they seem distant, bureaucratic, and impersonal, if people are even aware that they exist.

People in congregations and the middle levels of the church understand mission as engaging with the world beyond themselves. That world is often nearby—a neighborhood down the street or across the city where people and conditions are very different. Or that world may be on the other side of the globe. Either way, there are two hooks for interest. One is the dimension of difference represented by that other world. The second is local engagement. If the mission frontier is nearby, people naturally engage on a local basis, but even if it is very far away, it is the local connection that elicits interest and commitment.[11]

Notes

1. See Edward Johnson's blog: http://jamesedwardjohnson.blogspot.com/2008/07/am-i-my-brothers-keeper.html. Text also draws on correspondence with Johnson.

2. See Melanie Jianakoplos's blog: http://melaniespineapplediaries.blogspot.com/2010/02/grace-kirkwood-youth-group.html.

3. See Ciona Rouse's website: http://www.umc.org/site/apps/nlnet/content3.aspx?c=lwL4KnN1LtH&b=5138783&ct=8044245. See also Ciona Rouse, *Like Breath and Water: Praying with Africa* (Nashville: Upper Room, 2010), http://www.praywithafrica.com/.

4. Material from St. John's and St. James's is derived from conversation and correspondence with the named participants.

5. Material on First United Methodist, Evanston, is derived from conversation and correspondence with participants and from the congregation's website, http://faithatfirst.com.

6. See Vinjeru's website: http://www.vinjerueducationmalawi.com.

7. Material on St. Thomas, Hackney, is derived from conversation and correspondence with William Taylor.

8. I attended the 2009 Mission Celebration.

9. Material on the mission work of the Diocese of West Texas is derived from conversation and correspondence with Betty Chumney and from the World Mission Department's website, http://www.dwtx.org/index.php/diocese/World%20Mission.

10. Material on the international work of the Diocese of New York is derived from meetings of the Congregational Life for Mission Commission, conversation and correspondence with participants, and the diocesan website, http://www.dioceseny.org.

11. For a sociological analysis of USAmerican churches' global engagement today, see Robert Wuthnow, *Boundless Faith: The Global Outreach of American Churches* (Berkeley: University of California Press, 2009), esp. chap. 5, "The Global Role of Congregations: Bridging Borders through Direct Engagement," 140–87.

CHAPTER TWO

From the Ground Up:
Mission Democratized

Going global with God is the story of the entire Christian movement, the historical process through which the gospel of Jesus Christ has been proclaimed in word and deed in ever wider concentric circles throughout the world from the first community of Jesus' followers in Jerusalem to our own day.

What is emerging today is how the initiative for global outreach has moved away from direction and control by the centralized church structures of the modern era, the denominations' headquarters and mission offices. Instead, the initiative for going global is coming increasingly from congregations, as individuals and small groups catch a vision for global engagement, make contacts in other parts of the world, journey to those places and then develop relationships with the people they meet and work with there.

Alongside congregations, initiative is coming from the geographical units the churches have developed for their life and work: the Episcopal diocese, the Lutheran synod, the Methodist conference and the presbytery in the Presbyterian system. These units represent a middle level of organization in the churches, midway between congregation and churchwide headquarters. Depending on the region of the country and the size of the churches as a whole, the regional units include anywhere from a few dozen congregations to hundreds. Today these regional structures are often supporting and channeling initiative from congregations, and sometimes they guide the efforts of congregations into initiatives shared on a regional basis.

Increasingly, the central structures of the churches are acknowledging the change and are adjusting their historic role to accommodate and support it. "Global mission is about to become more local," declared a United Methodist News Service story in April 2010 in a dramatic illustration of the emerging movement. The story went on:

> Officials at the United Methodist Board of Global Ministries are signaling a "cultural shift" in how the denomination does mission.
>
> Instead of acting as an implementer of mission for the denomination, the agency must be "a resource to those individuals, churches, conferences and institutions already in mission," Ohio West Area Bishop Bruce Ough, board president, told directors during the April 12–14 spring meeting.
>
> Building a capacity for mission among all parts of the connection [the Methodists' interconnected church system] should be the standard for all the board's activities. "I think we could begin by strengthening our partnerships with annual (regional) conferences and devoting significantly more staff time to helping conferences build their capacity to be in global mission," he said.
>
> Part of that effort would mean strengthening ties to the largest congregations by attendance. Staff representing two of those churches, along with a conference mission leader, were part of a discussion on ministry with the poor.[1]

Striking in this announcement was recognition that a shift had already occurred. Leaders were not urging congregations and conferences to shoulder more of the burden. Instead, they were recognizing the accomplished fact that local levels were already carrying out much of the church's international mission. The real news was how the role of churchwide staff would change as a consequence, namely, that they would function as a "resource to those individuals, churches, conferences and institutions already in mission." Equally notable was the recognition that this would entail a "cultural shift"—a change in Methodists' worldview of mission, a change in their customary instincts and habits in thinking about how mission could and should be done.

In a similar vein, Hunter Farrell, director of world mission for the General Assembly Mission Council of the Presbyterian Church (U.S.A.), wrote in 2010, "In recent decades, as globalization has increased international communication, travel and awareness, U.S. Presbyterians haven't waited on the denominational offices to engage in mission—they've gone themselves!"[2]

This is a major change from the mission world of a hundred years ago. Those who gathered in Edinburgh for the World Missionary Conference in 1910 included church leaders, heads of denominational mission boards and missionary societies and missionaries, all of them from Europe and North

America with the exception of a very few Christian leaders from Asia. There was considerable ecclesial and theological diversity among the conferees, but the centralized mission structures of the churches and societies were virtually the only channels of global mission initiative, and there appeared to be no reason to anticipate change in that pattern. Conference chair John R. Mott, a Methodist layman from the United States, had been instrumental in energizing the Student Volunteer Movement, which since the early 1890s had drawn more than four thousand students into international mission service through ecumenical activism on college and university campuses. While the movement was and continued to be one of the largest and most impressive grassroots mobilizations for mission in modern times, its recruits were channeled into service directly through the central mission boards of their churches or the freestanding societies such as the China Inland Mission. We are now in a different era.

Democratization of Mission Initiative Today

There are several ways to describe how mission initiative is germinating from the ground up today. As the initiative for global engagement has moved away from central church headquarters, we can say that it has been *decentralized* and *localized.* Central headquarters still have important roles in encouraging, networking and organizing churchwide programs, but they are no longer where most of the action is. More people are going out to other parts of the world under local and regional auspices. More money is being raised and spent from local and regional church communities. More communication is being initiated by local and regional entities, both within the churches and with international companions. And more mobilization of awareness and involvement is happening in the local and regional orbits. So the sheer volume of personnel, funding, communication and mobilization expresses how going global with God has been decentralized and localized.

Another way to describe the process is that global engagement has been *deprofessionalized* and *democratized.* It used to be that most of the global engagement of the churches was managed by fulltime professional staff working at denominational headquarters. The denominational offices still have such staff, though many fewer than they used to because the diminishing size of the mainline denominations over the decades has forced successive budget cuts that, in turn, have reduced staff for many ministries, including international mission. The professional status of the staff is derived from a combination of their experience and their employment in fulltime administrative work. Many have been missionaries or development workers in other parts of the world, and they develop a generic knowledge of mission simply from working fulltime in church headquarters. Some have undertaken focused study in missiology, anthropology, sociology or specialties like Asian or African or Latin American studies.

It used to be that new initiatives in the global mission of the churches would be conceived by churchwide boards or commissions, developed by denominational staff and then implemented on a churchwide basis. If initiatives were conceived at more local levels, they would need to be funneled up through the central boards and staff. If approved, an initiative would be implemented churchwide, perhaps with the endorsement of the churchwide governing body, like the Episcopalians' General Convention, the Presbyterians' General Assembly, the Methodists' General Conference or the Lutherans' Churchwide Assembly. If an initiative was not approved up the line, it died.

Now that the bulk of global engagement is being undertaken by congregations and regional groupings, there are few professionals in charge. Instead, individuals in congregations and regions pool whatever experience they have and learn along the way, often assisted by returned missionaries. Pastors, district superintendents and bishops get involved, and sometimes they have veto power over particular initiatives and projects. Often they are simply learning alongside their parishioners and regional lay leaders.

Combined with mission's localization, this deprofessionalization has democratized global initiative in the churches. "Government by the people" and "a state of society characterized by formal equality of rights and privileges" are two definitions of democracy. Another is equally relevant: "The control of an organization by its members, who have a free and equal right to participate in decision-making processes."[3] The distribution of power and participation is an important issue in any system of organization. Who has authority to make decisions? Which people get to participate in making decisions that affect the whole? In the democratization of mission, decision-making authority has passed from the few in denominational hierarchies to the many in the congregations of the churches.

Diversification of mission initiative has been an inevitable result of the democratizing dynamic. More people involved in the myriad settings of congregations and mid-level units of the churches bring exponentially larger numbers of personal connections, life experiences and group priorities to bear on the tasks of discerning mission and planning initiatives. Reading a book about a particular place of suffering in the world, meeting a church leader at a conference, visiting a congregation while on vacation in another country, being captivated by a speaker—any of these experiences can prompt and have prompted not only an individual initiative but conversations with fellow church members that blossom into a congregational project or a regional program launched by a diocese, synod, presbytery or conference. The types of work undertaken become almost as diverse as the number of places around the world that are touched by these initiatives. On one hand, the diversity among projects large and small is so great that it bewilders and appears incoherent. On the other, behind each initiative is not only goodwill but the testimony of a few or many that this sewing micro-enterprise, that church planting, this scholarship program or that home for battered women is the fruit of a God-given vision that is transforming not only the people reached around the world but the people at home in the sending church as well.

Mission Management in the Centralized Past

In looking at the democratization of global engagement in the churches, and comparing it to earlier patterns, it may be helpful to think of circles of influence. Around each congregation there was traditionally a circle of influence confined to a particular village or town, or a particular neighborhood of a city. In the Roman Catholic and Anglican parish systems, geographical boundary lines were drawn to divide one parish from another. Clergy could minister legitimately within those boundaries, but evangelizing or offering programs in the territory of another parish was off limits.

The mid-level judicatories—the conference, diocese, synod or presbytery—continue to be defined geographically today: the North/West Lower Michigan Synod of the Evangelical Lutheran Church in America, the Dakotas Annual Conference of the United Methodist Church, the San Francisco Presbytery of the Presbyterian Church (U.S.A.) or the Episcopal Diocese of Virginia. The primary circle of ministry and jurisdiction is within the geographical boundary of each such unit, and it relates as such to its immediate neighbors and to the other such units in the church.

Relating to the wider world beyond national boundaries, however, was long a role assigned to the churchwide organizational expressions of any of these churches. Other nations, other groups with distinct cultures and languages—all this looked like ministry of a different order, requiring skill, expertise and experience beyond the reach of individual congregations or mid-level units. It seemed to the churches that reaching out internationally to other countries and relating to very different cultures was best handled by churchwide staff through headquarters or by specialized societies formed to carry out these functions on behalf of the churches.

Specialized societies to promote and carry out mission had precedent in the Roman Catholic tradition. From the medieval period onward, monastic orders such as the Benedictines, Franciscans and Dominicans made enormous contributions to Roman Catholic global engagement through preaching the gospel, forming new congregations and establishing schools in many parts of Latin America, Asia and Africa. The Jesuits have been one of the most influential groups, founded as the Society of Jesus by Ignatius Loyola in 1534. Although many today associate Jesuits primarily with education and the intellectual life, the society was founded primarily for mission work, and it is fair to say that the Jesuits' discerning interaction with other cultures around the world has shaped profoundly their contributions to scholarship.

In 1622 the Vatican established the Congregation for the Propagation of the Faith, commonly called the Propaganda, which directed cross-cultural work alongside the continuing work of Roman Catholic orders and societies. Over the centuries, Roman Catholic societies and men's and women's orders devoted to global engagement have multiplied. The Missionaries of Africa, for instance, were formed in Algeria in 1868 to evangelize north and central Africa, and today they have over three thousand lay and ordained members, including an active branch in the United States. The Maryknolls, formally the Catholic Foreign Mission Society of America, were founded in 1911 in Ossining, New York, with an initial focus on China, and today their more than five hundred members have significant social justice and teaching ministries around the world. Each of the many Roman Catholic mission groups has developed a complex history of deep engagement with the peoples of the world. The role of congregations and dioceses has been mainly to send recruits to be trained by the groups and money to support the work.

In the Church of England, the centralization and professionalization of global engagement followed the specialization side of the Roman Catholic tradition, as expressed through the orders, rather than the centralization side represented by the Propaganda. Mission was pursued by especially interested clergy and lay people. The process began with the formation of the Society for Promoting Christian Knowledge in 1698 and the Society for the Propagation of the Gospel in 1701, and it diversified with the founding of the Church Missionary Society in 1799 and a number of other groups during the nineteenth century. These groups ultimately reached many parts of Asia, Africa and Latin America.

Early Calvinist efforts in cross-cultural mission included Geneva's brief outreach to Brazil in 1557 and, in the seventeenth century, John Eliot's work among Massachusetts Indians through the Society for the Propagation of the Gospel in New England and Dutch Reformed work in southeast Asia. The Baptist Missionary Society, founded in London in 1792, supported William Carey's mission to Calcutta in 1795, the same year that saw the founding of the ecumenical London Missionary Society. British Presbyterian and Methodist societies followed in the early nineteenth century. Such societies expressed the principle of voluntarism in Protestantism, the conviction that people with a shared commitment had the right and even the obligation to organize to promote their particular common cause. Hence such societies are often called "voluntary societies."

Early mission efforts in North America focused on Native Americans and the settlers on the western frontier. For other parts of the world, the founding of the American Board of Commissioners for Foreign Missions in Boston in 1810 brought together the cross-cultural vision and enthusiasm of Congregationalists, Presbyterians and Baptists, but the ecumenical cooperation was short-lived. The American Baptist Missionary Union formed in 1814 to send Ann and Adioniram Judson to Burma. Methodists formed a mission board in 1830, and the Presbyterians founded their own Board of Foreign Mission in 1837.

Thus began the mission board phenomenon, in which major USAmerican churches established centralized agencies to pursue global engagement on their behalf as organic wholes, not missionary societies operating alongside the central structures, as had been the case in the Roman Catholic Church and the Church of England. This was a centralizing trend that contrasted with principle of the voluntary societies. The Episcopal Church followed suit, putting its Domestic and Foreign Missionary Society on a churchwide footing in 1835. Indeed, for Episcopalians, Presbyterians and Methodists, it was the felt need for global engagement through world mission that prompted previously loosely connected church structures—dioceses, presbyteries, conferences—to develop a level of organization that would enable them to work together.

For many churches, world mission was their first major churchwide initiative. Conceptually, churchwide organization for global engagement seemed appropriate as a matter of scale. "We as a people here" were going to relate to "those people over there." Just as nations relate to nations, it seemed that churches organized on a national basis should relate as whole church bodies to peoples in the wider world. At that stage, primary evangelization was seen as a major initial task, with medical and educational ministries coming quickly alongside. The magnitude and complexity of the work naturally called for the resources of entire churches, not their smaller units. Moreover, individual groupings such as synods, conferences, dioceses and presbyteries were not strong enough financially to engage globally on their own. The logistical difficulties of travel and communication called for a broader mobilization of resources for the focused efforts of denominational mission boards and voluntary societies.

As they developed histories of global engagement and reflected on their work through consultations and conferences, each of the mission boards and voluntary societies ripened into expert agencies. They had vision and strategies for their work and developed distinctive processes for recruiting, training, sending and supporting workers in what was known as "the mission field." Through mission periodicals they communicated with and enlisted the support of their church members in congregations, synods, dioceses, conferences and presbyteries. Women's groups coalesced in the denominations to support world mission in the nineteenth century by raising money and recruiting missionaries, and these vital resources were channeled principally through the mission boards.

Most important for catalyzing grassroots support, the mission boards and societies sent their global workers, the missionaries, to visit the congregations and report on their work. International travel was arduous and time-consuming, with missionaries traveling by sailing ships and pack animals in the early days, and later by steamship and railroad well into the twentieth century. It made sense that they served for five years at a time before going on leave or furlough, and the time home was then typically a year. Much of that year would be spent in "deputation," moving around to report on the work to individual congregations and regional groupings. Home itineration continues today, though it is usually for a couple of months after a term of three years. The typical missionary on deputation in the mid-twentieth century would cover thousands of miles by bus, train and automobile; give perhaps hundreds of talks to congregations, women's groups, men's groups and mission committees; screen hundreds of slides and sometimes 8-mm films; and eat innumerable potluck suppers.

Such contact with individual missionaries and their work educated congregations about other parts of the world and the outreach of their church there. It provided a biblical and theological framework for the church's work across cultures, whether in evangelization, church planting, education, healthcare or agriculture. It formed personal connections between home-side Christians and the missionary. It galvanized enthusiasm for the work. The inward fruit of this was prayer and continuing concern, with many congregations undertaking to pray for the work on a regular basis and to correspond with the missionaries. The principal outward fruit was two-fold. Some individuals were inspired to consider international service, ensuring a continuing flow of recruits. And many people contributed financially, so that the work was supported by the gifts of the faithful at home.

New recruits, however, did not go directly from the congregation to the mission field. Rather, they applied to the central board or to the missionary society to be accepted for service. A memorable cinematic depiction of this process and its aftermath is the 1958 film *The Inn of the Sixth Happiness*, which shows how Gladys Aylward, a domestic worker, was rejected for service by the China Inland Mission in London because of her lack of education. Convinced she was called to China, she went on her own in 1930 to assist an aging missionary in Shansi province, and the two established an inn for mule drivers whom they evangelized. She was later drawn into prison and orphanage ministries, and a dramatic high point of her story was a harrowing trek through mountains with the orphans to escape the invading Japanese. Her determination made Aylward a notable exception to the rule, for most would-be international missionaries served through mission boards or, if rejected, they contented themselves with serving at home.

Similarly, funds did not go directly from the congregation to the missionary. Offerings collected by the congregation for mission were sent to the mission board or society, where they were pooled with the offerings of many other congregations and directed as the board or society deemed advisable. Some of the funds were designated to support the missionaries and their families and were disbursed through complex personnel policies designed to ensure equity among missionaries and, depending on a board's specific guidelines, rough parity with indigenous colleagues in places of service. Some funds were used to support ministries and institutions on the ground, whether directed by missionaries or by indigenous leaders, and some funds supported the overhead of the boards and societies.

Thus the role of congregations and mid-level judicatories—whether in the Roman Catholic outreach over the centuries, or in Anglican and Protestant global work from the eighteenth century on—was to contribute funds and encourage members to offer themselves for international service. Vision, strategy, particular initiatives, decisions about where to be involved and what kind of work to undertake—all this was recognized, indeed assumed, to be the purview of the experienced mission societies and boards. Congregations and the mid-level judicatories saw the global as an important part of their discipleship. Direct involvement, however, was not generally included in their role.[4] Now much of that has changed. In explaining a major strategic shift of the Presbyterian Church (U.S.A.) announced in 2010, Presbyterian mission leader Hunter Farrell wrote:

> In 1960 Presbyterians worked primarily through one centralized international mission agency. Today there are literally thousands of Presbyterian "mission agencies": congregational mission committees, international presbytery partnerships, and numerous Presbyterian mission organizations. This new context requires that in addition to continuing to partner with churches around the world, Presbyterian World Mission partners with congregations and church members in the United States who are involved in God's mission.[5]

As with the United Methodists, the Presbyterians are focusing the denominational mission office's work not so much on initiating mission but on supporting the mission already being carried out by the congregations and regional expressions of the church.

Today's democratization of mission initiative radicalizes the principle of voluntarism that earlier gave rise to multiple mission societies in Anglican, Protestant, and even Roman Catholic settings. Although more accessible to individual initiative than the denominational mission boards, the voluntary societies developed their own hierarchical bureaucracies and became centers of authority to which congregations were secondary. Today the principle of voluntary initiative in mission has truly moved to the grassroots of congregations and the individuals who constitute them.

Democratization's Parallels in the Information Age

The contrast we are experiencing in mission today is between the centralization of mission initiative in the recent past of the modern era and its current decentralization, localization, deprofessionalization, democratization and diversification. This shift parallels similar changes in contemporary life, especially the way we negotiate information technology and social networks.

Not long ago I was mystified about how to install a sharing button on my blog. Displaying such a button would mean people could with one click place a link to the blog on their social networking site of choice: Facebook, Twitter, Buzz and more.

How was I going to insert such a button? My blog hosting company offered two options in small type at the bottom of my screen: "Support" and "Forums." Accustomed to relying on experts, I first clicked Support. What greeted me was an extensive list of standard topics, each of which opened to an essay, but my query did not quite match any of the topics. There was the option of e-mailing my question to the support staff, but experiences of no replies at other websites prompted me to consider Forums instead of Support. Yet I did so reluctantly, wondering to myself, "What are these 'forums,' anyway? I'll bet the people on the forums know just as little as I do. Talk about the blind leading the blind!" What I found on Forums was a long list of conversations underway, not between customers and expert staff at headquarters, but among bloggers themselves. In under two minutes I came across a conversation between "Jennifer" and "Time Thief" about almost exactly the question I was pursuing.

Time Thief seemed to be an answer person. I entered the conversation, and within ten minutes Time Thief was back to me. She—and I knew it was a she from the picture—suggested a couple of solutions, explained them a bit and referred me to a website that provided a very full explanation of just how to install a Share button. I tried it, got partway through, encountered a glitch, then went back to Time Thief, who explained how to sidestep the glitch. In minutes it was done.

The problem got solved through a process that was decentralized, deprofessionalized and democratized. The expertise Jennifer and I needed from Time Thief was not sitting behind a desk at headquarters, but out somewhere else at home or in a coffee shop. Time Thief was not a paid professional, but simply someone who enjoyed getting really good at cyber stuff and sharing her wisdom. The process can also be seen as localized, though in an odd way. Anything on the web is universalized rather than localized, because it is accessible to all people across vast stretches of space and time. Yet each of us was able to stay local to where we were as the problems got solved, even as we encountered one another in a public space.

The web provides many examples of this flattening of hierarchical pyramids of expertise and power. Job, travel and real estate websites have taken the place of people in offices whom you have to wait to see. Wikipedia, "the free encyclopedia that anyone can edit," illustrates how even defining the content of knowledge has been democratized. Anyone can register to revise an article or initiate a piece on a new topic. While this has led to wry faces about unreliable research based on Wikipedia articles, the phenomenon is only growing in volume and sophistication, with now more than 3.2 million articles in English, versions in a remarkable number of other languages, and numerous sister projects such as Wikibooks, Wikiquotes, Wikicommons, Wikisource, and Wikiversity.

"We believe that the creation and documentation of knowledge is a collaborative process but not a democratic one," countered Jorge Cauz of the Encyclopedia Britannica in insisting on the continuing importance of experts and objectivity.[6] We will want to wrestle with the distinction between democracy and collaboration in our consideration of mission. Yet Cauz made his statement while explaining Britannica's own move to allow readers to edit the encyclopedia's free online version, clearly an effort to match Wikipedia's appeal. Thus the documentation of knowledge, much of it very sophisticated, is being decentralized, localized, deprofessionalized, democratized and diversified—not only as has never *occurred* before but as has never before been even *imagined* possible.

The democratizing dynamic of the digital revolution is dramatized by efforts made by authoritarian political systems to limit access to the Internet and web-based communication. Such control is routine in China and Myanmar, and shutting down social networking sites was a major way the Iranian government sought to disrupt pro-democracy demonstrations in 2009. Web dominance and manipulation are obvious in open societies and free markets as well, as major players like Microsoft, Google, Amazon and Apple jockey for power and concerns grow about privacy in online advertising and communication of all kinds.

Nevertheless the undertow of our historical moment is obvious. It is *away from* centralized structures where access to knowledge and power is concentrated and cordoned off from others. It is away from a vertical orientation where people look upward for direction and authorization before they feel empowered to engage and act. It is *toward* the experience-based expertise of individuals and groups and their participation in forming communities of knowledge and action. It is *toward* a horizontal orientation as people look alongside to their peers for help in understanding situations and doing something about them.

From a simple web search to the power politics of knowledge and entire political systems, we can see that what is happening in the world mission work of the churches reflects the intensifying patterns of how we work in society and even how we think about thinking and assembling knowledge. As in these other areas, mission activists today are looking sideways, not up, for help. Mission is being understood as people learn in collaboration with one another.

Mission Politics in the New Testament

We have looked at what is happening on the ground with mission's democratization today, and we have seen how it contrasts with the centralized past. It is clear that it fits with how people are collaborating with one another to build up knowledge bases in the information age. How does it fit with the biblical picture, especially as we find it in the New Testament?

I frame this topic as mission *politics* in the New Testament, because the phenomena of decentralization and localization, deprofessionalization and democratization, are political phenomena. Defined most simply and neutrally, politics consists of the patterns by which people use power to accomplish work. Such use of power includes the distribution, accumulation and sharing of power as well—all to get work done. Looked at this way, politics, far from being a bad thing, is a necessary and unavoidable feature of being human. Virtually every human interaction has a political dimension because every human interaction involves relations of power. This is true in the home, on the street, in the workplace, in neighborhoods and, obviously, in governments. In the mission of the churches, power is now more evenly distributed, and the bulk of power can be said to have shifted away from denominational centers to the congregations and regional bodies. This is a political shift.

Mission politics in the New Testament gives generous room for the kind of local initiative we are seeing today, yet it also warrants the central structures that continue to function amid the flourishing of local initiative.

A number of instances illustrate Jesus' mission politics, that is, his practice in the distribution of power and initiative for mission. When he sent out seventy disciples, he was exercising initiative as the sender of those whom he felt he had formed sufficiently for mission through his teaching and example. He sent them to "every town and place where he himself intended to go," so he was preparing for his own arrival. Yet he handed over to them the fullness of his own mission: declaring peace, curing the sick and announcing the arrival of God's reign (Luke 10:1–9). I hear deep relief in Jesus' exultant rejoicing in the Holy Spirit when the disciples returned saying, "Lord, in your name even the demons submit to us!" (Luke 10:17–22). He had risked his reputation and credibility in devolving his mission on them, for they could have been ineffectual or, worse, derelict and deceitful. Sharing power with them had paid off, and now he could be confident that his mission had a future beyond himself.

Jesus' inner circle, by contrast, quickly developed a proprietary attitude. "Master, we saw someone casting out demons in your name, and we tried to stop him, because he does not follow with us," reported John. Jesus answered by endorsing God's evident working through an outlier and thereby shared power with someone he presumably did not even know: "Do not stop him; for whoever is not against you is for you" (Luke 9:49–50). Jesus' response echoed that of Moses when Joshua encouraged him to stop Eldad and Medad from prophesying in the wilderness camp because they were not among the seventy Moses had commissioned to adjudicate disputes. "Are you jealous for my sake?" Moses retorted, "Would that all the Lord's people were prophets, and that the Lord would put his spirit on them!" (Numbers 11:29). Jesus' rejection of ownership claims for his mission resonated with how he rejected the drive of the religious authorities of his day to own God's covenant and exclude tax collectors, prostitutes and other "sinners" from it.

A couple of Jesus' sayings could be interpreted as restricting leadership authority, and hence mission authority, to a chosen one or a chosen few. After Peter acknowledged him as the Messiah, the Son of the living God, Jesus declared that Peter was the rock on which he would build the church and went on to give him the keys to the kingdom with power to bind and loose (Matthew 16:13–20). This incident contributes to the continuing Roman Catholic view that the pope occupies the "chair of St. Peter" and thereby has unique authority. Another such saying is the risen Jesus' commissioning of the disciples in John's gospel: "As the Father has sent me, so I send you. . . . Receive the Holy Spirit. If you forgive the sins of any, they are forgiven them; if you retain the sins of any, they are retained" (John 20:21–23). In the wider testimony of the gospels, however, it is clear that the continuing presence of Jesus is conferred on the whole company of Jesus' followers, and that the entire company—including "those who will believe in me through their word" (John 17:20) —have continuing responsibility for the mission.

This is especially clear in the patterns of the early church, which also illustrate the tension between centralized authority and democratized initiative. The extravagant abundance of the Holy Spirit, beginning at Pentecost, created an empowered and empowering group of people among whom gifts of preaching, healing and community life were startlingly present (Acts

2:42–47). Appointed to be a serving deacon, Stephen instead preached with such challenge and eloquence that he was stoned to death (Acts 7). Philip was compelled by the Holy Spirit to meet an Ethiopian eunuch on the road and testified with such conviction that the African pilgrim sought baptism on the spot (Acts 8:26–40).

Most significant for the church's future, a brutal harasser of the movement received his own vision of the risen Christ. Paul responded by carrying the gospel beyond the bounds of Judaism and accepting those who received it gladly as Christ's own people without requiring that they conform to Jewish law. The ensuing dialogue between Paul the missionary and the Jerusalem monitors unfolded as a conflict between localized and democratic initiative on one side and centralized authority on the other. Discernment as well as control was at issue: Can God's will be ascertained only from the traditional centers of articulation, or is God revealing new, startling and possibly contradictory insights in the sprawling and disorderly growth of the church?

At the Jerusalem conference that tried to sort the issue out, Peter, Paul and Barnabas are not recorded as having appealed to scripture—probably because the bulk of Jewish scripture was against them. Instead, they proclaimed that the Holy Spirit had been lavished on Gentile as well as Jew, a claim they said was verified by "all the signs and wonders that God had done through them among the Gentiles." In a move for which we all can continue to give thanks, the council affirmed the open mission, and the few caveats they included seem quickly to have been ignored (Acts 15:1–21).

The communities that Paul, Barnabas and others established around the Mediterranean were birthed with a DNA for mission, for both the New Testament documents and the record of rapid Christian growth in the Hellenistic world demonstrate that local churches reached out in missional word and deed that multiplied themselves many times over. We get a sense of this from Paul's earliest surviving letter, written to the Christians at Thessalonika, on the east coast of what is now Greece: "For the word of the Lord has sounded forth from you not only in Macedonia and Achaia, but in every place your faith in God has become known, so that we have no need to speak about it" (1 Thessalonians 1:8).

Tension between the internal authority of communities and outside authority continued. Ironically, we see it vividly in Paul himself, who railed against what he regarded as the Galatian Christians' backsliding into Jewish law. He threatened to visit the Corinthian Christians with a metaphorical rod in response to transgressions that horrified him, and he exhorted the Philippian Christians, whom he dearly loved, to join him in trying to reconcile two church leaders at odds with each other. Even as he left elders in charge of each congregation he founded or guided, Paul resented challenges to his authority as an external arbiter of gospel truth and ethical behavior. We see a similar dynamic in the Revelation to John, where the writer reviews the life of seven churches in what is now Turkey and rebukes most of them (Revelation 2–3).

The overall picture is that the early church spawned both tremendous mission outreach from its congregations and the beginnings of the regional groupings led by overseers, presbyters and deacons that later became dioceses. Power was present and authority was exerted from the twin poles of the local and the regional. It may be helpful to see the local and the regional in a symbiotic relationship. The local is where the church lives and grows, yet it has no frame of reference if it acts entirely alone. Worse, it can become anarchic and go astray, which is what Paul feared was happening in Corinth. General oversight helps parts relate to one another, and it maintains consistency. Put another way, the church's history demonstrates that often the greatest vitality is at the edges, where the gospel is encountering new peoples, new movements and new situations. That is where mission innovation breaks out most powerfully. Innovation in mission from the center is not only less likely to happen—such is the nature of central structures—but it is less likely to be successful because it relates inadequately to local conditions. Yet the church on the edges needs a center to relate to, for a sense of identity at the very least, but also as a convening point so that the church's many expressions in mission can be correlated and coordinated.

Mission and the Church's Catholicity

Mission ferment at the grassroots level has the capacity to draw people into renewed awareness of what it is to be the church through time and space. "We believe in one, holy, catholic and apostolic Church," Christians profess in the Nicene Creed. That is the only statement the creed includes about the church, but it articulates essential elements of a theology of the church. The local and global mission undertaken by many congregations and mid-level judicatories is connecting their lived experience with what the creed means in declaring the church to be one, holy, catholic and apostolic. Those offering leadership in mission should help missionaries and mission teams to see their work as an expression of the oneness, holiness, catholicity and apostolicity, or sentness, of the church.

Aside from shared liturgies in Holy Week and at Thanksgiving, mission is the main activity that most congregations undertake ecumenically as they reach out to the suffering in their immediate neighborhoods. Meals ministries, the most common expression of such concern, often require time, people and money beyond the resources of a single congregation, so Roman Catholics, Methodists, Pentecostals, Congregationalists—whatever churches inhabit a neighborhood—share the work of preparing, welcoming, serving and cleaning up. The same goes for homeless shelter ministries. Youth mission trips are often undertaken ecumenically. In all these ventures, Christians who ordinarily stay within their denominational boundaries confirm experientially what they know intellectually—that the church is one. "Yes, I'm a Presbyterian," someone might say, "but by working side by side with Baptists and Methodists in the Loaves and Fishes Food Pantry I've really come to appreciate their gifts and perspectives."

In global mission the *oneness* of the church that people rediscover focuses on the community they experience with Christians in other parts of the world. Not only is the language different, but worship, biblical interpretations, community life, ethical standards and responses to societal conditions may differ, often in startling ways and even with Christians who share their global communion, whether Lutheran, Methodist, Reformed, Roman Catholic or Anglican. Yet missioners often celebrate how beneath the differences they discover a shared faith in the triune God. Sometimes there is ecumenical collaboration, as with the many Presbyterian medical teams that help at the Episcopal L'Hôpital Sainte Croix in Haiti. People in mission often discover churches they never knew existed, for indigenous churches are springing up in virtually all settings, whether in India or China, Mexico or Brazil, Nigeria or Zambia. In all these ways, Christians in mission are able to profess with renewed conviction their belief in the oneness of the church.

The *holiness* of the church derives from the holiness of God, which the Old Testament depicts as the purity of being that distinguishes God from all other beings, even as God is present in and committed to the world. In calling Israel to be holy, God was inviting God's people to share God's otherness and separateness from the mixed motives and behaviors of the world. As the ones called out by God, Christians gathered as the church share the call to holiness. They are able to fulfill that call through being indwelt by God's presence through the Holy Spirit, who shares God's holiness with its members and guides them in carrying out God's work.

One of the most frequent testimonies of church members in mission today is their thrill in experiencing the worship and prayer life of fellow Christians in different parts of the world. Returning from worship experiences in the Two-Thirds World, North American Christian often say things like, "They're so into their worship! . . . The presence of God was so powerful in their services. . . . I was touched by the nightly family prayers, with everyone kneeling down in the living room." In my own experience, the worship of Shona Christians in Zimbabwe continues to open hitherto unknown spaces of worship in my soul, whether I'm with mission-founded churches or African-initiated churches.

The dynamic is also at work for those visiting the West from the Two-Thirds World. "I am so impressed by how people come well before the service to pray quietly alone," said Charles Masina, an Anglican priest from Malawi about his experience of ministry at St. James Episcopal Church in New York City. "I did not expect that from what I had heard about Christians in the United States before coming here." Individual devotion to prayer apart from the public liturgy authenticated for him the personal faith of USAmerican Christians, especially in the context of doubts expressed in Africa. People in mission often rediscover that, despite its weaknesses and failures, the church is yet holy.

The *catholicity* of the church consists in its extension across both time and space and its validity as an expression of Christ's presence in all the circumstances and cultures of that extension. The Episcopal Catechism conceptualizes catholicity in an intrinsically missional way: "The Church is catholic, because it proclaims the whole Faith to all people, to the end of time."[7] The church's *apostolicity* consists partly in its faithfulness to the pattern of life established by the apostles, what theologian Mark Dyer has called the Apostolic Quadrilateral found in the earliest Christian community in Jerusalem: "They devoted themselves to the apostles' teaching and fellowship, to the breaking of bread and the prayers" (Acts 2:42). The other aspect of apostolicity is faithfulness to God's call that we be sent, for sending is the root of the Greek-derived word "apostle." The church's qualities of being catholic and apostolic are intertwined. Those sent to proclaim as apostles extend the church's reach, so that its catholic nature becomes more evident over time. The mission lives into and makes real the world-embracing catholicity that God eternally envisions for the church.

Recently I saw vividly the oneness, holiness, catholicity and apostolicity of the church in mission during a chance meeting with two young Indian missionaries after Sunday morning worship at the ecumenical Church of North India's Cathedral of the Redemption in Delhi. Since 2000, Deva and Sudha Subir have been working to commit the language of the Bhilodi people in Gujarat, a western India state, to written script for the first time and to translate the Bible into that language. In their mid-thirties with two young children, the Subirs themselves are from Tamil Nadu, the region around Chennai in south India. Their work requires them to cross linguistic and cultural boundaries—of which there are many in India—so the Subirs readily identify themselves as missionaries. They spent the first five years of their ministry simply living with the Bhilodi, learning the language and exploring how to commit it to writing. Now they are working on Bible translation in order to strengthen the 1 million Bhilodi Christians and to share the gospel with the other 3.5 million.

The Subirs illustrate how the mission dynamics we have been exploring are at work in diverse parts of the world. Their concern for the Bhilodi came out of simply becoming aware of a people group who did not have the Bible in their own language. They initiated the mission themselves, founding a new organization, Life Giving Word, which receives contributions and publishes news of the work.[8] Yet throughout this very complex and demanding task, they have had technical assistance from Wycliffe Bible Translators, the world's premier scripture translation agency. As longtime members of the cathedral, they receive substantial support from its parishioners, as well as from other congregations. Their mission work is localized, decentralized and democratized. They have become translation professionals on their own, and their ministry certainly exhibits diversification in the church's mission.

As the Subirs link both with the indigenous Bhilodi church and with their home church, they highlight the church's oneness. In their dedication they exemplify the holiness of the people of God. Their sentness expresses the apostolicity of the church and extends its catholicity, which is the church's presence and validity in all times and places.

Notes

1. Linda Bloom, "Mission Agency Stresses Collaboration," United Methodist News Service, April 20, 2010; http://www.umc.org/site/apps/nlnet/content.aspx?c=lwL4 KnN1LtH&b=5847611&ct=8198457&notoc=1.

2. Hunter Farrell, "We're Better Together: Each Member of the Body of Christ Has a Vital Role in God's Mission to the World," *Presbyterians Today*, May 2010, 14; http://www.pcusa.org/ [May 3, 2010].

3. *The Random House Dictionary of the English Language* (New York: Random House, 1987), s.v. http://encarta.msn.com/encnet/features/dictionary/DictionaryResults .aspx?lextype=3&search=democracy.

4. For details of the proliferation of missionary orders and societies, see Stephen Neill, *A History of Christian Missions*, 2nd ed. (New York: Penguin, 1986), esp. 120–334.

5. Hunter Farrell, "We're Better Together," 15.

6. Http://www.britannica.com/blogs/2008/06/collaboration-ownership-and-expertise/; http://en.wikinews.org/wiki/Encyclop%C3%A6dia_Britannica_fights_ back_against_Wikipedia,_soon_to_let_users_edit_contents; http://www.britannica .com/blogs/2008/06/britannicas-new-site-more-participation-collaboration-from-experts-and-readers/.

7. *The Book of Common Prayer* (New York: Church Publishing, 1979), 854.

8. See the Life Giving Word website: http://sites.google.com/site/lifegivingword/ home.

PART II

What Does It Mean to Go Global with God?

"Have you understood all this?" Jesus asked his disciples after shar-ing parables about the reign of God. With a show of confidence they replied, "Yes." Jesus' concluding comment was suggestive and intriguing: "Therefore every scribe who has been trained for the kingdom of heaven is like the master of a household who brings out of his treasure what is new and what is old" (Matthew 13:51–52).

It is through mission that the reign of God is proclaimed and enacted. That was Jesus' mission, and it continues to be God's mission, in which we now join. So a scribe training for the kingdom of God was substantially a scribe training for the mission of God in the world.

Jesus' ministry and teaching startled many through its apparent newness. Yet he built on the old, and said as much many times. So in suggesting to his disciples that they treasure both new and old, Jesus was reflecting on the interplay of tradition and innovation in his own mission.

The themes in Part II set out the nature of mission, the terrain over which mission travels, the direction of God's mission and the emerging mode of mission today. These elements are grounded in the lived experiences of individuals, congregations and the churches. This part's discussions of sent-ness, difference, reconciliation and companionship are shaped by the per-spectives of our day and respond to the needs of the contemporary world. In that sense I am bringing out or surfacing some emphases that may sound or feel new.

There is nothing new, however, that does not build on the old—on the biblical witness, on the record of history, on the wisdom of Christians in cen-turies past. If anything said about the gospel, about God's reign, about going global with God in mission is true, it has at least as much old in it as new. But what is true in the old always calls out for renewal. That is the project we take up now.

CHAPTER THREE

Sent by God:
The Nature of Mission

Amid all the flourishing of mission initiative throughout the churches, Christians are sometimes unclear about what mission is.

Preparing for a mission conference to be held the next day, a regional mission committee told me what they needed most. "It would be helpful to have a definition of mission," said one member. "I'd like people to know the difference between checkbook mission and personal mission," said another. "What's the difference between evangelism and mission?" asked a third.

The committee and the many congregations they were convening were involved in a great deal of what looked like mission to me, so in one sense it might not matter how they were defining mission in their minds. Yet they rightly sensed that over time their vision could blur and their energy dissipate if their understandings of mission were vague and inarticulate.

Jostling for a Mission Focus

People often have differing views about mission's proper focus, so they discuss it and even argue about it. Congregations, regional units, even entire churches and global communions encounter conundrums as they ponder mission, especially when facing the advocacy of partisans of this or that particular emphasis.

"Mission shouldn't be about cramming the gospel down people's throats anymore," say some. "It should meet people's real needs, like food, education, healthcare and sustainable incomes. We're called to care compassionately for the world. The Millennium Development Goals are a good guide for mission today."

"If that's the sum total of Christian mission," say others, "how is the church any different from a development agency? Only we probably won't do it as well as an NGO. How can it be that sharing the good news is outdated? Mission has got to include helping people come to a relationship with Christ."

"You're both too programmatic," a third group weighs in. "Mission is not about doing but about being. We're called simply to be with people and form relationships. If a microenterprise loan program comes out of that, fine. If we're moved to talk about Jesus, that's fine too. And who says it's all one way? We need mission as much as others do, and we'll receive gifts in simply growing together."

"What's wrong with program?" another group retorts. "Jesus certainly proclaimed a program for his ministry at the synagogue in Nazareth, and it's a program about justice, just like Amos proclaimed in the Old Testament. The church needs to get beyond charity and be a force for systemic change that brings justice for the oppressed, both in our own society and around the world."

"Speaking of program," another group puts in, "Jesus gave his disciples a program to preach not only in Judea and Samaria but to the ends of the earth. Evangelism and church-planting have got to be central in the mission of the churches today, especially in a world so alienated and torn by strife. There wouldn't be a worldwide Christian community if people hadn't been faithful to that call."

"But a lot of that strife is between religions, with a good deal of it fomented by us Christians," replies yet another group. "Evangelization and the cultural imperialism that came with it have left lasting wounds all over the world. Now is the time for people of the many religions to listen to each other. Let's take time out for dialogue, and we'll probably discover that's mission, too."

This kind of discussion has been common in mission circles since the early twentieth century and before as Christians have sought to discern the proper direction of mission. The conversation continues in the mission committees of congregations, synods, presbyteries, dioceses and conferences, as well as in scholarly journals and international gatherings.

Approached to sponsor a would-be missionary who felt called to evangelize in Kazakhstan, members of a regional committee wondered how this project fit with the denomination's refrain that evangelism was now the task of the local church, not of outsiders. They wondered about the "frontier mission" agency that the missionary was affiliated with and about what the stance of the proposed mission was toward Islam.

Another committee had money specially designated to achieve the Millennium Development Goals (MDGs) and wondered whether it should go directly to church agencies in the Two-Thirds World or be funneled through missionaries serving there because they function as a bridge between the church at home and the church abroad. Members wondered whether only church agencies doing MDG work directly should be funded or whether supporting the local church itself would be a way of continuing the MDG work that churches have been doing for centuries.

Some members of a short-term mission team getting ready to build houses through Habitat for Humanity in Honduras felt that building the homes was mission enough. Others were anxious because so far there was little sign that local Honduran church members were going to work alongside them, so the mission felt like a parachute jump. Still others wanted to feel free to talk about Jesus with local villagers. The parish mission committee was wondering what guidance to give the team leaders among these competing priorities.

Mission discernment jumped notoriously to the top of secular news coverage when Baptist missionaries based in Idaho sought to rescue orphans after the 2010 earthquake in Haiti and were arrested for kidnapping when they attempted to cross into the Dominican Republic. Cultural presumption and lack of preparation were written all over the situation, but it also provoked widespread press and online discussion about mission priorities. Was rescuing orphans the business of a church in Idaho, or would that be done better by local agencies? Would it be right to take such children out of their country for economic advantages, or should they be cared for within their home culture, even if it meant continuing poverty? Did the missionaries intend to evangelize the children, and if so did they intend to erase possible backgrounds of Catholicism and indigenous Haitian religion?[1]

The various mission options and the adversarial tone in discussions can be confusing for activists in congregations and regional church groupings. Is God's mission just one kind of activity, or can it include various kinds of activity? If we choose one, does it mean we are rejecting the others? Is there a unifying theme in God's mission that can help us sort out different expressions of mission?

Such questions are on the right track because they highlight problems in the debate. Some imagine that mission choices are either-or, when in fact they are often both-and. Mission activists sometimes talk past each other, setting up caricatures of each other and then knocking them down. "Stuffing the gospel down people's throats" is a caricature of evangelism, while "secular do-goodism" is a caricature of concern about poverty, hunger and clean water. The reality is that Christian mission has been remarkably multifaceted over the centuries.

Intense advocates of a particular focus sometimes imagine that their own particular approach to mission is entirely new, a break with the benighted past that will usher in a new era of faithful and authentic Christian mission. The reality is that there is no contemporary direction in Christian mission today that does not have significant precedent in Christian history. Whatever we are enthusiastic about, we are likely to find forebears from fifty years ago, five hundred years ago or fifteen hundred years ago. In fact, that helps account for the long staying power of the Christian mission enterprise and for the deep and wide impact that it has had around the world.

This brings us to an essential question: What is God's mission? Put another way, What is God up to? Is there a theme in God's purpose that brings together the many and diverse ways in which Christians have sought to express God's mission through the ages?

What Is God Up To?

The content of Christian mission has everything to do with what God is up to in the world. Jewish and Christian scriptures testify everywhere that God is up to *something*. Many things are said about the character of God—for instance, that God is loving, patient, eternal, angry, vengeful, forgiving, powerful and so on. Many more things are said about what God *does*. God speaks and hears, creates and destroys, calls and sends, delivers and teaches, abandons and tends. These generic kinds of action are attributed to God in scripture, and even the static qualities that biblical writers attach to God tend to be based on God's record of dynamic action.

Moreover, God's generic actions are expressed through innumerable specific acts: bringing things into being through speaking; flooding the world and then resolving never to do so again; talking with many individuals; delivering the Hebrews from Egypt; bringing down Jericho's walls; allowing the Jews to be taken captive—at least as the scriptures see it—and then delivering them. The New Testament testifies to God sending Jesus and working through his miracles of healing and deliverance; restoring relationship with humanity through the cross; overcoming the power of sin and death through the resurrection; sending the Holy Spirit at Pentecost; calling Peter to the nations through Cornelius the centurion; knocking Saul off his horse to send him to the wider world—just to list a few.

In all that acting, what was God up to? Is there an overall purpose we can discern in what God was up to? If so, what was that purpose, and what does that purpose tell us about what God is up to today?

Framing the first mission question this way clarifies that mission does not begin with us, or even with the church. Mission begins with God. God is the envisioner and initiator. God is where mission begins. Mission likewise is not ours, but rather God's. We do not own mission, nor does the church. God is on mission in the world, so if ownership is an issue, that ownership is God's.

Being on mission, then, is a matter of joining in what God is up to in the world. This means that the first task in mission is not doing but discerning. Discernment involves meditating on the scriptures and listening to the voice of God in prayer. Discernment equally involves opening our eyes to what Jesus called "the signs of the times" and to the signs of God acting amid those times. So any mission work by us must derive from God's mission, whatever it is that God is up to in the world.

What God is up to in the world can be framed as God's *mission,* God's *sending,* because the biblical record makes it clear that God sends God's very self to engage with humanity.[2] Creation itself can be seen as an act of self-sending as God projected God's self into that which had not existed in order to catalyze a community of being in a newly conceived universe. Occasional ambiguity in the Old Testament about whether presences sent by God are simply angels or manifestations of God's own presence—as with Abraham's visitors by the oaks of Mamre (Genesis 18–19) and Jacob's nocturnal wrestler (Genesis 32:24–30)—strengthen the impression that God is eager, even pressing, to be sent into the human situation. Prophets describe their experiences and claim their authority in several expressions—"the word of the Lord came to me," "the hand of the Lord was upon me," and "the Spirit of the Lord was upon me"—all of which convey God's self-communication and self-sending into the human story.

God's self-sending climaxes in Jesus, the Word become flesh and living among us. The sending of the Holy Spirit at Pentecost universalizes and perpetuates God's self-sending. It echoes the many prophetic witnesses to the Spirit's coming in the Old Testament, only now the Holy Spirit's coming is identified with a specific historical outpouring on the entire community of Jesus' followers in Jerusalem. "Repentance and forgiveness of sins is to be proclaimed in his name to all nations," Luke records Jesus as saying, ". . . so stay here in the city until you have been clothed with power from on high" (Luke 24:47–49). The sending of the Spirit, God's self-sending into the Jesus movement, was intended to empower the movement for the work it was to do as a *sent* community, that is, for mission.

Congregations today often celebrate Pentecost as "the birthday of the church." That, however, is secondary to God's self-sending through the Spirit into the company of Jesus' followers so that his work would continue through the community God was now sending into the world. Yes, an entity that soon was called the church, the "called out ones," came into being. Yet it was called out, called into being, for the sake of that which it was sent to do, the mission of God in the world. As Emil Brunner, a Swiss theologian of the twentieth century, said, "The church exists by mission as fire exists by burning; if there is no burning there is no fire; if there is no mission there is no church."[3]

The self-sending of God, the sending of Jesus, the sending of the Spirit and the sending of the church are all intimately related. They can be seen as one continuous out-breathing of God that began with God exhaling into the first earth creature in the second creation story, continued through the prophets' many in-fillings, culminated in the Word made flesh, and then continued as the Spirit came on the disciples and blew them out into the world in a movement continuing through our own day. No wonder Jesus *breathed* on his disciples in conjunction with saying, "As the Father has sent me, so I send you. . . . Receive the Holy Spirit" (John 20:21–22).

Sent across Boundaries to Witness

With this vista on the biblical saga of God's mission, we can offer a comprehensive definition of the nature of Christian mission. *Christian mission is the activity of sending and being sent, by God and by communities, across significant boundaries of human social experience to bear witness in word and deed to God's action in Jesus Christ in the power of the Holy Spirit.*

This definition is grounded in Christianity's scriptural, theological and historical tradition. Mission concerns the sending and being sent that are core to the very meaning of the word "mission." God originates the sending, and the community's sending follows.

The word "mission" comes from the Latin verb *mittere*, which means "to send," and from one of its principal forms, *missum*, which means "I have been sent." In all instances of mission there is some element of sending and being sent. In Christian thought, mission historically concerned the sending within the Trinity: God the Father sent God the Son on mission into the world, and the Holy Spirit was likewise sent to empower the church.[4] The original Greek of the New Testament uses the verb *apostellein* when Jesus sends out the twelve disciples, who are consequently termed *apostoloi*, apostles, meaning "sent ones" (Luke 9:1–2, 10). In the sixteenth century, especially with the founding of the Jesuits, the word "mission" began to be used to denote sending people to other parts of the world on errands of Christian witness, and those sent began to be called "missionaries."

Mission, then, has to do with sending and being sent. People are sent, the senders being church communities, and typically both the senders and the sent ones have faith that God is deeply involved in the sending. Thus missioners often say in the same breath both that they feel sent by God and that they were sent by particular churches or agencies. In this perspective we can restate today's developments in terms of sending and being sent: The tasks of sending are being shared more widely in the churches today, and the number of people who are being sent and who feel sent is larger than it once was.

The specification of significant boundaries of human social experience expresses the essential criterion of difference as the terrain of mission. I will discuss this marker at greater depth in the next chapter, setting out a functional understanding of mission as ministry in the dimension of difference. For now, it is critical to note that being sent across boundaries is what marks the cutting edge of mission and sustains the element of challenge always implicit in mission. This criterion applies to the work of churches in all contexts, among all cultures and ethnic groups, in all parts of the world. Reaching out across boundaries into difference marks off the specifically missional work of churches, regardless of their setting. Thus the definition does not assume any particular geographical directionality, whether North to South, East to West, or vice versa. The only requirement is that the action be directed outward. The ecumenical Friends Missionary Prayer Band, for instance, terms its work "mission" because it sends missionaries, currently more than a thousand, from its base in Tamil Nadu in south India to evangelize and plant churches in north India, where its personnel must learn languages very different from their own and make cultural adjustments similar to those encountered across national borders in western Europe. The Church Mission Society of Nigeria sends missionaries to evangelize in northern Nigeria and in countries such as Mauritania, contexts that are different in both religion and culture. Korean church groups now have almost thirteen thousand missionaries on all continents, the vanguard of the growing majority-world mission movement.[5]

Closer to home, many USAmerican congregations that sent teams to minister in New Orleans after the devastation of Hurricane Katrina in 2005 called their groups "mission teams," a reflex based in the reality that they were being sent to minister to and with people who were very different from themselves and in circumstances very different from their own. The criterion of difference supports the World Council of Churches' 1963 slogan, "Mission In Six Continents," and Michael Nazir-Ali's mission summary, "From Everywhere to Everywhere."[6] When people from one setting are sent to minister in a different setting among people who are different in some major way—that is mission.

The content of what Christians do in mission is stated in terms of Jesus' parting charge, "You will be my witnesses" (Acts 1:8). The content of that witness includes all the activity God pursued in the world in Christ. This formulation is specific enough to have theological content, yet broad enough to include most or all contending views about Christian mission's proper focus, from saving souls to the Millennium Development Goals, from inter-religious dialogue to planting churches.

Mission in Relation to Ministry

The comprehensive definition affirms a common impression about mission and clarifies a common confusion between ministry and mission. The common impression it affirms is that mission concerns initiatives and activities of religious communities beyond their own boundaries, boundaries defined by membership and particular characteristics the membership may have. For example, if someone asks you about your congregation, you may tell her about how fulfilling the worship is or how adult formation forums are excellent but poorly attended. If the inquirer then asks, "And does your church have a mission program?" or "Is your church mission-minded?" you are likely to understand immediately the meaning of the question: "Does your congregation reach out beyond itself to others? Are you involved in the life of the wider community in the town or city? Is the parish connecting with people in other countries and cultures?" The term "mission" is widely understood by church members to refer to the church's engagement with the other who is different from whatever characterizes the social group of the church itself. Thus "outreach" is rightly the most common synonym for mission, and "reaching out" is the phrase most commonly used to signify mission activity.

Sometimes theologians equate mission with the full breadth of God's action in the world, and this can be useful in summing up God's intent in interacting with humanity. More problematically, the full breadth of action to which God calls the church and the human community is said to derive from the mission of God. As a result, all activities that support the church's faithfulness in fulfilling God's call to mission are seen as equally part of the mission. Thus opening the church door, revising a worship book and holding an annual congregational meeting are just as missional, on this view, as engaging refugees in the community, evangelizing in the city square and caring for AIDS orphans in Africa.

An example of this comprehensive understanding of mission is found in the Catechism of the 1979 *Book of Common Prayer* of the Episcopal Church. Its answer to the question, "What is the mission of the Church?" is: "The mission of the Church is to restore all people to unity with God and each other in Christ." This statement can be summed up as reconciliation, and in Chapter Five I suggest that reconciliation is indeed the fundamental direction of

God's mission. But then, to the question, "How does the Church pursue its mission?" the Catechism responds: "The Church pursues its mission as it prays and worships, proclaims the Gospel, and promotes justice, peace, and love."[7] These activities constitute such a comprehensive summary of the church's work that it becomes unclear what in particular makes them all equally missional. Is there no missional difference between a weekly men's prayer breakfast in the fellowship hall and prayers that the evangelism team offers in door-to-door visitation? Between Sunday liturgy in the sanctuary and a liturgy offered at the local psychiatric hospital? Between the youth group's weekly meetings and its summer trip to paint houses of the elderly in Appalachia? Between Sunday School in the church and a parishioner spending three years teaching ex-combatants in a postwar setting in Asia?

One result of refracting God's comprehensive mission into the existing spectrum of the church's activities is that the phrase "the church's mission and ministry" appears often in church leaders' sermons and publications, with no differentiating explanation of the two terms. Everything is comprehended in mission, but ministry still seems a relevant term, so the two are thrown together as a convenient catch-all lest anything be left out. Possibly latent in such usage is the notion that mission is the full range of God's vision and the church's task, and ministry is the operationalization of God's mission through the church's work: worship, education, proclamation, justice and so on. What God is up to is mission, and what we do in participating in God's mission is ministry. This terminology, however, does not do justice to the biblical, historical and theological traditions of reflection on ministry, nor does it recognize adequately the considerable weight that most churches give to ministry, whether that of the baptized or that of the ordained. Similarly, this theoretical assignment of terms tends not to be implemented in practice, for churches continue to highlight as "mission outreach" such initiatives as baskets for the needy at Christmas or a collection for famine victims, and they continue to designate as "missionaries" their members who minister in other cultures.

A more useful way to distinguish ministry and mission is to include within ministry the full range of service to which God calls the church. Ministry thus includes both the work that builds up the community within itself and the work that extends the community's work beyond itself. It is this latter kind of ministry, ministry that travels into the dimension of difference, that is the mission work of the community. Likewise, particular kinds of ministry are found in both the work of the community within itself and in the boundary-crossing work that is mission, whether those are prayer, worship, proclamation, education, healthcare, eldercare or administration. A church is on mission when it is ministering in any of these ways beyond itself, with people and communities who are different from its own. Typically, visiting parishioners in homes and hospitals is inreach, whereas visiting inmates of the local prison is outreach. A physician's work at the local hospital is her ministry, but when she joins a parish group in offering a two-week clinic in Haiti she is on a mission. And a few ministries—evangelization, church-planting and justice work—are intrinsically and always missional in their import and impact, whether in the local area or abroad.

Yet another confusing contemporary use of the term "mission" is found in the mission-statement exercise that corporations, service organizations and government agencies undertake and that has now become common in congregations and church judicatories as they seek to focus on what God is calling them to be and do in their contexts. Microsoft Corporation, for instance, claims this mission: "Create experiences that combine the magic of software with the power of Internet services across a world of devices."[8] In a perhaps over-caffeinated mission statement, Starbucks Coffee states its mission thus: "To inspire and nurture the human spirit—one person, one cup and one neighborhood at a time."[9] Such declarations could more accurately be termed "purpose statements." If "mission" trumps "purpose" in corporate parlance, it is probably because "mission" connotes the urgency and sense of vocation that we know so well in religious mission.

Such blurring of purpose and mission characterizes some churches' adoption of the mission-statement exercise. For instance, St. Mary's Episcopal Church, Laguna Beach, California, articulates its mission as follows:

> To be open to God's love and guidance,
> To embrace all in the name of Jesus Christ,
> To be free to use God's gifts for the daily expression of our faith,
> To work in the power of the Holy Spirit.[10]

With such fusing of the concepts of purpose, mission and sometimes vision, it is natural for the term "mission" to become vague and diffuse, as well as comprehensive.

Some church statements, by contrast, are clear in distinguishing purpose from mission and ministry from mission. Saddleback Church in Lake Forest, California, says that "its purpose is to lead people to Jesus and membership in his family, teach them to worship the Lord and magnify his name, develop them to Christlike maturity, and equip them for ministry in the church, and a mission in the world."[11] Here one of the largest congregations in the U.S. states not its mission but its purpose, not surprising for a church led by Rick Warren, author of two popular "purpose-driven" books.[12] Once the missional activity of making disciples is articulated, the congregation's community life is elaborated as the environment that prepares them for ministry, which is termed as set "in the church," and for mission, which is set "in the world." Such conceptualization accords well with defining mission as the activity of being sent across boundaries of difference to bear witness to Christ in word and deed. The definition, in turn, grounds the particular use of "mission" in this purpose statement, for "in the world" is an environment different from the church community itself.

In contrast to conceptual uses of the term "mission," as in mission statements, practical uses of the term "mission" in secular discourse are premised on a sending into difference. "Space mission" came into common usage because rockets and then astronauts were being sent to explore the radically different environment of outer space where there is no air, no light, no heat, no sustenance. A "diplomatic mission" involves sending a nation's representative to negotiate with a different nation. "Trade missions" involve sending representatives to other countries to discuss international commerce. A "military mission" involves sending armed forces into combat against those of a different nation or nonstate entity. In all these uses, being sent to encounter difference is what prompts use of the term "mission," a premise consistent with the understanding of Christian mission suggested here.

Mission involves sending and being sent. Significant boundaries of human social experience are crossed in mission. With this understanding we are in a position to explore at greater depth the dimension of difference that is mission's terrain.

Notes

1. Much material on the incident is available online. One place to start is: http://titusonmission.wordpress.com/2010/02/04/haitian-orphan-rescue-mission-brings-disgrace-to-christian-mission/.

2. The concepts of God's mission and of God being the source of mission are widely embraced in ecumenical missiology under the Latin term *missio Dei*, literally "mission of God." In addition to being committed to vernacular communication, I do not use that term because the shift to Latin often prompts mission theologians to buttress a particular missional emphasis by associating it with what looks like a technical term. For a brief overview of the rise of *missio Dei* in missiology, see David J. Bosch, *Transforming Mission: Paradigm Shifts in Theology of Mission* (Maryknoll, NY: Orbis, 1991), 389–93.

3. H. Emil Brunner, *The Word and the World* (London: SCM Press, 1931), 108.

4. See, for instance, Thomas Aquinas, *Summa Theologica*, Part I, Question 43, "The Mission of the Divine Persons" in *Basic Writings of Saint Thomas Aquinas*, ed. Anton C. Pegis (New York: Random House, 1945), 1:413–25. "Self-sending" by God is not cited as such by Aquinas, but he argues that a divine person can be sent through a procession in which a divine person "begins to exist where he was before, but in a new way, in which sense mission is ascribed to the divine persons" (Question 43, Article 6).

5. *Christianity Today*, March 2006: http://www.christianitytoday.com/ct/2006/march/16.28.html?start=2.

6. Michael Nazir-Ali, *From Everywhere to Everywhere: A World View of Christian Mission* (London: SCM, 1990).

7. *The Book of Common Prayer* (New York: Church Publishing, 1979), 855.

8. http://counternotions.com/2008/09/22/mission/.

9. http://www.starbucks.com/mission/default.asp.

10. http://www.stmaryslagunabeach.org/.

11. http://www.saddleback.com/aboutsaddleback/index.html. Many congregations define their mission outwardly, among them First Methodist Church in Seattle, which declares, "We're out to change the world," and then clearly distinguishes ministry from mission: http://www.firstchurchseattle.org/who-we-are.html

12. Rick Warren, *The Purpose-Driven Church: Growth Without Compromising Your Message and Mission* (Grand Rapids, MI: Zondervan, 1995); *The Purpose-Driven Life: What on Earth Am I Here For?* (Grand Rapids, MI: Zondervan, 2002).

CHAPTER FOUR

Ministry in the Dimension of Difference:
Mission's Terrain

"I want to meet Jesus!" exclaimed Ranjit Mathews in response to a seminarian's question about why he was interested in international mission. Students were having dinner together after a mission class I was teaching at General Seminary in New York City, and Ranjit had joined us after being interviewed uptown for mission service.

"Can't you meet Jesus here?" asked a young postulant from Atlanta. "Yes, but Jesus wants to get me out of my comfort zone," Ranjit replied. He had grown up in Massachusetts as the child of Indian immigrants, he explained, and the previous year he had gone back to India with his family. At the steps of the Roman Catholic cathedral in Mysore, a young woman about Ranjit's age came to beg from him on a makeshift skateboard because leprosy had taken away her legs. "She put her hand to my bare foot and then to her mouth. I saw Jesus in her, and she saw in Jesus in me. I felt my call to priesthood then." Ranjit told the story with tears.

So Ranjit went to South Africa through the Young Adult Service Corps of the Episcopal Church, worked with the AIDS crisis, and returned to enter Union Seminary in New York, after which he was ordained. Ranjit's life has been defined by difference. Growing up as an Indian American in Massachusetts, he was always aware of the difference embodied in his background, including Malayalam, the mother tongue of his parents' native state of Kerala. He encountered disturbing difference when he visited

India, and out of that turmoil he embraced an African context of difference in God's mission.

Now Ranjit and his wife, Johanna Kuruvilla, are serving as missioners in theological education in Tanzania, and they are still reflecting on difference:

> The exotic tribal dances, sumptuous food and an extraordinary array of people in colorful Tanzanian garb, made us realize the richness that exists in this particular culture. It was such a gift to be a part of the [wedding] celebration. . . .
>
> Life here is different, rather the pace is. We experience a lot less stimulation than what we have been accustomed to—no television (we are very happy about that), sporadic Internet connection, and our conversations on the cell phone are not very clear. We don't have a car so that makes us a lot less independent . . . but it's really, really nice just having time. Time to be, time to think, time to read, time to reflect, spending time with each other, time spent in silence, taking time to say *Habari* to someone. There's something about finding comfort in something new and different.

Insights about spirituality are surfacing out of that experience of difference. A Tanzanian friend named Michael fell into step with Ranjit and Johanna during an afternoon walk in the country:

> We started talking about African spirituality and he said something that has really stayed with us: "People in the West want to know who God is, whereas people here in Africa want to know what God can do. We want a God who can provide us with crops, otherwise our people will starve." His statement was so real, and it cut to the chase of what faith means here in Tanzania: faith not being an appendage, but something so absolutely important to one's survival.[1]

Here we see how difference is the terrain of mission. Disconcerting and magnetic, difference both draws and challenges. Difference stimulates, and paradoxically it can comfort as well. Through difference comes insight into religious experience, insight into God.

Beverley Booth

"As part of our language and orientation experience, we spend time living with a Nepali family," Beverley Booth wrote on arriving in Nepal as a mission coworker of the Presbyterian Church (U.S.A.):

> I spent two weeks living with a middle-class Hindu family here in Kathmandu Valley. The Bisnets are of the Chetri caste, which is just below the highest (Brahmin) caste. It was a fascinating experience to live intimately (and I mean intimately!) with a family of another faith. Much of family life is dictated by the rules of maintaining oneself free of pollution. In fact,

one morning I absentmindedly polluted an entire basin full of clean dishes merely by placing my used tea cup on one of the clean plates in the basin and thereby requiring the entire basin full of dishes to be rewashed.

Having just arrived as a health adviser to the ecumenical United Mission to Nepal, Beverley wanted to convey to her friends and supporters what life in Nepal was like. She did that by highlighting not the similarities but the differences she encountered: a social system arranged by caste, a religious environment of Hinduism—"here in Kathmandu there are temples and idol worship everywhere"—and particular norms of personal hygiene formed by both.

Difference marked this setting off from others. Difference was interesting. Difference was also jarring when she stumbled into an infraction she was not aware was there to commit. Obviously, one of the goals of the orientation experience was to sensitize her to differences so that she would understand her environment better and be able to minister effectively in it. Overall, what was the experience of difference like? "Fascinating," she said.[2]

Melanie Jianakoplos

After three months among the Igorot people in the mountains of the Philippines, Melanie Jianakoplos of the Episcopal Young Adult Service Corps listed "first-timers," or experiences she had had for the first time in her life. They included:

- Home-based funerals with the coffin holding the deceased kept in the home for ten to twelve days of rites and socializing before it was added to other coffins suspended by ropes over a cliff.
- Encounters with rabid dogs that bit people, and later hearing that the dogs were eaten after they were killed.
- Riding on the roofs of vehicles not only for space but because it could be safer than riding inside when mishaps occurred on Filipino roadways.
- Being asked to stand up and introduce oneself in a church service, instead of simply being greeted at the door and asked to sign a guestbook.
- Feeling homesick: "All of the people here would like for me to extend my stay, and I told them that if I could bring my friends and family to Besao I could stay forever, but I can't do that, so I can't stay for more than a year."[3]

The entire environment was different for Melanie, and the external differences prompted particular reactions: fear, interest, exhilaration, acceptance, loneliness, joy. Some of the experiences were disconcerting, but she was intrigued by the differences she was seeing. "I truly feel that this experience as a whole was much more enriching than it was stressful or uncomfortable," she said. Equally significant, Melanie went seeking difference:

> I was planning to apply to seminary for the summer after I finished my undergraduate degree, but having lived in Missouri my entire life, I felt that I really needed to be out of my comfort zone and gain some life experiences before entering the seminary. I am so happy that I made that leap. This experience has been amazing. I have learned so much about myself and this new world.[4]

These reflections from people who have gone global with God highlight a central defining characteristic of mission—the encounter with difference. This feature is what marks off mission from other kinds of ministry. When we are reaching out to different kinds of people in different settings—that is when we are on mission. The different need not be exotic, and it need not be criticized or dismissed as focusing on clichés of the especially traumatic, beautiful or bizarre. No, the different is simply *different* from ourselves, different in some way that is broadly identifiable.

Mission Defined by Difference

As this book focuses on mission that seeks reconciliation in a world of difference, understanding just how fundamental difference is to mission helps us to see that addressing differences in the world is not an optional direction for mission to take. Instead, the encounter with difference defines the basic environment of mission. Whatever particular directions mission activists may emphasize, they pursue those trajectories across boundaries of difference.

We have seen the significance of difference in the previous chapter's definition of the narrative of mission: *Christian mission is the activity of sending and being sent, by God and by communities, across significant boundaries of human social experience to bear witness in word and deed to God's action in Jesus Christ in the power of the Holy Spirit.*

I now take this definition a step further by offering a *functional* definition of mission: *Mission is ministry in the dimension of difference.* It is functional in that it provides a criterion that marks mission off from other kinds of ministry. The difference criterion asserts that Christians and our communities are engaged distinctively in mission when we are reaching out beyond who we are and where we are to encounter and form community with people and communities who are different from ourselves. When we are ministering to and with the other who is different, that is the hallmark of Christian mission.

This criterion of difference helps our reflection in a number of ways. It ties our understanding of mission to one of the most prominent features of life, which is the phenomenon of human difference, whether we find such difference attractive, neutral or repellant. The definition makes explicit the distinctive character of mission that is implicit but often unacknowledged in many discussions that focus on particular theological or practical emphases, such as evangelization, church-planting, social justice or infrastructure development. The criterion of encountering the different is a useful way to compare the practices of churches and the thoughts of theologians. Though I do not explore this here, the definition is useful even among religions—Islam, Hinduism, Buddhism and others—for it provides a measure for comparing mission emphases across the range of human religious experience.

The formulation focuses a commonplace impression about mission, namely, that it concerns engagement with the other. It provides a marker for types of ministry in local and global settings alike, for it applies equally to work around the corner and to work across the world. Similarly, it applies equally to the work of local churches on all continents in distinguishing their mission work, whether those churches are located in Caracas or Cameroun, Cambodia or California. Finally, in highlighting difference, it connects missiology with a major feature of postmodern thought in the twentieth and twenty-first centuries.

Difference Embedded in Mission History

The term "difference" as used here has ordinary meanings: a state of unlikeness, a point of dissimilarity or a distinguishing characteristic. This commonsense understanding is empirically based, yet difference is itself a relative term in two senses. First, it subsists in the relation between phenomena, so something is not different in itself but only *in relation to some other thing.* Second, the recognition of difference depends on observers' perception and assessment of whatever it is that they are experiencing.

This relativity alerts us to the inherent subjectivity of judgments about difference, a subjectivity in which ability to perceive distinctions, and especially social distinctions in the world addressed by mission, is shaped, limited and extended profoundly by personal experience. For instance, a person whose experience has mostly been in a single ethnic community is likely to experience going to a different ethnic community differently than someone who grew up in a cosmopolitan environment in a multiethnic city. People who are used to certain particular differences with groups living nearby can nevertheless be startled when they encounter the differences presented by other groups. Moreover, understandings of identity may depend on prior perceptions of difference: we do not know ourselves until we know the other as well. This point is important as we connect mission with contemporary philosophical thought later in this chapter.

It may seem ironic at this historical moment to suggest difference as a clarifying criterion of mission. Much mission thought and practice in the Global North from the sixteenth through the nineteenth centuries was premised on the view that mission, itself a new concept at the time as applied to the church's work rather than simply to the inner life of the Trinity, concerned only those in cultural groups different from one's own. From the North Atlantic standpoint, mission designated ministry with people groups in Latin America, Asia, Africa and Oceania, where the principal tasks were thought to be gospel proclamation, church planting, infrastructure development and, most ambitiously, the transformation of so-called "pagan" or "heathen" cultures. The emissaries were designated as missionaries, a term understood to apply to persons who ventured beyond their home societies to initiate, continue or extend the church's work in societies other than their own. Missionaries, in other words, were people who engaged difference in the name of Christ.

Many mission organizations were premised on the understanding that mission concerned Christian work in other places in the world, an understanding especially explicit in the full name of the first such Anglican group, the Society for the Propagation of the Gospel in Foreign Parts, founded in 1701. Similarly, the London Missionary Society's aim at its founding in 1795 was "to spread the knowledge of Christ among the heathen and other unenlightened nations." "Domestic" and "home" appeared in the names of some mission societies and boards for work within a church's national borders, and here the primary initial reference was to outreach among groups beyond a church's historic constituency, such as, in the case of the United States, the western frontier or among African slaves and Native Americans.

Mission addressed the not-us, the different, the other, whether at home or abroad. The common plural term "missions" designated both such missionary-sending groups and the multiple institutions they established on frontiers at home or in other parts of the world. In such areas the terms "mission school," "mission hospital"—or simply "the mission" as applied to a complex of church, school, hospital, training center and monastic community—indicated that these institutions had been established by missionaries, people who came from a different culture into a society not their own. Such usage continues today in the receiving societies, long after the churches and their institutions have come under indigenous leadership. Thus the dimension of difference was constitutive in the understanding of what mission was.

Missionaries' letters, travelogues and books detailed the many religious and cultural differences they encountered in their places of work, much as missionaries continue to do today. They also shared their own responses, which included puzzlement, fascination, horror, amusement, fear, distaste, attraction and a desire to understand—a range similar to responses that people in virtually all cultures have today as they encounter human differences. A distinctive of the Global North mission encounter was that it occurred within the historical framework of the impact of the colonial and imperial power of missionaries' home societies on the host societies in the Two-Thirds World. This accelerated a process in which hosting cultures began to adopt some features of the arriving culture so that similarities began to emerge among the differences—use of English, French and other colonial languages; adoption of European dress and diet; spread of capitalist economic patterns; legal prohibitions against practices such as the burning of widows; a common educational system, and the like. Missionaries actively aided some changes that lessened difference and mourned others as the effacement of indigenous culture.

Difference in the Century of Self-Criticism

Difference was assumed as the environment of mission at the 1910 World Missionary Conference in Edinburgh a century ago, though there was little probing inquiry into difference as a category. A number of factors broadened missional understanding in the twentieth century, what I call the Century of Self-Criticism in the mission of Global North churches. The barbarity of World War I and the genocide perpetrated by the Nazis during World War II prompted European and USAmerican Christians to realize anew that their own cultures, supposedly steeped in Christian values, were sources of evil as well as good, and that there might be good in cultures that had different roots. The degree to which Christian mission had benefited from and sometimes collaborated with the colonial expansion of Europe and the United States in other parts of the world undercut the positive view that people previously had of mission's reaching over boundaries of cultural, ethnic and geographical difference. Now such reaching seemed like an imperial overreaching. Moreover, longstanding distinctions between the "civilized" and the "uncivilized" were undermined as North Atlantic peoples realized there were gifts to be received from peoples in other parts of the world. Frontiers of societal difference were no longer borders where Europeans and North Americans were simply conferring gifts on others.

With increased exposure to other religions, North Atlantic Christians could grant that different faiths were valid disclosures of the divine. This undermined positive assessments of Christian mission's reach into religious difference and its traditional concern with conversion. Transformation of "the missions" in the Two-Thirds World into indigenous churches—self-governing, self-supporting, self-propagating and self-theologizing—brought those Christian communities into peer relationships with Global North churches. Here liturgical, musical, theological and even ethical differences were phenomena to explore and, in time, even celebrate, rather than obstacles to overcome and suppress.

The new environment for mission thought prompted significant shifts in the standing of difference. Missiology's grounding became theocentric—focused on God—rather than ecclesiocentric—focused on the church. The churches' mixed record helped to push mission reflection back to God as the source and author of mission. God's mission in the world became determinative theologically, so that the church's mission was seen as derived from God's mission. God was on mission in the world, and the church's role was to discern that mission movement and participate in it. Correspondingly, mission thought became more comprehensive, reflecting on the whole of God's intention and action through the church and in the world.

Mission thinking from the mid-twentieth century onward produced a number of comprehensive views of God's mission. Dutch missiologist J. C. Hoekendijk summarized mission in a triad of proclamation, community and service. Witness has long been a central theme in conferences of the World Council of Churches. Church mission programs focused increasingly on economic and infrastructure development as integral to societal wholeness. In contrast, sheer Christian presence was emphasized as central to mission by Anglican mission leader Max Warren and others. Wholistic evangelization that addressed social conditions as well as spiritual commitments was recovered by the Second Vatican Council of the Roman Catholic Church, the World Council of Churches and, eventually, the Lausanne Movement among evangelical Christians. Liberation was lifted up as key by Peruvian Gustavo Gutiérrez, and liberation theology was elaborated by many theologians in Latin America, Asia and Africa. More recently, reconciliation and its implications for ethnic and political conflict have come to the fore, and currently many people emphasize the Millennium Development Goals as a practical urgency in the twenty-first century. All these emphases have been articulated as grounded in the nature and action of God and as therefore framing the nature of the church's work in the world.

Human differences tend to be pushed to the background in such comprehensive characterizations of mission. For Euro-American mission activists, this served to soothe widespread unease and guilt about the ignorance, insensitivity and arrogance with which the Euro-American mission movement sometimes responded to the cultural and religious differences it encountered in other parts of the world. For mission activists in the Two-

Thirds World, comprehensive themes marked a theological coming of age that transcended historical wounds that could otherwise be fixating.

The advance of secularism in the West also prompted the leveling and even denial of historic assignments of difference in the area of evangelization. The difference between Christian and non-Christian remains, but historic associations have been scrambled when Christian commitment in many African countries far exceeds that of many European countries, signaling that the geography of mission as understood historically in the Euro-American tradition has shifted. "We in the West shouldn't be evangelizing the rest of the world," goes the emerging North Atlantic refrain. "Instead, we need *them* to send missionaries to *us.*" Indeed, traditionally missionary-receiving parts of the world have actually become missionary-senders, and this is especially true in Korea, India and Nigeria.

A subtext implicit in comprehensive reinterpretations of mission has been: "We need to get beyond us-them thinking. And we certainly need to get beyond seeing mission as focused primarily on the exotic. God's mission is to all of us, to all human groups equally, and to the planet. All of us need God's mission." At the same time, a particular emphasis—such as "development," evangelization, interfaith dialogue or liberation—is lifted up as the mission priority for all human groups equally. Particular human differences are considered a minor theme in the face of such a mandate.

Moreover, human difference is experienced as relativized in a polycentric world, for in itself every human group is equally different from every other. Tying mission to the experience of human difference *can* seem a vestige of the rightly outmoded parochial worldview in which Euro-American peoples saw themselves as the standard human beings and others as the different ones who needed to see how they should conform to the standard. But it is not.

The fact of human difference—religious, ethnic, cultural, linguistic, social and so on—is an irreducible premise in all the comprehensive conceptualizations of mission I summarized earlier. Emphasis on God as the source of mission assumes the self-projection of God from the world of spirit (at least in traditional conceptions) into the temporal and material world. This movement into a dimension of difference culminates in the incarnation of God in Jesus Christ. A missional stress on witness is premised on gospel testimony in word and deed to a world that needs such proclamation and that thereby is different in otherwise not being aware of the gospel. The vision of mission as quiet and simple Christian presence proposes a way of encountering and living with difference that may diverge from other modes of mission, but it is no less premised on the fact of difference. Evangelization assumes differences in religious profession. Liberation addresses differences in the distribution of power, and reconciliation responds to differences that have provoked alienation and enmity. Current emphases on mutuality in partnership and companionship suggest that difference should be explored and embraced in community rather than accentuated by competition and effaced by domination.

Likewise the phenomenon of enculturation—the process by which the gospel makes a home in a particular cultural setting—takes place in environments of cultural difference. The study of enculturation in mission wrestles with difference as its basic raw material as it analyzes the mutual perceptions of difference between peoples and missionaries, and peoples' perception of the differences between biblical revelation and their preexisting worldview. Similarly, formation programs for missionaries preparing to serve cross-culturally tend to focus chiefly on how missionaries should perceive, understand, adjust and respond to differences they encounter in their places of service.

Exploring the Difference Criterion

Mission is ministry in the dimension of difference. But what kind of difference?—the differences experienced in crossing significant boundaries of human social experience. This means mission involves crossing boundaries, boundaries that are significant by virtue of being sociologically identifiable— easily identifiable in the society, as Ranjit, Beverley and Melanie noted in the stories at the start of this chapter.

The boundaries may be religious, cultural, linguistic, racial, ethnic, sexual, economic, political, national, educational, professional and geographical—any one of these, any combination of these, and others as well, so long as they are major and socially identifiable. The inherent relativity and subjectivity of assessments of difference and identity mean they should not be ossified in rigid and static categories.

Yet the importance of these differences at any particular point of time is clear from the fact that the great oppressions in the human community are grounded precisely in such differences. We see that in gender violence, sexual slavery, tribal warfare, ethnic cleansing, interreligious conflict and, as ever, war between nations. In all these cases, people have responded to perceived differences in ways that caused conflict, broke relationship and built oppression.

The phrase "dimension of difference" invites reflection on difference as a category of human experience. It prompts us to reflect not only on specific differences but also on difference as an existential and social experience and on questions of perspective and identity that it raises. How do I experience and define my social location and the group or groups of which I understand myself to be a member? What assumptions about identity operate in our experience? What particular privileges and disabilities do we experience in our group, relative to other groups? How do our concepts of difference relate to our concepts of commonality with other human groups? What anxieties and fears do my social group and I experience as we engage the prospect of encounters with people who are different from us in major ways? What joys and discoveries do we anticipate as we engage such difference? Beyond the particulars of one's own group, the concept of the dimension of difference invites historical, sociological and philosophical reflection on difference within one's society and on the world stage.

Engaging these questions honestly encourages us to take full account of the integrity of other persons and groups and of ourselves. This stance keeps us from avoiding the gravity of human differences. It is such avoidance that sometimes prompts people to say, even before a genuine encounter has occurred, "Oh, I just know we're going to get along, because really we're all the same." This is "cheap grace" that conceals a fear of acknowledging difference and a desire that the other conform to oneself. A joy of cross-cultural encounter is the realization of shared community in a common humanity, but difference must be explored and accepted if that experience of community is to be authentic.

There is a common negative association of mission that the difference criterion engages head-on. The most prevalent critiques of Christian mission today concern quite precisely how missionaries and their churches responded to difference, that is, to the differences they encountered in the societies to which they went. Challenge is launched mainly on two fronts: religion and culture. It is commonly thought that missionaries condemned wholesale the different religions they encountered in the Two-Thirds World and in North America, and that they insisted that the peoples they found both become Christian and embrace the particular missionaries' brands of Christianity. It is also commonly thought that missionaries condemned wholesale the different cultures they encountered and insisted that the peoples they found adopt the missionaries' languages and ethics and their styles of eating, housekeeping, dressing and the like.

The charges are often inaccurately universalized to include all missionaries in all times and places. Yet the substantial truth of the charges in many instances has prompted the missionary movement to critique itself thoroughly along these lines, especially since 1900. The point here is that differences among human groups and how to approach them are the issues at stake in the critique. The difference criterion does not seek to shift the ground of mission's definition to some other criterion. It rather accepts the encounter with difference as the pivotal criterion of mission both in the past and going forward. It assumes the need to discuss further how we encounter and respond to difference.

We know intuitively the importance of difference in the life of the church. A common self-critique in many congregations is that their prayer, worship, education and fellowship are flourishing but that the community is not reaching beyond itself to encounter others, with the result that the congregation is becoming complacent and self-absorbed. Here the congregation is identifying a failure to cross the boundaries of difference that are peculiar to mission. Often people intuit that personal growth is a fruit of responding to the challenge to minister "outside their comfort zone," as Ranjit Mathews and Melanie Jianakoplos put it.

A less common self-critique is that a congregation is so engaged in outreach—that is, in difference-engaging mission—that it is neglecting its mutually supportive community life, with the result that members are becoming fatigued and jaded. Community and mission are symbiotic: community without mission dies out, and mission without community burns out. The distinction between community and mission is clear, and it is grounded in the criterion of difference.

A related dynamic is the aspiration of many North American congregations and church institutions to become more *diverse*. Racial diversity is the most frequent reference, but cultural, national, linguistic and economic diversity are often included, as well. This aspiration expresses an intuition that fulfilling the mission of the congregation, denomination, school or seminary involves engaging difference and drawing in people different from the existing majority group. If the congregation or school is monochrome— whether white, black, Asian or Hispanic—there is a nagging sense of a neglected mission frontier. Conviction that the whole people of God should include all available local ethnicities prompts conversation about outreach to the groups not represented. Conversely, a congregation that includes an ethnic, international and linguistic rainbow often exults in the fulfillment of its mission, because it has succeeded in crossing boundaries of difference and drawing a diverse range of people into its midst. Again, people realize instinctively that difference is the cutting edge of mission and that it is integral to the community's health and fullness.

The difference criterion affirms the now commonplace relativizing of the geography of Christian mission. A frequent critique of preoccupation with "overseas mission" or "foreign mission" is the observation, "Well, mission is not only over there but here in our backyard too." This is true, so long as the criterion of difference is fulfilled. A congregation may be very missional while never venturing beyond the county line, because it is reaching out to, say, the unchurched or an immigrant group or victims of an apartment building fire or a particular addiction group. In practice, however, missional congregations tend to reach out both locally and globally, because they find that mission in one context stimulates mission elsewhere, and multiple and diverse mission experiences inform and enhance each other. The difference criterion applies to both the local and the global, and it prioritizes neither.

Highlighting the difference criterion acknowledges the conflicted state of the world as we know it. The world is dying of difference. I mean this in the sense that millions of people die because of socially constructed differences to which life-and-death valuations have been attached. The implicit human attitude behind such social constructions and valuations is something like this: "You and your group are different from me and my group, so you are not as important as I am. So it's all right if you have less food and shelter, less security, less freedom, less opportunity—even a lot less. You do not deserve these things, because you are different. Maybe you don't even deserve to live." The successive genocides of Jews, Cambodians, Bosnians, Rwandans and Darfuris since 1940 are instances, as are the wars in Korea, Vietnam, Sri Lanka, Liberia, Congo, Iraq, Afghanistan and Israel/Palestine. Discrimination and violence based on race, ethnicity, gender, age, national origin, sexual orientation and religion express perceptions of difference. These are equally though more subtly active in the world's continued toleration of abject poverty and its many attendant ills. As Christian mission seeks to participate in God's healing of the world, understanding itself in terms of engaging difference is a crucial starting place.

Biblical Resonance for Grounding Mission in Difference

Sending and being sent are essential to Christian mission, as we have seen in the previous chapter. Scriptural grounding for the difference criterion of mission is found in the biblical stories of sending and being sent. There we find that encounters with difference are the terrain of major biblical instances of sending and being sent. Missional sending in the Bible tends to be directed into environments of difference.

The call of Abram articulates God's promise and blessing in the context of a sending in which leaving the familiar and going to the new and different are intrinsic: "Go from your country and your kindred and your father's house to the land that I will show you." The world of difference becomes explicit in the promise's conclusion, where God assures Abram that he will make a difference in a world defined by difference: "And in you all the families of the earth shall be blessed" (Genesis 12:1–3).

Jonah was sent into an environment of difference: Ninevah. In this Assyrian city he expected that Yahweh's call to repentance would be greeted with the contempt due to a local deity with no sway beyond local borders and certainly not in the great temples of the Assyrian cults. The fear that encounter with difference evokes in the prospective emissary, especially when on a religious errand, is spelled out in one of scripture's more vivid narratives, the marvel of which is that a people so different are said to have repented so immediately (Jonah 1:1–3; 3:6–9).

Missional sending into difference is prominent in John's reflection on the very event of Jesus in the prologue to his gospel. The incarnational declaration—"The Word became flesh and lived among us" (John 1:14)—brings together two terms that were regarded as categorically incompatible with each other: ordinary human flesh and the exalted Greek philosophical concept of the eternal Word (*logos*) in the universe. That Word, understood by John to be the Word of God, entered, took the form of, actually *became* that from which it could not be more different: flesh. John's prologue echoes the creation story of Genesis 1: as God created humanity in God's image at the beginning of time, so now God embarks on humanity's re-creation and renewal in Christ. The connection between the two narratives reminds us that God's primordial creative activity was a venture into difference, as God who is spirit brought into being a universe rich in both matter and spirit.

John's use of the phrase "into the world" (*kosmos* in Greek), in conjunction with the concept of sending, emphasizes the embrace of difference that the incarnation embodied. "I have come as light into the world," says Jesus (John 12:46). Martha exclaims, "Yes, Lord, I believe that you are the Messiah, the Son of God, the one coming into the world" (John 11:27). In prayer Jesus connects his own being sent with that of his disciples: "As you have sent me into the world, so I have sent them into the world" (John 17:18). The identification of Jesus as the Word who was with God and was God (John 1:1) means that his being sent into the world constitutes a self-sending by God, God sending God's very self in the Word who was the Son. This self-sending constitutes movement across a boundary of difference.

Jesus' preaching of the reign of God was shared with all equally, but a disproportionate number of the stories of encounters with particular individuals are devoted to his ministries with those residing on the other side of a boundary: the Gerasene demoniac, the Roman centurion's servant, the anointing sinful woman, the Samaritan woman, the woman caught in adultery, Zaccheus the tax collector, numerous lepers and others.[5] The synoptic gospels record that this boundary-crossing ministry was so intrinsic to Jesus' ministry that he developed a reputation for consorting with tax collectors and prostitutes, people whose Jewishness was compromised by the moral failings of enemy collaboration and sexual promiscuity.[6] From Jesus' standpoint, his difference-engaging ministry was extending and redefining God's covenant community, but for the religious authorities this involved boundary violations that polluted community purity and faithfulness to God. In defending his outreach in parables—the Good Samaritan, the Pharisee and the tax collector, the lost sheep—Jesus portrayed God as reaching people over differences. He sought to persuade people that salvation lies in true faithfulness, not in inherited identities and purity codes.[7]

In his account of the Canaanite woman's faith in the district of Tyre and Sidon, Matthew records Jesus confining his sentness to Israel—"I was sent only to the lost sheep of the house of Israel" (Matthew 15:24)—but this understanding of a purely local calling is challenged immediately and successfully by the foreign woman's importunity. She is not only characterized as different ethnically and nationally, a Gentile Syrophoencian (Mark 7:26), but also as a Canaanite, which in Israelite history evoked religious abhorrence and national enmity (Matthew 15:21–28). It is fair to conclude that she expanded Jesus' understanding of his calling to include a sending to the Gentiles. Looking to the future, Jesus saw God's reign culminating in a judgment over all the nations (Matthew 25:31–46) and consummated in an embrace of human differences at the messianic banquet: "Then people will come from east and west, from north and south, and will eat in the kingdom of God" (Luke 13:29).

Sending is explicit in Luke's account of Jesus dispersing the twelve disciples: "He sent them out to proclaim the kingdom of God and to heal" (Luke 9:2). No geographical extent or limitation is mentioned, but it is understood that they would be arriving as strangers, and the disciples became apostles in the act of being sent. Their initial trajectory, like Jesus' own, was "to the lost sheep of the house of Israel" (Matthew 10:1–6), but the elaborated instructions clearly envisage proclamation to nations beyond Israel, for the disciples would be "dragged before governors and kings because of me, as a testimony to them and the Gentiles" (Matthew 10:18). Matthew ends his gospel with Jesus saying to the disciples, "Go therefore and make disciples of all nations" (Matthew 28:19). Luke reiterates this sending to "all nations" in closing his gospel (Luke 24:47), and his second account of the ascension extends it "to the ends of the earth" (Acts 1:8). All these dominical sendings are into environments of difference where the people to be encountered are different in major ways from those in the originating community.

The outpouring of the Holy Spirit at Pentecost presaged the church becoming a transcultural Mediterranean entity, as people of different languages and nationalities heard "about God's deeds of power" (Acts 2:11). This vision was fulfilled initially not so much through obedience to being sent but through the geographical dispersion of the Jesus Movement following the persecution that began with the stoning of Stephen (Acts 8:1–4). Yet the initiatives of Peter and John in Samaria and Philip with an Ethiopian official, each encounter on a frontier of difference, resulted from explicit sendings by the community or by the Holy Spirit (Acts 8:14, 26, 29).

The boundary-crossing initiative of the early Christian community that was both its greatest challenge and its lifeline to survival was the incorporation of Gentile believers into the body of the faithful without the intermediate step of entering Judaism. For Jews, Gentiles constituted a boundary of difference of the greatest magnitude. Peter's venture with the Roman centurion Cornelius at Caesarea emerged from sendings by the Holy Spirit, as Cornelius sent servants to Joppa and Peter accompanied them home (Acts 10:5–8, 17–22). The commission Paul received through Ananias at his conversion explicitly affirmed proclamation to Gentiles: "He is an instrument whom I have chosen to bring my name before Gentiles and kings and before the people of Israel" (Acts 9:15).

In defending to the Galatians his work among Gentiles, Paul characterized both Peter's errand to Jews and his own to the nations as prompted by God's sending: "He who worked through Peter for an apostolate for the circumcised worked through me also [for an apostolate] for the Gentiles" (Galatians 2:8; my translation). "Apostolate" here represents the Greek *apostolen*, a "sending" or "mission" (as in the Revised Standard Version translation).[8] Clearly Paul saw himself as sent to the Gentiles, an understanding that grounds the historic association of the word "mission" with Paul's outreach and supports the association of mission with engaging difference. When at the far end of his ministry Paul summarized to Roman Christians the story of his mission, it was clear that crossing geographical boundaries and their associated ethnic and cultural boundaries was central—"from Jerusalem and as far around as Ilyricum"—as was the crossing of religious boundaries— "not where Christ has already been named" (Romans 15:19–20).

Sending is intrinsic to the concept of mission of any kind. The biblical data indicate that major developments related to the extension of God's reign in the world are closely associated with God, Christ or the Holy Spirit sending individuals to undertake particular initiatives. The more major of these sending initiatives concern encounters with persons and groups who were different from those who were sent, different in ways that are sociologically identifiable. Indeed, environments of difference seem to call forth narratives of sending and being sent. It is around this dimension of difference that historically the term "mission" has gathered. Thus testing mission according to the criterion of difference has solid biblical warrant in scripture's association of sending with encountering human difference.

Difference and Mission in Contemporary Thought

Valuing and cherishing difference stands against the forces of the world that use difference as a basis for competition, exclusion and violence. It is striking that progressive movements today join the churches in valuing diversity of all kinds in education, government and the full range of workplaces. This drive appeals to basic ideals of justice and evokes eschatological visions of a peaceable kingdom, a reconciled world.

The global advertising campaign of HSBC, which bills itself as "the world's local bank," provides an interesting instance of reflection on difference. The campaign features many tableaux of three identical photographs, each of which bears a different single word or phrase indicating different potential responses to the image. The three responses to a photograph of a backpack are debt, fear, adventure; to a couple on their wedding day: fate, fear, fairy tale; to a passport: adventurous, proud, elusive; to a car: polluter, status symbol, freedom; and so on. On explanatory panels, HSBC says, "We recognize how people value things differently," and "The more you look at the world, the more you recognize that what one person values may be different to the next." These meditative pieces resonate well with how the exploration and acceptance of difference is part of the global cultural agenda today.

Any observer can see that the universe is an environment of infinite difference, a reality that biblical faith says proceeds from the infinite creativity of God. Emphatically nonreligious postmodern philosophy suggests that identity and difference as categories of human experience may not only be mutually dependent. If anything, the identity of any particular thing, including the human self, may be knowable only on the basis of prior experience of things that are different. "Conceiving the same on the basis of the different" makes identity secondary to and derivative from difference, according to French philosopher Gilles Deleuze.[9] Moreover, postmodern philosophy speculates that difference may be prior to identity not only in the order of knowledge, or epistemology, but in the order of being, or ontology.

Philosopher and theologian Jonathan Sacks, chief rabbi of the United Hebrew Congregations of the Commonwealth, writes with urgency about difference in the wake of the attacks of September 11, 2001. Hoping to stall "the clash of civilizations," he calls for a shift away from a Platonic view that true knowledge is to be found in universals that generalize from particulars. Universalist cultures, Sacks argues, have historically viewed particularities as "imperfections, the source of error, parochialism and prejudice," and therefore have marginalized and diminished difference in favor of universal categories and goals. Instead, he says, knowledge and wisdom are accessible from the particulars of human communities that distinguish them from other human communities, that is, in difference. Sacks declares, "We need . . . not only a theology of commonality—of the universals of mankind—but also a theology of difference: why no one civilization has the right to impose itself on others by force: why God asks us to respect the freedom and dignity of those not like us."[10]

Where past philosophical stress on the reality of the particular, as opposed to the universal, has entailed religious skepticism, Sacks argues instead for the integrity of the particular and the different in the revelation and work of God. Certainly a theology of difference would begin with the diversity intrinsic to the creative work of God and would develop the ways in which humanity has distorted God's abundance of difference to create a virtual taxonomy of sin, of which the urge to dominate and suppress difference is a major expression.

The Christian mission enterprise is the world's most extensive and longest sustained intentional engagement with human difference. The recent philosophical insistence on the integrity and autonomy of difference calls on us in mission to think about our stance toward difference, given that mission's errand in a world of difference is founded on a revelation that celebrates both the universal and the particular. Further, postmodernism's exploration of the priority of difference over identity may be helpful in explaining the perennial Christian conviction that engaging the other who is different is intrinsic to Christian faithfulness, a conviction that is evident in scripture and in Christianity's missional reflex over two millennia.

The other who is different presents a frontier over which the journey of understanding is both outward and inward, both receptive and reflexive. Knowing the other authentically requires mature self-knowledge, yet such maturity is not accessible to the isolated self, or the isolated society or the isolated culture—or the isolated church. We do not and cannot know ourselves truly without knowing the other as well. That, I believe, is a major intuition and motivation for many or most who go out in Christian mission.

Similarly, the gospel understanding that Christians of any particular setting have—and the setting may be a region, culture or church—is intrinsically and inevitably partial and incomplete. Every Christian community, regardless where it is located, needs the perspective and insight about the gospel that other communities can offer from experiences and worldviews that are shaped differently. The truth of what God has done in Christ Jesus in the power of the Holy Spirit is ultimate, universal and final, but our apprehension of it is limited, contextual and provisional. This very provisionality draws us into a pilgrimage into difference through which we hope to see less dimly, toward that place where we will see face to face.[11]

Difference, in sum, is foundational in human experience, which includes our religious experience. As the criterion of Christian mission, difference must be similarly foundational in the reflection of those who feel called to join God in mission.

Notes

1. The website of Ranjit Mathews and Johanna Kuruvilla: http://www.joranjtanza nia.blogspot.com/.

2. Beverley Booth's blog: http://www.pcusa.org/missionconnections/letters/boothb/boothb_0007.htm.

3. Melanie Jianakoplos's complete list of "first-timers" appears at: http://melanies pineapplediaries.blogspot.com/2009/10/first-timers.html.

4. Melanie Jianakoplos, personal correspondence with author.

5. Mark 5:1–20; Matthew 8:5–13; Luke 7:35–50; John 4:1–42; John 8:3–11; Luke 19:1–10; Mark 1:40–45 and Luke 17:11–19.

6. Luke 15:1–2.

7. Luke 10:25–37; 18:9–14; 15:3–10.

8. NRSV represents the sense, though not the syntactical form, of the Greek: "He who worked through Peter making him an apostle to the circumcised also worked through me in sending me to the Gentiles."

9. Gilles Deleuze, *Difference and Repetition*, trans. Paul Patton (London: Continuum, 2005), 50–51. See also Michel Foucault, "Theatrum Philosophicum," in *Language, Counter-memory, Practice: Selected Essays and Interviews by Michel Foucault*, trans. and ed. Donald F. Bouchard (Ithaca, NY: Cornell University Press, 1977).

10. Jonathan Sacks, *The Dignity of Difference: How to Avoid the Clash of Civilizations*, rev. ed. (New York: Continuum, 2003), 19–20, 21.

11. Part of this chapter appears in Titus Presler, "Mission Is Ministry in the Dimension of Difference: A Definition for the Twenty-first Century," *International Bulletin of Missionary Research* 34, 3 (2010).

CHAPTER FIVE

Reconciliation:
The Direction of God's Mission

"Apartheid was a terrible time. I don't how I can explain it. Klerksdorp was a white town. Blacks were not allowed to stay in town. Blacks were not allowed even to walk on the pavement." William Lolwane was talking about his hometown, which is about a hundred miles southwest of Johannesburg. He went on to describe his church and what happened there in the first decade of the twenty-first century: "St. Peter's was a white church. I was not allowed to worship there. Today at St. Peter's, things have changed. In one short year, Father James has succeeded in uniting the different racial groups in the church, so that now we are able to worship the Lord as one."

James and Lorine Williams have been Episcopal missionaries in South Africa since 1999. Hailing from Buffalo, New York, they serve in the Anglican Diocese of Matlosane, where Lorine is a deacon and James pastors St. Peter's Anglican Church and handles various diocesan responsibilities.

"South Africa is a model for the rest of Africa and for the entire world in that there was not a bloodbath and slaughter at the end of apartheid," James says in the *Windows on Mission* film series. "And this is due to a very large extent to the capacity of the African population to forgive—not necessarily to forget—but to forgive and to reconcile the differences that they had. We constantly see this sense of forgiveness each and every day."

Here James focuses on difference, which we have seen is a fundamental element of human experience and thus of mission. He identifies one response to difference as the root of apartheid and another response to difference as the root of the new South Africa's reconciling witness to the world. Instead of repaying the former oppressors with fear, suppression and exclusion, black South Africans are responding to the history with forgiveness and reconciliation.

Longtime white parishioner Isobella Marais celebrates in the film what she calls "the day the door of this church was opened to all nations, because that's what the Lord Jesus said in Matthew. His last words were, 'Go into all the world and make disciples of all the nations.' That's where the blessing lies—all the nations and us, worshiping together."

In uniting racial groups at St. Peter's, James and Lorine brought with them their experience as African Americans working through racial crises in the United States. They went out of their way not only to welcome all racial groups—blacks, whites, Indians, coloreds—but also to get to know and cherish each individual in the parish. They turned that cherishing into a physical artifact as they inscribed the names of parish households on a giant "Scroll of Thanks" that they hung in the sanctuary. Then at a parish *braai*, or cookout, they gave each household an individual scroll of thanks with comments of tribute to each. There were tears of joy. People were experiencing and celebrating reconciliation.[1]

Reconciliation amid difference, I suggest, is the direction of God's mission in the world. Reconciliation is what God is up to.

From Alienation to Restoration

The verb "reconcile" comes from the Latin verb *reconciliare*, and it means most basically to restore persons and communities to friendship or harmony. Restoration implies previous disturbance, so reconciliation is premised on a situation in which relationship has suffered. The degree of disturbance can range from alienation and estrangement to enmity and hostility, and it may be expressed in acts ranging from silence and shunning to covert and overt relational subversion and to verbal and physical violence.

Reconciliation in itself is the healing of relationship. In ordinary conversation, metaphors abound for the transformation that reconciliation brings. What is torn is mended. What is broken is repaired. What is wounded is made whole. Those walking away now walk toward. The brush-off becomes an embrace. Closeness replaces distance. People walking apart now walk together. Those who looked away now look each other in the eye. In relational terms, there is movement from suspicion to trust, from alienation to cordiality, from isolation to collaboration, from hostility to friendship.

The joy of reconciliation is that of joy restored. Something good and loving used to exist, and then it disappeared, or it was withdrawn or destroyed, whether by one's self, the other or a combination of the two. What was a garden became a relational wilderness, with no particular hope surviving that it would ever be restored. Something previously vital is missed and mourned. Then it comes back. The return may be sudden and inexplicable, or it may be the result of a drawn-out and even tedious struggle. But when the relationship is restored and friendship or love returns, there is an extra measure of joy compounded of recognition, reentry and relief.

Bernie and Farsijana Adeney-Risakotta are Presbyterian "mission coworkers" who teach in Indonesian universities. Farsijana directs a center for research and community development and leads the Indonesian Women's Coalition, which works to empower women and mobilize for relief after natural disasters. Bernie directs the Indonesian Consortium for Religious Studies, the only cooperative program worldwide among secular, Christian and Muslim universities.

Working together with Christians and Muslims to build a just society in the world's third largest democracy, Bernie and Farsijana built their home in an all-Muslim neighborhood and use it for hospitality and community outreach. Clearly the Christian-Muslim divide is one of the major fissures in the world community in the twenty-first century, with political, ideological and military ramifications, as well as theological issues. Not only do the Adeney-Risakottas teach about interreligious relations and carry out projects with both Muslims and Christians, they have offered their home life for the project of building bridges between communities and fostering friendships between individuals who might not otherwise have contact with one another.[2] In the contemporary environment, that is a work of reconciliation.

"If you know and respect my religion, you respect the deepest part of me," said a child at one of the summer camps of Kids4Peace, an interfaith initiative that brings Jewish, Christian and Muslim children together for mutual understanding in programs in Jerusalem, Atlanta and Vermont. "What began as a reaction to violence and suffering is now much more proactive," says founder and former missionary Henry Carse. "The interfaith learning that these children inspire is the first step in a new culture."[3] Clearly in the context of the Middle East but also on a global scale we might term it a new culture of reconciliation.

Amid the disputes that are afflicting Christian world communions today, people yearn to restore relationships that have been strained or broken by controversies such as the turmoil about different approaches to human sexuality. Following the 2009 decision by the Evangelical Lutheran Church in America's Churchwide Assembly to allow people in committed same-gender relationships to be on the church's official ministry rosters, Presiding Bishop Mark Hanson said, "We finally meet one another not in our agreements or disagreements, but at the foot of the cross, where God is faithful, where Christ is present with us, and where, by the power of the Holy Spirit, we are one in Christ."[4] Making the theme of reconciliation more explicit, a Lutheran congregation in Charlotte, North Carolina, held what it called a service of reconciliation to bring together people who had a variety of responses to the assembly's decision.[5]

The Indaba Mutual Listening Process of the Anglican Communion, roiled by the sexuality controversy now for more than a decade, does not seek or encourage persuasion by either side, much less unanimity. Based on a Zulu model of consultation, Indaba's purpose is to develop patterns of listening and conversing over the divide of deep differences so that relationship can grow and Christians collaborate in mission together. Disagreement may continue, but the aim is to build the relational capacity that will support shared mission amid disagreement. Such flourishing in mutual listening and mission collaboration requires reconciled relationships.[6]

Reconciliation is more explicitly on the agenda of the world community today than it has been before. Spurred by the Truth and Reconciliation Commission that sought healing in South Africa after apartheid, people in many communities are recognizing reconciliation as central to healing after mass atrocities and violence. Rwanda's National Unity and Reconciliation Commission was designed to illuminate the decades-long ethnic tensions that built up to the 1994 genocide and to develop a national reconciliation strategy. Given the large number of imprisoned perpetrators, *gacaca*, a traditional community-based healing process, was activated to help establish truth, explore the trauma and offer justice.[7]

Canada's Truth and Reconciliation Commission was appointed in 2009 to discuss experiences and impacts of the residential schools' earlier oppression and abuse of First Nations children and to work toward respect and reconciliation between Aboriginal and non-Aboriginal Canadians.[8] Canadian churches, some of which participated in the residential schools system, have reconciliation efforts that work alongside the national initiative. Anglicans, for instance, are committed to ongoing efforts to "live out" the public apology made in 1993 by then-Archbishop Michael Peers for the church's role in the Indian residential schools that it operated between 1820 and 1969.[9]

Commissions to clarify truth and foster reconciliation have worked with varying success to bring healing after oppressive regimes and civil wars in Chile, El Salvador, Guatemala and Peru. Some have suggested similar efforts in the wake of communal violence in Northern Ireland and slavery in the United States. Today leaders in government and civil society call for reconciliation after and even during wars, such as those in Sri Lanka, Congo, Iraq and Afghanistan. An often-cited diplomatic achievement of USAmerican foreign policy after World War II was that former enemies Japan and Germany became major allies. While "reconciliation" as a term did not appear so often in that era, the shift would have been impossible without many and widespread steps to reconcile.

Reconciliation is the theme underlying all forms of Christian mission, whether evangelism or poverty reduction, social justice or medical care. Reconciliation is key whether the mission is expressed in South Africa or South Central Los Angeles, whether it is addressing race, religion or gender relations, and whether it is happening in the drama of warring parties or in the anonymous and oppressive injustice of long-term poverty.

Reconciliation in Scripture and Theology

Both scripture and the theological tradition of reflection on scripture testify that the fundamental fact of the human condition is estrangement from God. We see it in the Garden of Eden, as Adam and Eve hide themselves from God after eating from the forbidden tree. Creatures bearing God's image and thus created for friendship with God now treat God as stranger and adversary. God's calling out to them in the evening breeze, "Where are you?" (Genesis 3:9) can be taken as the cry of God throughout the drama of biblical revelation. We are used to hearing the question posed from *our* side as people in desperation cry, "Where *are* you, God?" The reality is not that God is hidden, but that God is seeking. *We* are the hidden ones, concealed in the effects of sin. "Sin is the seeking of our own will instead of the will of God," says a contemporary catechism, "thus distorting our relationship with God, with other people, and with all creation."[10]

The estrangement brought by sin inspires much of God's action throughout scripture, as God consistently seeks reconciliation with humanity. Enslaved but skeptical Hebrews cried out for deliverance in Egypt, so Yahweh released them through the ministry of Moses. Despite their persistent doubt and criticism, God gave them water, manna and quail to assuage thirst and hunger in the wilderness. Entering the promised land, God intervened on their behalf before the walls of Jericho, but the Chosen People continued to vacillate between faithfulness and rebellion. Even as prophets read Israel's exile in Babylon as God's punishment for sin, they also described God as longing for restored relationship with Israel.

The nature of reconciliation is dramatized in one of the most moving reunions in all of scripture, the return of Jacob, son of Isaac, who stole the birthright of Esau by deceiving their father and then fled his brother's wrath. On his way back to Canaan, family and wealth in tow, Jacob attempted to sleep and instead experienced a night of wrestling. In those painful and lonely moments, he confronted how cavalierly he had treated both God and his brother and entered the wasteland of his own sin. He was terrified to imagine how Esau might receive him, so he sent his possessions and family ahead and bowed and scraped his way toward his brother. Against all expectation, Esau ran to meet him, and embraced him, and the two of them wept. Overwhelmed by being forgiven, Jacob exclaimed, "Truly to see your face is like seeing the face of God—since you have received me with such favor" (Genesis 33:10).

The onerous prophecy Hosea is asked to make depicts God's longing for reconciliation with particular sharpness. The prophet is told to marry a prostitute and an adulteress as an image of God's forgiving and persevering faithfulness. Along the way he proclaims harsh things about Israel's perfidy, but the keynote is sacrificial work for healing: "Therefore I will now allure her, and bring her into the wilderness, and speak tenderly to her. . . . The Lord said to me again, 'Go, love a woman who has a lover and is an adulteress, just as the Lord loves the people of Israel, though they turn to other gods and love raisin cakes'" (Hosea 2:14; 3:1).

It is in Paul's Second Letter to the Corinthians that the centrality of reconciliation in God's purpose is set forth for Christians with unequalled succinctness. In defending his leadership as an apostle to a fickle audience that was not impressed with either his credentials or his personal style, Paul wrote passionately:

> For if we are beside ourselves, it is for God; if we are in our right mind, it is for you. For the love of Christ urges us on, because we are convinced that one has died for all; therefore all have died. And he died for all, so that those who live might live no longer for themselves, but for him who died and was raised for them. (2 Corinthians 5:13–15)

He then moves on to the relational and cosmic implications of what he describes as Christ dying for humanity:

> From now on, therefore, we regard no one from a human point of view. . . . So if anyone is in Christ, there is a new creation: everything old has passed away; see, everything has become new! All this is from God, who reconciled us to himself through Christ, and has given us the ministry of reconciliation; that is, in Christ God was reconciling the world to himself, not counting their trespasses against them, and entrusting the message of reconciliation to us. So we are ambassadors for Christ, since God is making his appeal through us; we entreat you on behalf of Christ, be reconciled to God. For our sake he made him to be sin who knew no sin, so that in him we might become the righteousness of God. (2 Corinthians 5:16–21)

This remarkable rhetoric brings together the pleading of a besieged missionary for restored relationship with a community he loved, a summary of the entire Christ event, and a vision of the Christian community's call in the world. "In Christ God was reconciling the world to God." The Greek verb

Paul uses for this work is *katallasso,* which means to reestablish friendly interpersonal relations after these have been disrupted or broken, or to reconcile those who are at variance. The verb builds on its root in the verb *allasso,* which means to make other than what is now, to change, to transform.[11]

Paul is claiming here that reconciliation was the intent and the desired fruit of what God was up to in the Christ event.[12] Reconciliation between whom? Between God and the human community. This claim is premised on the import of the entire biblical saga of the relationship between God and humanity. God created humanity for community with God. People turned away from God in pride, narcissism and rebellion. And God has been seeking reconciliation with humanity ever since.

For Protestant theologian Paul Tillich, humanity's estrangement from God resonated with the alienation that twentieth-century philosophical existentialism discerned in modernity. Roman Catholic theologian Karl Rahner described "man [sic] as a being threatened radically by guilt," saying that "the situation of our freedom is inescapably co-determined by guilt, and this guilt touches everything which exists as individual elements within this situation of freedom."[13]

"Truly to see your face is like seeing the face of God," exclaimed Jacob. So the face of God is primarily a *reconciling* face, not a rule-giving face or a punishing face or even a long-suffering face. From a Christian standpoint, this takes us back to Jesus, the human face of God, as theologian John A. T. Robinson termed him,[14] and to Paul's reflection on the Christ event. *How* was it that "in Christ God was reconciling the world to God"? Christ "died for all," says Paul, "not counting their trespasses against them." In that dying of Christ, says Paul, "all have died," meaning that Jesus, who himself knew no sin, suffered the consequences of sin on behalf of all sinners. So sinners— meaning all people—would not need to suffer sin's consequence, that eclipse of God that Jesus experienced as he cried out on the cross, "My God, my God, why have you forsaken me?" (Mark 15:34).

Christian tradition has never settled on a single view of the nature of the atonement that Jesus offered humanity on the cross of execution, but his suffering for the sake of reconciliation has riveted attention. Christian devotion has interpreted the suffering in two ways. Jesus suffering *for* humanity stresses the depth of sacrifice Jesus undertook to suffer the consequences of sin and thereby remove the obstacle of sin between humanity and God. Jesus suffering *with* humanity stresses his solidarity with the human experience of suffering, which gains depth and meaning as God in Jesus suffers with us, even if the suffering is not alleviated. In both understandings, the cross receives and represents the estrangement posed by human sin and suffering and answers with reconciliation.

Whether Jesus saw his own death in the sin-atoning way that Paul and others did has been disputed in biblical scholarship. Amid all the indications and counterindications, Jesus' words over the cup at his last supper with his disciples—words attested in three gospels and in 1 Corinthians—confirm that Paul's understanding began with Jesus' self-understanding: "Drink from it, all of you; for this is my blood of the covenant, which is poured out for many for the forgiveness of sins" (Matthew 26:27b–28).

The cosmic event of the cross, completed in the victory of Jesus' resurrection and the glory of his ascension, removes the offense, the obstacle, the grudge of sin in the relationship between God and humanity and opens the way of reconciliation. From the New Testament's standpoint, that way of reconciliation involves repentance for sin, which means acknowledging and confessing how we have, in another of Paul's phrases, "sinned and fall short of the glory of God" (Romans 3:23). God's forgiveness is a grace, which is to say that it is given freely without regard to merit or work, and in that forgiveness we are invited into a restored relationship with God through the love of Christ in the power of the Holy Spirit. Reconciliation is accessible through that life of faith, which consists primarily in a relationship of trust.

Reconciliation with God is the foundation of Christian ministry, according to Paul, as ministers catalyze in others reconciliation with both God and neighbor. "If anyone is in Christ, there is a new creation," exclaims Paul. Having received the transforming gift of reconciliation with God, all in Christ are called to and entrusted with God's own ministry of reconciliation in the world. Paul's passion for the topic is sharpened by his own need for reconciliation with the Corinthian Christians. Hence his outburst: "We entreat you on behalf of Christ, be reconciled to God" (2 Corinthians 5:20), a plea that implies that an unresolved human relationship includes an unresolved relationship with God.

In the wider environment of Paul's ministry he was deeply concerned to promote reconciliation between Gentile Christians and Jewish Christians, and it was to that end that he gathered money from the Gentile churches for the suffering Jewish Christians in Jerusalem and Judea. It was to try to reconcile Jews in Jerusalem to the Jesus movement that Paul journeyed there, prompting the predictable arrest that ultimately sent him to Rome and, we think, to martyrdom. These initiatives in reconciliation were across boundaries of difference.

Reconciliation was a major dimension of Jesus' own ministry as he crossed boundaries of difference to reach people on the margins—tax collectors, prostitutes, lepers, demoniacs, and sometimes Romans and other Gentiles. He sought to catalyze reconciliation between them and God *and* between them and the community that had pushed them into untouchable status. Recent theology and biblical criticism have tended to see these initiatives in terms of the liberative justice of the reign of God that was central to Jesus' preaching. Yet that liberative justice was itself in service to the cosmic reconciliation that is the ultimate intent and fruit of the work of God in Christ.

Thus the entire biblical narrative depicts God's unending quest to overcome our estrangement, a quest that culminates in God's incarnation in Christ Jesus, who comes among us as the ultimate solidarity, the ultimate sacrifice, the ultimate renewal. The vision and fruit of God's quest is reconciliation: reconciliation between God and humanity, and reconciliation within the human community. Reconciliation is the principal and overall concern of the story. Reconciliation is the mission of God. Reconciliation is the divine mission in which we participate. Again as Paul wrote to the Corinthians, "All this is from God, who reconciled us to himself through Christ, and has given us the ministry of reconciliation" (2 Corinthians 5:18).

Reconciliation and Diverse Expressions of Mission

In April 1993 a lorry bomb was detonated by the Irish Republican Army in the old City of London, England. Damaging the targeted banks and other financial institutions, the bomb also left in ruins the tiny medieval church of St. Ethelburga's, which had survived the Great Fire of London in 1666 and the Blitz during World War II. The church's insurance did not cover terrorism, so there was a financial incentive to sell the site to wealthy institutions. Instead, Richard Chartres, the Anglican Bishop of London, embraced a vision to found there a ministry to heal the enmity and violence that had destroyed the church.

Money was raised, and a creative architect designed a sanctuary incorporating what remained of the church. In 2002 the church was reconsecrated, and St. Ethelburga's Centre for Reconciliation and Peace opened to focus on the religious dimensions of conflict and the role of faith communities in resolving conflict. The center convenes people across religious differences, often meeting in a goat-hair tent imported from north Africa and installed in the courtyard. St. Ethelburga's had a major role in communal healing after the July 2005 terrorist bombings in London, which aggravated tensions between Christians and Muslims.

St. Paul's Chapel has played a similar role in New York City since the September 11 attacks of 2001. After ministering to rescue workers for many months, St. Paul's became an international pilgrimage site for commemoration and prayer. Walking in the way led by Coventry Cathedral after its destruction in World War II, St. Paul's is a center of the international Community of the Cross of Nails, which is dedicated to reconciliation in many settings around the world.

We humans are authors of horror: local and world wars, torture and degradation, mayhem and terror on every continent. We can cower, shielding our eyes from the self-image these events impress on us. Visionaries at St. Paul's, St. Ethelburga's and Coventry Cathedral refused to accept that inflicting horror defines the essence of being human. Instead, they raised up countersigns that say, "No! There is a face of God to behold, an image of God to live into. We are called to build community and live in reconciliation."

Although not including the word "mission" in its name, St. Ethelburga's is clearly missional. We have seen that difference is a criterion of mission, and the chapel is reaching out across boundaries of difference, even from a place of woundedness. There is clearly a sense of sending and being sent to bear witness in word and deed to the triune God's action, and its guiding vision is reconciliation—between Protestant and Catholic and among Christians, Muslims and Hindus in London and beyond.

If reconciliation is the overall theme of God's mission in the world, how are the many particular expressions of that mission grounded in reconciliation? How do the many things Christians do in mission hold together with reconciling the world in Christ?

Convinced that each person needs reconciliation with God, *evangelism* focuses on telling our story in the light of God's story, or telling the story of God's reconciling work in light of how we have experienced that reconciling gift in our own lives. Centering the narrative in reconciliation focuses the evangelistic conversation on the healing of relationship. This direction may be experienced as invitational by the person being approached and disarming by Christians wary of the demanding tone often associated with evangelism. Salvation and redemption are important biblical categories, but in an evangelistic appeal they can sound like commodities to be acquired, concessions to be negotiated. Reconciliation, by contrast, speaks to the heart's longing.

Church-planting extends evangelism strategically to a group of people. God's mission activity is not limited to the church, for God can and does work far beyond the confines of what the church can touch. Yet gathered communities of the called out ones are precious to God, and churches are major avenues of God on mission. Why? Because churches are entire communities of people who at least are reaching out for the reconciliation that God offers through Christ and seeking to live into such reconciliation with their neighbors, however partially and imperfectly. The church is the one group of people that proclaims the triune God explicitly and mobilizes for God's mission explicitly. The church is called to live and work as a sign of God's reconciliation in the human story—though, of course, this makes it especially tragic when churches instead nourish bigotry and foment conflict.

Reconciliation must be key in *interreligious relations*, a major source of tension in today's world. Interreligious conflict has taken many people by surprise in the twenty-first century, for societies in the North Atlantic region thought that the influence of religion would fade with the intellectual and social impact of Darwinian evolution, Freudian psychology, Marxist communism and market consumerism. The method of dialogue, long a cherished approach in ecumenical and interreligious relations, is being dusted off anew, especially in contacts between Christians and Muslims. Mutual learning and discussion of points of contact and conflict are essential between people of different religions. In the case of Islam and Christianity, conversation about the missional energy that the two religions share is important, especially since it is also a source of friction between them. Simply the name of the Center for Interfaith Reconciliation initiated by St. Stephen's Episcopal Church in Richmond, Virginia, is instructive in highlighting that reconciled relationship between people of differing religions is a crucial and inviting vision that takes us beyond tolerance and mutual coexistence.

There are many expressions of Christian mission that fall under the rubric of *social justice and service*. All address conditions in human societies that impoverish and disfigure the lives of individuals and communities. All are equally related to reconciliation as their ultimate aim. Oppression and injustice express the estrangement between humanity and God, the underlying alienation that distances people from their neighbors and from themselves as people created in the image of God. From this estrangement arises the disregard for God's image in the other that treats him or her as a thing rather than as a person, as a commodity to be exploited rather than as a gifted individual with creativity to contribute, as an obstacle to overcome rather than as a friend with whom community can be formed.

Poverty eradication, to take the most ambitious form of mission that addresses poverty and injustice, is intimately bound up with reconciliation. With the exception of the sudden poverty that results from disasters such as flood, fire and earthquake, virtually all poverty is the result of inequalities built systematically into human communities in order to benefit the few at the expense of the many. Systemic inequality is what defines injustice and constitutes oppression. Typically oppressors have seized on an existing difference and have succeeded in making that difference a reason to deprive groups different from themselves of equal access to economic power and basic human rights.

In this way, social constructions of difference become the basis for structures of sin in which grasping avarice on behalf of one's own group is the rule, and exclusion of other groups from sharing the fruits of the earth and their own human toil is the means. Sexism, the most widespread oppression, builds on the difference of gender to concentrate economic power in the hands of men at the expense of women. Racism seizes on differences of skin color to concentrate power in particular ethnic groups and exclude other groups. In the global community, nationalism, often combined with ethnocentrism, consigns entire nation-states to the status of the poor, the excluded, those who for specious reasons are regarded by the privileged as not deserving an equal place at the table. The collateral damage of these vast systems of oppressive injustice concentrates illiteracy, disease and violence among the excluded. And this calls forth the historic and continuing efforts of Christian mission in education, healthcare and economic sustainability, with the overarching hope for genuine reconciliation.

Mission and God's Reconciliation

Understanding reconciliation as the fundamental vision of God's mission in the world has several important implications for our participation in God's mission.

First, reconciliation radicalizes mission. We have long been aware that simply giving money to provide the poor with food, clothing and shelter—what is often called "charity"—does not respond to the fullness of God's vision. While it benefits recipients for a day or a week, it does not address underlying conditions of injustice that perpetuate their poverty, the exclusion that deprives them of the right to flourish as human beings. Working for justice, therefore, has become more central in mission, and today empowerment and capacity-building are keywords in that struggle.

If we then ask, "Is this a reconciled community?" we realize that even justice is a penultimate goal, a milestone on the way but not the destination. When we ask the reconciliation question, we are forced to address not only the situation of a particular group in its setting, but the life of all groups in the society or the nation, and even the life of all societies in the global community. Reconciliation as the vision keeps us attuned to all discordant notes of estrangement and keeps us from complacency when intermediate goals are fulfilled.

Second, reconciliation retains relational focus. Reconciliation may be expressed in diverse ways, but its essence is a healing of relationship that builds community. In situations of estrangement, the vision of reconciliation keeps us asking the relational question after people have been empowered and capacity has been built, after the school or clinic has been constructed, after every woman in the village has her microenterprise underway, after the historic wrong has been righted, after some approximation of justice has been achieved. We keep asking and encourage others to keep asking, "How are we living together? How are we seeing each other? Are we truly neighbors? Are we building a shared community?" If relationships between individuals and communities are indeed being healed, then reconciliation is on the way and the restoration of the community has a chance to endure. Otherwise, not only is the work incomplete, but from a systemic perspective latent dynamics of estrangement, enmity and even violence are likely to be activated later with destructive force.

Third, discerning reconciliation as the focus of God's mission dissolves the artificial boundaries between diverse forms of mission and the competition among their advocates. We see that concern for reconciliation among human communities is continuous with reconciliation with God. Reconciliation is one continuous stream of God's action in the world. It touches and revives body and soul, individual and community, so it is mistaken and futile to elevate one dimension of God's reconciling work and dismiss the others. Mission that devotes more attention to sharing the gospel story of God's reconciling work through Christ is an important support to mission that devotes more attention to the societal conditions that express estrangement. The converse is equally true. Over the past centuries and today, those involved in evangelism have typically found themselves drawn into addressing poverty, illiteracy and disease as well, and often in quite systemic ways. Often those involved in education, medicine and economic development have found that attention to reconciliation with God is an important dimension of their work.

Fourth, a focus on reconciliation confirms the centrality of difference as a criterion of mission, the marker that functions to distinguish mission as one kind of ministry. As we have seen, estrangement from God and neighbor tends to fixate on difference and use it as the pretext for sin, a platform on which to construct entire systems of sin that oppress other people and groups of people because they are different. The pretext may be language or nationality, skin color or physical disability, sexuality or caste. Whatever the pretext, it is being used as an occasion for sin—personal sin, communal sin, societal sin, global sin. God's mission is to reach across those differences to care, form relationship, liberate, work justice and reconcile. God invites us to join in that mission.

The mission is into difference. The mission is to reconcile.

Notes

1. "The Scroll of Thanksgiving: James and Lorine Williams in South Africa," in *Windows on Mission* video film series, directed by Philip Carr, produced by Jane Butterfield (New York: Domestic and Foreign Missionary Society of the Episcopal Church, 2006).

2. Bernie and Farsijana Adeney-Risakotta's blog: http://www.pcusa.org/mission connections/profiles/adeneyb.htm.

3. Kids4Peace's website: http://www.kids4peaceusa.org.

4. http://www.elca.org/Who-We-Are/Our-Three-Expressions/Churchwide-Organization/Communication-Services/News/Releases.aspx#&&a=4258.

5. http://www.elca.org/Who-We-Are/Our-Three-Expressions/Churchwide-Organization/Communication-Services/News/Releases.aspx#&&a=4287.

6. http://www.anglicancommunion.org/ministry/continuingindaba/about.cfm.

7. Phil Clark, *The Gacaca Courts, Post-Genocide Justice and Reconciliation in Rwanda: Justice without Lawyers* (Cambridge: Cambridge University Press, 2010); http://www.foreign policydigest.org/Africa/April-2010/phil-clark.html.

8. http://www.trc.ca/websites/trcinstitution/index.php?p=3.

9. http://www.anglican.ca/rs/.

10. *The Book of Common Prayer* (New York: Church Publishing, 1979), 848.

11. H. G. Liddell and R. Scott, *Greek Lexicon*, 9th ed., with revised supplement (Oxford: Oxford University Press, 1996), s.v.

12. Reconciliation is similarly central in the summary of Christ's work in the Paulinist Letter to the Colossians: "For in him [Christ] all the fullness of God was pleased to dwell, and through him God was pleased to reconcile to himself all things, whether on earth or in heaven, by making peace through the blood of his cross" (Colossians 1:19–20).

13. Karl Rahner, *Foundations of Christian Faith: An Introduction to the Idea of Christianity*, trans. William V. Dych (New York: Crossroad, 1986), 115.

14. John A. T. Robinson, *The Human Face of God* (London: SCM Press, 1973).

CHAPTER SIX

Accompaniment and Companionship:
The Mode of Mission Today

"Now," said Desmond Tutu in filmed remarks about mission, "I think that almost all missionaries come as people who want to be servants. Now the exchange of missionaries tends to affirm the good that is in each culture and also allow Christ to judge every culture, as Christ does.

"Some of the most eloquent witnesses to the Christian gospel," Tutu went on to say, "are those who are side by side with people in need, incarnating God's concern and love. If they do that with integrity people may ask, 'What makes you want to do this?' And then you have the opportunity to say, 'I am here really because I love Jesus, and Jesus has impelled me to come here, and I hope that my touch will be to some extent his touch.'"[1]

At a church gathering a teenage girl from the Episcopal Diocese of Pennsylvania testified to what a trip to the Anglican Diocese of Guatemala meant to her in the context of a companion diocese relationship between the two. "It was the most amazing experience of my life," she said. "I will never be the same, and I know the friends I made there will be friends for life."

In preparing people to serve in mission I begin by asking, "What is mission? How do you understand the mission that you're undertaking?" Over a number of years I worked with groups of up to sixty outgoing missionaries from the Lutheran, Presbyterian, Episcopal, Reformed and Roman Catholic churches. Groups included lay people and clergy, women and men, people in their twenties and thirties, those in midlife, and some in retirement from other vocations. Typically, they were on their way to medical, pastoral or educational work in Africa, Asia, the Middle East, Latin America, the Pacific or Europe.

The missionaries' responses to the question of what mission meant to them can be summarized in four general statements: Mission means being with people. Mission means forming relationships with people. Mission means being before doing. Mission means meeting Christ with another people group.

The missionaries all had specific assignments such as teaching in a school, nursing or doctoring in a hospital, pastoring a parish, organizing a microenterprise or accessing solar power. They knew *what* they were going to be doing, and they had thoughts about how that activity fit into the overall purposes of God and the commitments of their churches. When asked what mission *is*, however, they shared from their concern, even anxiety, about *how* they anticipated doing their work. What would their style be? What approach to other people did they envision? What quality of relationship did they hope for in their work?

The concern about the *how* of mission expressed their desire to work differently than they felt some of their predecessors in mission history had. They wanted to stress quality of relationship rather than accomplishment of goals, celebration of being rather than intensity of activity. "With," not "to," was and continues to be the favorite preposition of missionaries as they talk about their ministry. They see themselves as being *with* people, rather than as going *to* people. Tutu echoes this in his phrase "side by side with people." What Tutu and these new missionaries are describing is a way or a mode of doing mission. That mode is accompaniment and companionship.

Rethinking the *How* of Mission

At this stage, it may be helpful to review the concepts that shape this section of the book. The *nature* of mission is sending and being sent by God and by communities to bear witness in word and deed to the work of the triune God. The *terrain* of mission is human difference, and the *purpose* of mission is reconciliation. But the *mode* of mission—interpreted as style, manner or approach, essentially *how* mission is expressed and carried out—is accompaniment or the similar concept of companionship.

In this exploration, I do not presume to announce the theme of accompaniment and companionship prophetically as a new mandate for mission that has been ignored and neglected. Instead I celebrate how companionship has come to the fore in missionaries' understanding of their experience, in the articulations of even very young people as they talk about their ventures in mission, and in Desmond Tutu's observations about the approach taken by missionaries today. So at the outset there is good news to be shared: companionship has emerged as a major expectation in mission, and it is flourishing in the relationships between churches in diverse parts of the world.

This commitment has worked its way into the official mission policies of churches and communions. Accompaniment is the keynote of the mission vision of the Evangelical Lutheran Church in America:

> The concept of accompaniment is becoming a central theme in an emerging vision of global mission. Its promise lies in inviting the ELCA to take seriously the contributions of other expressions of the global church. . . . We understand accompaniment as walking together in a solidarity that practices interdependence and mutuality. . . . It is a walking together in Jesus Christ of two or more churches in companionship and in service in God's mission.[2]

With such an emphasis it is not surprising that a network of "companion synod relationships" has grown up among the 140 churches of the Lutheran World Federation. "Through these companion relationships," says the ELCA, "members of ELCA synods live out the accompaniment model of global mission and experience the rich gifts and witness of Lutheran churches in Africa, Latin America, Asia, Eastern Europe, or the Middle East." Companionship is emerging as the major mode of mission among Anglicans, who for forty years have had companion diocese relationships. Presbyterians of the PC(USA) have developed companion presbytery relationships, and United Methodists have recently begun the In Mission Together Partnership Program, which links congregations, districts and conferences.

The two terms, accompaniment and companionship, are obviously linked: a companion is one who accompanies another, accompaniment is the action that is undertaken, and companionship describes the relationship. Missiologically, accompaniment and companionship are equivalent terms, one stressing the action, the other the relationship. Lutherans highlight accompaniment as the approach of mission, as do Roman Catholics, and speak of companion churches around the world. Anglicans stress companionship, a term used by Presbyterians for their presbytery links. Methodists tend to speak in terms of partners and partnership.

The statements I have recounted contrast with the tone of some missionaries in earlier periods. Writing of early twentieth-century missionaries, Stephen Neill observed in his 1986 *History of Christian Missions*, "Missionaries were extraordinarily slow to recognize and trust the gifts of indigenous Christians. Even when ordained to the ministry, they were still regarded as no more than assistants to the missionary."[3]

"The disillusionment of the East and Africa with the West's betrayal of its own spiritual heritage," was on the mind of Max Warren, general secretary of the Church Mission Society in the mid-twentieth century, as he wrote about the personal impact of many westerners during the colonial era. "This betrayal," Warren said, "beginning with the attitude of contempt for the Asian and African on the part of individuals from the West, has been, beyond question, the main source behind the bitterness which has characterized so much of the struggle for independence."[4]

The motif of companionship was never entirely absent, for various missionaries laid the foundation for relationships of equal status and shared vision with colleagues where they ministered. For instance, at the height of nineteenth-century colonialism, Edward Steere, the third Anglican bishop of Zanzibar, wrote of the African Christians nurtured by the Universities' Mission to Central Africa:

> Our desire is to cultivate an independence of spirit. We don't want them under our orders, but we think that the sound principle is that they should be able to rely upon [their] individual efforts, so that if the whole European superintendence were withdrawn, the Church we have founded and the society we have founded might be able to stand by itself.[5]

These words did not express a fulfilled companionship of peers, for European superintendence continued for another seventy-five years, but Steere was recognizing human equality and anticipating that the African church would eventually be led by Africans.

What is new and welcome today is how companionship has become an aspiration shared by all sides in the mission encounter—the people who are sent, the sending community and those in the receiving community.

Growing toward Accompaniment and Companionship

Human difference is the major challenge that Christian mission has had to wrestle with in its struggle to develop an ethos of companionship. As we have seen, the principal challenge of the first Christian communities was the question of whether the Jesus movement would be a sect dominated by the norms of its Jewish members. The alternatives were, on one hand, a requirement that every Gentile become a Jew on the way to becoming a Christian and joining the *koinonia*, the community, and, on the other hand, an invitation that Gentiles join the *koinonia* from right where they were.

The first option entailed the effacement of difference, for all would have become similar through the domination of the originating group. The stance that prevailed was initially the toleration and ultimately the embrace of difference in true companionship in the *koinonia*. In this light, Paul's declaration to the Galatians is truly extraordinary, even twenty centuries later: "As many of you as were baptized into Christ have clothed yourselves with

Christ. There is no longer Jew or Greek, there is no longer slave or free, there is no longer male and female; for all of you are one in Christ Jesus" (Galatians 3:27–28). The differences were not effaced but embraced. They persisted, but they did not affect salvation, nor were they to correlate with preference or priority in the church's life. The gospel according to Paul relativized radically all human differences and invited all into the gospel of Jesus. It was this move that determined whether the Jesus movement would grow, as it did, or would continue simply as a Jewish sect or disappear altogether, as it might have.

Similarly, difference was the intellectual and theological puzzle Europeans confronted when they arrived in the Americas. If all humanity were descended from common ancestors, as the Bible said, how were they to explain the diversity they were encountering in the Americas and beyond? One solution was to conclude that other peoples had declined from a primeval state in which they were more similar to Europeans. Another was to wonder whether the peoples of what was called the New World were really human. The treatment they received at the hands of mine and plantation owners in Central America and the Caribbean expressed this latter view. In contrast, Dominicans Antonio de Montesinos and Bartolomé de Las Casas argued passionately in the sixteenth century that the indigenous inhabitants must be acknowledged as fully human.

We rightly cry ethnocentrism at the fact that such matters could be considered debatable, but we do so only with the benefit of the last five centuries of experience with difference in the global community. It was only in the nineteenth century that anthropology emerged to think systematically about the differences among human cultures. Various human groups on all continents at various historical times have seen themselves as the only humans or, at least, as special humans, and have viewed other humans as lesser humans or as not human at all. White ethnocentrism claims particular attention today because the hitherto unequalled power of Europe and later the United States made their ethnocentrism especially far-reaching, touching most parts of the globe.

Despite the Pauline charter of equality in Galatians, the mission movement that accompanied Euro-American global influence inevitably shared some Euro-American assumptions about the status and value of other people groups. Attitudes of superiority and condescension persisted in Western mission groups, as they did in their wider societies, long after the common and shared basis of the human family was established and accepted on an intellectual basis. A pervasively Western-centric worldview made it difficult for an ethos of mutuality and companionship in mission to emerge.

Roland Allen, an Anglican missionary to China in the early twentieth century, criticized in 1912 what he saw as the alien character, the dependency and the uniformity of indigenous churches formed by mission work in Asia and Africa. In contrast to the Western models he saw being reproduced, Allen was one of the first Westerners to see and celebrate the possibility that the Christianity of converts in Asia or Africa might be a new revelation of the gospel of Jesus Christ. "Everywhere we see the same types," he complained. "There has been no new revelation. There has been no new discovery of new aspects of the Gospel, no new unfolding of new forms of Christian life."[6] Later history demonstrated that indigenous innovation was taking place even then, as it always does, but it was not obvious to Allen and other missionaries. It remains significant that Allen anticipated the possibility that new Christianities could emerge as peers of Christianities in Europe and North America.

In 1925, American Presbyterian Daniel Johnson Fleming, a former India missionary then teaching at Union Seminary in New York, saw eradicating a sense of superiority as the first necessity of Western mission. He felt that a sense of racial superiority was what lay behind the West's confidence in its cultural superiority, and this in turn, he said, formed the basis of its sense of religious superiority. Fleming introduced much of today's missiological vocabulary, for he spoke of mutuality in giving and receiving; an interpenetration of East and West; interdependence, mutual learning and mutual obligation. He counseled a struggle of love in which missionaries would seek to discern what was good in other cultures that could supply what was deficient in their own.[7]

In the same year, American Methodist E. Stanley Jones published *The Christ of the Indian Road*, a remarkable polemic premised on confidence that Christ would be understood uniquely in the Indian context. "Every nation has its peculiar contribution to make to the interpretation of Christianity," Jones wrote. "The Son of Man is too great to be expressed by any one portion of humanity. Those that differ from us most will probably contribute most to our expression of Christianity."[8]

In Allen, Fleming and Jones we see Western mission's assumption of the superiority of its home culture being challenged and dismantled. They were laying a theological and cultural foundation for an exploratory and accepting missional response to human difference to take hold in the churches. Difference was now being seen not as a problem but as an opportunity; not as an alien element to be dominated, suppressed and extinguished, but as a frontier for new ways of seeing the self, the other and the world. Difference was being interpreted not as a threat to gospel truth, but as a threshold for fresh gospel revelation. It was this new response to difference that made possible the exploration of true companionship in mission.

Anglican thinking along these lines in the mid-twentieth century was led by three major figures. The historical mission scholarship of Stephen Neill, conditioned by his work as a missionary bishop in South India, assessed modern mission developments substantially according to whether and how they nurtured the maturing of indigenous churches toward mutual relationships with the Global North churches that had initiated work in their societies. This developed further the nineteenth-century ecumenical "Three-Self" concern that mission work aim for the establishment of churches that would be self-governing, self-supporting and self-propagating.

Max Warren of the Church Missionary Society was influential ecumenically as a practitioner of mission vision and organization. He wrote during a period that spanned the gathering momentum and fruition of political independence movements in the Global South and the accompanying ecclesial impulses toward autonomy in areas that hitherto had been mission fields of churches in the Global North. In his 1956 book, *Partnership: The Study of an Idea,* he explored partnership's application in ecumenism, mission and the life of a multiracial society. In mission, Warren wrote, "Partnership means involvement between real people in real situations. It means committal of oneself in trust to the genuine integrity of the other person. It calls for a responsible attitude to the other by each. It means the acceptance of a host of liabilities. And all this is completely mutual or it is not partnership."[9]

It was in the environment of such thinking that Mutual Responsibility and Interdependence in the Body of Christ (MRI) took root as the watchword of the 1963 Anglican Congress in Toronto, in the vision and organization of which Stephen Bayne had a strong role as the first Executive Officer of the Anglican Communion. "The full communion in Christ which has been our traditional tie has suddenly taken on a totally new dimension," the congress declared. "It is now irrelevant to talk of 'giving' and 'receiving' churches. The keynotes of our time are equality, interdependence, mutual responsibility."[10] Bayne recounted the moving words of Bishop Goto of Tokyo:

> Formerly a giver and receiver faced each other, each preoccupied with the reactions of each to the other, each ashamed, both with anxious eyes fastened on the gift. Now we are released from this, for we are to stand hand in hand facing one great missionary task. . . . Where before, some of us felt we had no gifts to offer because we were confronting those whom we thought had everything, now we shall discover that all have gifts that are needed, and in giving, shall receive.[11]

The great gift of the initiative was simply the watchword, Mutual Responsibility and Interdependence in the Body of Christ. Apart from a few memorable statements, the congress's theology was thin. Even as the conferees called for "the rebirth of the Anglican Communion" and insisted that one-way giving and receiving were over, they persisted in the old paradigm and got busy trying to raise $15 million, equivalent to more than $100 million today, to fund a directory of projects among poorer provinces of the communion. The concept of MRI itself, however, has abiding cogency, and it awaits fulfillment in our own day across the denominations.

Accompaniment as Lived in Mission Today

The meaning of companionship and accompaniment today is best accessed through the experience of those living it in cross-cultural mission relationships.

Francis Wilson in Belize

Francis Wilson is an Episcopal missionary serving as manager of Holy Cross Anglican School in Belize, where her husband Vernon also serves. She writes candidly of her experience under the theme of transparency, one of the Ten Principles of Partnership formulated in 1993 under the auspices of a pan-Anglican mission and evangelism commission:

> I feel like an outsider, an interloper at a family event. I am aware—a little uncomfortably—that I am a white face in an environment filled with vibrant shades of color; that I am an American living in a community that has long suffered exploitation at the hands of the developed world.
>
> I am financially comfortable by the standards of my native land but outrageously wealthy in comparison to the vast majority of people living in this region. And my feelings of being outside are furthered by the fact that I am an official representative of the Episcopal Church U.S.A. at a time of turmoil within the Anglican Communion as a result of the consecration of Gene Robinson as a bishop of the Church.
>
> Yet after four years . . . I feel as much a part of this community as I feel apart from it. This is where I have chosen to live and move and have my being—where I seek to know God and my neighbor—where I long to learn the often painful lessons of loving and serving. I have come to Belize and sought to be a Companion in Ministry with people who view the world through distinctly non-American eyes and are products of cultures—Creole, Garifuna, Mestizo, Mayan—very different from my own. More amazingly, I have asked those same people to be in companionship with me—to somehow live with all my different-ness and allow me to walk with them as a fellow pilgrim. . . .
>
> Each morning finds me praying once again for guidance and wisdom. Each day I continue to struggle to be "quick to listen and slow to speak." Each evening I ask God to transform my less-than-Christ-like actions into something that will bring honor and glory to his name and benefit to his people.

Being a companion in mission and ministry with God's people in Belize continues to be an up-close and personal encounter with my own imperfections, often magnified through the lenses of cultural diversity and my own cultural fatigue. It isn't always easy or pleasant to see myself as others see me; to be involuntarily transparent. . . .[12]

Francis offers us much of what we want to know and need to hear about accompaniment in mission and about a spirituality of companionship. I suggest that spirituality is the habitual orientation toward God that one expresses in prayer and faithful action. Francis makes it clear that she is in Belize not simply to do a job but to travel with God and find God, to be a pilgrim, as she says. Hers is a spirituality of discovering God, others and herself in relationship. Far from imagining herself as someone whole who is in a position to offer wholeness to others, she is intensely aware of her weaknesses and of her need to grow through relationship. She does not claim that the Belizeans were immediately her companions, for at first they and everything else in the environment seemed strange and perhaps threatening. Indeed, the strangeness has not worn off entirely, for she still feels very different—racially, socially, economically, nationally—and, as a result, she sometimes feels alone.

Yet she sees the Belizeans as companions and her relationship with them as companionship. What might she mean by that? She does not highlight particular friendships, nor does she claim to know people intimately. Instead, her use of the concept expresses a quality of commitment. Companions are those who accompany one another, and accompaniment implies travel, a journey. Francis's Belizean colleagues are companions because she and they are committed to sharing a journey, a journey with God and a journey in one another's company.

Ben and Bobbie Chase in the Middle East

Ben and Bobbie Chase, who served as Episcopal missionaries in the Middle East, reflect on the resonance between the prayer they brought with them as Christians and the prayer they found among Muslims:

One of the clearest memories of our twelve years on the Arabian Peninsula is the Muslim response to their call to prayer. Whether it was closing their shops and making their way to the local mosque to worship in community or stopping their cars to pray by the side of the road, their response was immediate and faithful. As soon as they heard the prayer call, practicing Muslims faced the Kabbah in Mecca to align themselves with every other Muslim in the world who paused with them to pray.

The Christian altar is equally a visible *axis Mundi* [axis of the world] for liturgical Christianity. Celebrating the Eucharist is the apex of the missionary experience, both defining its purpose and establishing its form. . . . the Eucharist is the fuel of missionary experience.[13]

The Chases cite three graces of eucharistic life in their mission experience, always in places where Christians were less than 1 percent of the population and where conversion from Islam was punishable by death: the grace of hospitality, the grace of being at home in foreign places, and the grace of communal authenticity. In settings where not only strangeness but often hostility were to be expected, the eucharistic *koinonia*, the community gathered with bread, was what defined Christian identity and Christian mission. Even as they center in Eucharist, they recognize that Muslims' habit of prayer is in companionship with their own.

The eucharistic note reminds us that the Latin roots of the word "companion"—*cum* meaning "with" and *panis* meaning "bread"—highlight bread shared on a journey. A companion is a person who is so with one on the journey that there is a sharing of bread, a sharing of the sustenance that makes the journey possible. In this perspective, Christian companionship is intrinsically eucharistic, as is the mission journey taken with companions. For the Chases, the journey with bread *was* the mission.

Justin Mutter in Haiti

A third element strong in contemporary mission companionship is solidarity with the suffering. Justin Mutter, a young adult missionary who served two years in Haiti before becoming a Rhodes Scholar, writes about his work with malnourished children and recounts the anguished death of a three-year-old of *kwashiorkor*, a disease caused by severe malnutrition. He continues:

> Three weeks after Celusim'ne's death her mother turned up at our nutrition office. She placed before me two bulging baskets of large, ripe Haitian grapefruits. She had walked six hours from Bouly in the hot sun just to offer me this gift. I was overwhelmed, speechless under the generous donation of such wealth out of such dire poverty. "But . . . we *failed*," I wanted to say. "We didn't save her."
>
> But then I saw the gift for what it was: her act of resurrection in the face of death. This was her work of hopeful solidarity. More pointedly, for me her gift was a sacrament of understanding and perception; through it I began to learn how it is that Christian solidarity can and should move from failure to serious hope, from hiddenness to revelation, and *through* death toward life.[14]

Here the missionary who saw himself as being in solidarity with the poor, as indeed he was as he labored in a poor and dangerous country, found himself moving to a deeper understanding of solidarity in Christ. It came through the solidarity expressed with *him* by a poor and bereaved mother bringing a basket of fruit—sharing sustenance on the journey.

From Partnership to Companionship

From these rich expressions of mission companionship and accompaniment, I return to the ecclesial developments that have formed the environment in which such a spirituality of companionship can and does now flourish.

When the Anglican Consultative Council (ACC) was formed to bring lay and clergy representatives of all Anglican provinces into regular consultation, its first meeting, in 1971, took place not in Europe or North America, but just south of the equator, in Limuru, Kenya. This signaled a recognition that the churches of Africa, Asia and Latin America were churches with their own vision and initiative to bring to the table, especially now that those regions were becoming Christianity's center of gravity in both numbers and vitality. Such recognition prepared the way for the companionship that we are experiencing today. MRI was much in the air at that first meeting, with various proposals for how the assistance programs launched through MRI could be organized and channeled. Ecclesio-bureaucracy was still the preoccupation.

The second meeting of the ACC, in 1973 in Dublin, Ireland, continued to take MRI as its point of departure, but it introduced Partners in Mission as the organizing principle for shared mission. Its eloquent introductory reflection has been influential:

> The missionary task of the Church continues to be that of reconciling man [*sic*] to God, man to man, and man to his environment. The oneness of the missionary task throughout the world has been emphasized in recent years in all parts of the Christian Church. The emergence everywhere of autonomous churches in independent nations has challenged our inherited idea of mission as a movement from "Christendom" in the West to the "non-Christian" world. In its place has come the conviction that there is but one mission in all the world, and that this one mission is shared by the world-wide Christian community. The responsibility for mission in any place belongs *primarily* to the church in that place. However, the universality of the gospel and the oneness of God's mission mean also that this mission must be shared in each and every place with fellow-Christians from each and every part of the world with their distinctive insights and contributions. If we once acted as though there were only givers who had nothing to receive and receivers who had nothing to give, the oneness of the missionary task must make us all both givers and receivers.[15]

MRI was an ecclesiological concept to which the communion could aspire, but Partners in Mission provided a relational model in which Anglican provinces could see themselves and one another. Parallel conversations were occurring in other world communions, so that partnership took hold as an ecumenically shared ethos of mission: "What are we as we seek to live in mutual responsibility and interdependence in the Body of Christ? We are partners in mission. We are a partner with you, and you are a partner with us." Individuals, congregations and regional expressions of the churches could enter into partnership as well. Meetings to nurture partnership took place at many levels. Among Anglicans they took the form of Partners in Mission (PIM) Consultations, in which one province would invite several other provinces to visit and confer about its life and mission. While PIM Consultations tapered off in the 1990s, they stamped the partnership concept on the communion as a whole.

Most influential, however, has been the phenomenon of companion relationships between the regional groupings of the churches—companion presbyteries, companion synods among Lutherans, the Methodists' In Mission Together Partnerships and the Anglicans' companion dioceses. What I call the Companion Church Movement is more responsible than any other development for making the world church real for ordinary church members in the denominations. Ordinary Christians have been getting to know their sisters and brothers in Christ in very different cultures through visiting companions and undertaking shared mission together. Each of the 65 ELCA synods has a companion synod, and the vast majority of the 110 Episcopal dioceses have a companion relationship, with some dioceses linking with several companions, often in widely dispersed parts of the world. Missionaries often serve in places that have a companionship with their own regional expression of the church.

True to the personal dimension of companionship, a substantial number of companion relationships between church entities arise out of personal friendships that develop between leaders who meet at international gatherings and other venues. For instance, a thirty-year link between the Diocese of West Ankole in Uganda and the Diocese of Oklahoma emerged out of a friendship between the respective bishops at the 1978 Lambeth Conference. The relationship between the Episcopal Diocese of Massachusetts and three dioceses in Zimbabwe that drew my wife Jane and me to be missionaries there grew out of a conversation between the Massachusetts bishop John Coburn and Desmond Tutu in Johannesburg in the 1980s. Tutu suggested that a stronger church in Zimbabwe could strengthen the new nation's witness to a South Africa still bound in apartheid. That proved to be true, though Zimbabwe has more recently been shackled again by despotic rule.

With the exception of the United Methodists, the "companion" terminology for these relationships often predates the language of "partnership"
as a guiding concept and has survived longer. Churches did not move to
such terms as "partner synods" and "partner presbyteries." Why did the concept of companionship persist in interchurch links despite the strong ethos
of partnership in mission thought? It was because companionship highlights
the sharing of life, as distinguished from the work to be done. The ELCA
offers a helpful analysis:

> As political colonialism declined after the Second World War, the word
> "partnership" was used to describe the relationship between the former
> sending churches and the emergent international churches. Some
> churches prefer this term and will continue to use it because it best
> expresses their concept of cooperation in God's mission. The implications
> of this term have come under scrutiny by other churches and often been
> found wanting. Critics note that the term "partnership" may mask an
> unequal yoking of a supposedly powerful giver and a weaker receiver; i.e.,
> it preserves the ecclesiastical counterpart of colonialism.[16]

With similar insight the Mission Commission of the Anglican Communion suggested in 1999 that the paradigm for mission shift from partnership
to companionship. The commission noted that, although in the New Testament the concept of partner, *koinonos,* is rooted in the shared life of
koinonia, Partners in Mission had increasingly been used to describe "specific
programmes or collaborative activity between agencies or dioceses." To some
it connoted a business relationship of doing rather than a gospel relationship of being. "Companionship," said the commission, "speaks of values,
trust, listening, generosity, encouragement, support and sharing; of journeying together in the movement of the Church."[17]

Although using the term "partnership," the Methodist program has a
similar intent:

> "In Mission Together" partnership relationships are based on a commit-
> ment among UMC congregations or faith communities in different coun-
> tries and cultures. They agree to listen to one another, understand and
> become sensitive to the other's culture, suspend judgment, share
> resources, and be open to God's transforming power through participation
> together in God's mission.[18]

Missional Companionship in the Bible

However theologically cogent the theme of companionship may be for mission, where might one look in scripture to ground such a theology?

Mark says that Jesus "appointed twelve to be with him." He chose the disciples first and foremost *simply to be with him.* The second reason was the mission task, that they "be sent out to proclaim the message, and to have authority to cast out demons" (Mark 3:14–15). But first came pure and simple companionship. Like anyone, Jesus needed friends so that he would not be alone, companions who would share bread on the journey. This reality is obscured when we see the disciples as convened exclusively to be taught, formed in the way of the cross and sent out on mission.

In Matthew's gospel it is striking how often Jesus returned to Capernaum, the home of Peter. Foxes had holes, birds of the air had nests and the Son of Man had nowhere to lay his head—except, however, when he was relaxing at the home of one of his best friends and enjoying the home-cooked meals of that friend's mother-in-law.[19] We might say the same of Jesus' friendship with Mary and Martha at Bethany (Luke 10:38–42; John 11:1–44; 12:1–11). When Jesus sent seventy disciples to proclaim and enact God's reign, he sent them out in pairs, replicating the companionship he himself had found so helpful in mission (Luke 10:1). It was in order to have companions in prayer that Jesus invited Peter, James and John to accompany him up the mountain where he was transfigured (Luke 9:28).

Jesus asked the question, "Who do you say that I am?" not simply to see if his disciples knew a "right" answer. Rather, amid vicious opposition that showed signs of becoming truly threatening, he needed confirmation of his own intuitions about his identity. Jesus was overcome with joy at Peter's response, "You are the Messiah, the Son of the living God" (Matthew 16:15–16). Not only did someone have breathtaking clarity about his role in the saving work of God, but that person was among those who knew him best, one of his companions, one of his journeying bread-sharers. It was out of a similar need for companionship that Jesus asked the inner three to pray with him in Gethsemane and then expressed hurt at their slumber: "Could you not stay awake with me one hour?" (Matthew 26:40).

Typically reifying the implications of Jesus' story, John has Jesus say, "I do not call you servants any longer, because the servant does not know what the master is doing; but I have called you friends, because I have made known to you everything that I have heard from my Father" (John 15:15). This occurred after Jesus himself had taken the role of a servant in washing his disciples' feet. Jesus leveled the formal role of rabbi, teacher and master by joining his disciples as a friend, as the companion that he had asked them to be with him.

Underlying my framing of Jesus' *koinonia* is a high but *kenotic*, or self-emptying, view of the incarnation. Jesus was truly the Word made flesh, the second person of the Trinity incarnate, but utterly emptied of the prerogatives of deity.[20] Jesus was not all-sufficient. Rather, he was needy, not more needy than you or I, but needing companionship and friendship just as much as you and I do, with the attendant desire for solace, humor, affirmation and the ordinary give-and-take of relationship. Jesus needed that companionship for his own personal wholeness, and he needed it for the mission. He was the leader, the envisioner, the sender, the empowerer through the Holy Spirit. That missional role was sustained and buttressed through the mutuality of companionship with his friends.

It is this incarnated companionship at the heart of our faith that is the fundamental basis of the companionship to which we are called in mission. Theologically, we can work off of both ends of the accounts of the evangelists. "And the Word became flesh and lived among us," says John at the beginning of his story, "and we have seen his glory, the glory as of a father's only son, full of grace and truth" (John 1:14). The phrase "lived among us" is "tabernacled" or "tented among us" in the original Greek. As Jesus called the disciples to be with him, so also the event of the incarnation is the event of Emmanuel, as Matthew puts it, God with us (Matthew 1:23). This with-us-ness is the heart of companionship.

At the other end of the narrative, Luke tells the story of the Emmaus road, where a companion, a traveling-with-bread person, joins two of Jesus' grieving friends on the way. It is a with-us-ness moment, an Emmanuel moment, and it ends with bread, *cum pane*. A popular evening prayer based on the Emmaus story gets it perfectly right: "Lord Jesus, stay with us, for evening is at hand and the day is past; be our companion in the way, kindle our hearts and awaken hope, that we may know you as you are revealed in Scripture and the breaking of bread."[21] Beyond the ministry of Jesus, we see companionship in the gregarious life of the earliest Jerusalem community: "Day by day, as they spent much time together in the temple, they broke bread at homes and ate their food with glad and generous hearts, praising God and having the goodwill of all the people" (Acts 2:46–47).

Especially important for us today are indications of genuine companionship between the sent-out ones and the receiving ones, between missioners and missionized. The "we" passages in the latter part of the book of Acts may be only a stylistic literary device or they may indicate that the writer actually accompanied Paul on his dramatic journeys. In any case it is striking that the first-person-plural accounts feature especially touching instances of the companionship between Paul and new Christian communities that he had formed, for instance the all-night discussion session in the upper room in Troas and Paul's heartrending farewell with the elders of Ephesus (Acts 20:7–12; 17–38).

In his letters Paul frequently expressed gratitude for the companions who were with him, longing for those he was missing and joy in the companionship of entire communities. His care for the Thessalonian Christians, for instance, certainly included the concern of a pastor anxious lest they backslide. His decision to send Timothy, his "brother and coworker," to strengthen and encourage them had the downside of leaving Paul alone in Athens, without a companion. The good news Timothy brought of the Thessalonians' faith and love prompted not only the commendation of an overseer but the celebration of an affectionate friend:

> He [Timothy] has told us also that you always remember us kindly and long to see us—just as we long to see you. . . . For we now live, if you continue to stand firm in the Lord. How can we thank God enough for you in return for all the joy that we feel before our God because of you? (1 Thessalonians 3:6, 8–9)

Paul expressed similar feelings in connection with various other individuals and communities.[22] And in 1 Corinthians 12, he makes an elaborate case for understanding the church as a body in which every part needs every other part and is incomplete without the others. They are one interdependent body, walking together, casting no one aside.

Accompaniment in Lutheran Reflection

"Don't walk in front of me, I may not follow. Don't walk behind me, I may not lead. Just walk beside me and be my friend." This anonymous saying encapsulates the quality of relationship that churches aspire to fulfill in accompaniment and companionship.[23]

More than other churches, the Evangelical Lutheran Church in America has articulated its understanding of accompaniment—and, by implication, companionship—in a detail and depth that is helpful to the ecumenical community.

"Accompaniment emphasizes relationship before resources," the ELCA said in 1999, when it declared accompaniment its paradigm for mission in the twenty-first century. "Development of programs and allocation of resources flow from how companions relate, rather than vice versa. Accompaniment is valued for its own sake as well as for its results. It is open-ended with no foregone conclusions." Implicit in this emphasis on quality of relationship is critical reflection on mission's history of emphasizing activist work and the achievement of results, whether in evangelization or in educational, medical and economic development. The ELCA was not saying that there is less work to be done today, but that now the work would be carried out within a relationship of companionship.

In the same statement, the church's leaders went on to say:

> A primary reality of accompaniment is the mutual respect of the companions. The conversation is no longer between a giver and a receiver but

between two churches, each of which has gifts to give and to receive. The difference in the gifts is not prioritized. Mutual respect also applies to regions. In accompaniment each church has the primary responsibility for mission in its area. In conversations between the churches, each will describe its gifts for outreach in its own country. A fruitful outcome of the conversation is the discovery of the outside church's gifts that may assist in mission in a church's own country.[24]

This new mode contrasts with an earlier approach when people from the missionizing West or Global North "took" the gospel and the techno-logical achievements of their societies "to" Africa, Asia, Latin America and Oceania as blessings they "gave" to "receiving" audiences. The transforma-tion of the former "mission fields" into indigenous and autonomous churches since the mid-twentieth century prompted people to recognize the need for equality and mutuality in relationship. That impulse birthed first the partnership and then the companionship model of mission. The model does not only respond to a changed situation with a new strategy, however. Instead, companionship is recognized as a more faithful model in all circumstances—yes, in settings where there are now fully formed churches in place, but also in situations where primary evangelization, basic healthcare and education might be appropriate concerns. From the start of mission work, going with an emphasis on relationship rather than work— being with people rather than doing things for them, discovering their gifts as well as one's own, receiving from them as well as giving to them—affects profoundly the communal faith that is birthed and the relationship that is formed with the companion community. Historically one can never be sure how things would have turned out if mission had been pursued differently, but it is likely that paternalism, dependency and cultural confusion would not be such issues today if companionship had been the mode of mission from the beginning of the modern period.

In planning how accompaniment would be expressed in its mission, the ELCA put forward twelve criteria or "signposts" of its mission accompani-ment in the twenty-first century. The list is heterogeneous in that in includes matters of mission content, such as witness in word and deed, justice and ecology, and programs between different parts of the Global South; core val-ues in all ministry and mission, such as racial diversity and gender equality; and desired qualities in how mission is carried out, such as transparency, col-laboration, and interchurch and interfaith ecumenism. In short, the sign-posts articulate the entire mission program of the church. Nevertheless accompaniment is lifted up as the *process* of mission that is to be expressed through the twelve signposts. For each of them, the ELCA articulates what the "implications for walking together" are for the various expressions of the church: the ELCA as a whole, missionaries, ecumenical partners and the Global Mission Unit. Rafael Malpica-Padilla, who directs the unit, calls accompaniment the *methodology* of the church's mission today, which, like the category of the *mode* of mission, highlights *how* mission is carried out. Elaborated through twelve signposts, however, it becomes clear that accompaniment and companionship touch on both the *what* and the *how* of mission.

In emphasizing relationship, the themes of accompaniment and companionship seek to deliver mission from purely functional criteria of effectiveness and validity. "We have made objects of one another," an African woman theologian told the ELCA at a global mission event. "Northern mission agencies made us objects of their evangelism programs and counted the numbers of us they converted to Christianity. We, in turn, made objects of you, seeing you as object, as source for the funds and resources we need."[25] This analysis can be expanded to include the Global North's view of the Global South as an arena of human need in which northern expertise can have free play, and the South's use of the North as a repository for blame in cultural and political turmoil.

Maturing in accompaniment has not been easy in Lutheran relationships. James Gonia, the ELCA's program director for work in west Africa, was serving as a missionary in Madagascar when accompaniment was coming to the fore in the late 1990s. "We were told, 'This is the new vision,'" he told me. "A lot of us said, 'This is what we've been trying to do all along. This is how we operate.' Accompaniment gave us language to express what we were already trying to do, but now we felt chastised and unheard. We also felt there had been little conversation about accompaniment with the local churches where missionaries were serving. Maybe there had been talk at the synodical level, but not with local churches. So the introduction of the theme of accompaniment became another non-accompaniment way of doing things."

Historic patterns of dominance and subservience made the transition difficult in obvious ways. "We keep saying we respond to the initiative of the companion church, but then we go ahead on our own anyway," Gonia said. There were also unexpected turns in the road:

> For awhile we thought accompaniment meant we should have no say or initiative, that we should only await our companions' initiative or voice. It was not accompaniment for us to have a strong opinion. So this was a growing experience, because that's not accompaniment. Accompaniment is when both companions have mutual conversation. . . . Power was a major concern in discussions of accompaniment: power relations and the exercise of power. We heard accompaniment as indicating that we don't ask for any accountability, but that's not accompaniment. It's important for us to be

fair to the people who made the offerings that fund the mission work. . . .
If one partner is silent, then it's not accompaniment. The silence factor has
flipped. It used to be our international companions who were silent. Now
the North Americans are silent.[26]

Malpica-Padilla likewise stresses that mutual advice and admonition are integral to true accompaniment.

Accompaniment has been experienced as central in infrastructure development as well. Megan Bradfield was initially puzzled by the accompaniment
emphasis when she went to the ELCA world mission unit's international
development office. "International NGOs historically have operated from
[a] standpoint of confidence in their own expertise and [a] perception of
proper priorities," she told me before continuing:

> So often they took programs into areas without the endorsement of the
> locals, assumed their priorities and methods were the right ones, and eval-
> uated success without the participation of locals. Accompaniment involves
> the spirit of giftedness: awareness of one's own gifts and the stimulation of
> others' awareness of their own gifts. In accompaniment, we all sit around
> the table and assess the gifts that are present: insight, talent, finance, time,
> experience. Sustainable development asks the question, How can all these
> gifts be activated and used for the flourishing of the community? It does
> not ask simply, Where is the money going to come from and what will it
> take to keep it coming?[27]

Yoshitaka Franklin Ishida, who directs the ELCA's work in Asia and the
Pacific, notes that no term for mission is perfect, that in some languages the
word "partner" avoids unfortunate local connotations of "companion," and
that the old patterns can persist despite new terminology. Nevertheless he
argues that the ethos of accompaniment challenges the churches to tran-
scend legalistic patterns of junior and senior partners and enter into relationships of mutual discovery. He points out that accompaniment puts into
practice the theology of the church as *communio*, or communion, which is,
in turn, the heart of accompaniment, so that accompaniment is a sacramental as well as a practical reality in the church's life.[28]

Stories Shared among Friends

Responding to human need is such a dominant reflex of Christians in
Europe and North America that the nature of companionship can quickly
get lost amid program and finance. "What do you hope for in this relationship?" I asked the newly appointed chair of a link committee for a relationship between a Church of England diocese and an Anglican diocese in
Africa. She immediately began talking about drilling wells and providing

bursaries for school children, both very much needed but not the first agenda items in true companionship.

Sharing stories was what reset a companion synod relationship between Colorado and Madagascar. "We asked ourselves, 'What do our Malagasy friends think about accompaniment?'" said James Gonia of the ELCA. "We realized we didn't really know what they thought." The Companion Synod Committee organized a weekend retreat for both sides of the companionship during a Malagasy visit to Colorado.

> We decided accompaniment meant that we share our stories. So we told our stories, and we spent hours sharing our stories. And we wrote them down. The theme was how we experience faith in our cultural experience. This created community and mutuality. We found points of uniqueness and points of sharedness. Projects are fine, but the heart of accompaniment is the ability to have conversation about things that matter. So the group discussed the question of evil and how it is addressed by the church, as in, for instance, Fifohazana [a new movement in Madagascar]. The group discussed the "sects," as in the African-Initiated Churches and various new religious movements in North America.

The result was discovery and the sense of truly knowing one another amid difference.[29]

There are numerous expressions of mission accompaniment and companionship in world Christianity today. Churches Together in Britain and Ireland has a Centre for Mission Accompaniment. Christian Peacemaker Teams places teams of trained volunteers in zones of armed conflict to "accompany" unarmed communities who are at risk of violence from armed groups. "To accompany means to be a companion," says Jesuit Refugee Service/USA, "We are companions of Jesus, so we wish to be companions of those with whom he preferred to be associated, the poor and the outcast."[30] The Anglican Communion's 2005 Covenant for Communion in Mission strikes many notes of accompaniment and companionship.[31] In relating to churches in Latin America and the Caribbean, the United Church of Christ feels called to "reaffirm our commitment for mutual accompaniment in mission with the churches and ecumenical partners in the region."[32] Thus the theme has become generalized in Christian communities.

Still, what is often missing in the bureaucratese of the churches, however well intentioned, is the sheer friendship to which the girl from Pennsylvania testified after her trip to Guatemala. "I know the friends I made there will be friends for life," she said. Such friendship, with its mutual knowing and sharing of life, must be the heart of the companionship we seek in mission.[33]

We lift up accompaniment and companionship for the sake of the gospel we are sent to share in word and deed, which is the very nature of mission.

Companionship in mission fulfills and energizes because it takes place across boundaries of difference, the terrain of mission. It is there that both the other and the self are discovered, explored and, however partially, understood. Boundaries divide. Companionship reconciles across difference and so fulfills God's mission in the world.

Notes

1. *The Gospel of Grace*, introductory film of *Windows on Mission*, directed by Philip Carr, produced by Jane Butterfield (New York: Domestic and Foreign Missionary Society of the Episcopal Church, 2006).

2. ELCA, *Global Mission in the Twenty-first Century* (Chicago: Evangelical Lutheran Church in America, 1999), 5–6.

3. Stephen Neill, *A History of Christian Missions*, 2nd ed. with Owen Chadwick (Hammondsworth, UK, and New York: Penguin, 1986), 384.

4. Max Warren, *Partnership: The Study of an Idea* (London: SCM Press, 1956), 87.

5. *Report of the Proceedings at a Meeting in Liverpool for UMCA, June 1882*, cited by Jerome T Moriyama, "Building a Home-grown Church," in *Three Centuries of Mission: The United Society for the Propagation of the Gospel, 1701–2000*, ed. Daniel O'Connor (New York: Continuum, 2000), 335.

6. Roland Allen, *Missionary Methods: St. Paul's or Ours?* (Grand Rapids: Eerdmans, 1962), 141–42.

7. Daniel Johnson Fleming, *Whither Bound in Mission* (New York: Association Press, 1925).

8. E. Stanley Jones, *The Christ of the Indian Road* (London: Hodder and Stoughton, 1925), 232.

9. Max Warren, *Partnership: The Study of an Idea: Being the Merrick Lectures at Ohio Wesleyan University, Delaware, Ohio, March 1955* (London: SCM Press, 1956), 92–93.

10. Stephen F. Bayne, Jr., ed., *Mutual Responsibility and Interdependence in the Body of Christ, with Related Background Documents* (New York: Seabury Press, 1963), 18.

11. Bayne, *Mutual Responsibility*, 14.

12. Francis Wilson, "Transparency" in *The Scripture of Their Lives: Stories of Mission Companions Today*, ed. Jane Butterfield (Harrisburg: Morehouse, 2006), 36–37.

13. Ben and Bobbie Chase, "Celebrating Eucharistic Community," in *The Scripture of Their Lives*, 117–18.

14. Justin Mutter, "Solidarity with the Suffering," in *The Scripture of Their Lives*, 76.

15. Anglican Consultative Council, *Partnership in Mission: Anglican Consultative Council: Second Meeting, Dublin, Ireland, 1973* (London: SPCK, 1973), 53.

16. ELCA, *Global Mission in the Twenty-first Century*, 6.

17. Eleanor Johnson and John Clark, eds., *Anglicans in Mission: A Transforming Journey: Report of Missio, the Mission Commission of the Anglican Communion, to the Anglican Consultative Council, meeting in Edinburgh, Scotland, September 1999* (London: SPCK, 2000), 80. For more current reflections on partnership, see Jonathan Bonk, "What About Partnership?"; Cathy Ross, "The Theology of Partnership"; and Leon Spenser, "Seminaries and the Challenge of Partnership" in *International Bulletin of Missionary Research* 34, no. 3 (July 2010): 129–30, 145–48, 150–54.

18. http://new.gbgm-umc.org/connections/partnerships/inmissiontogether/resources/partner-guidelines/?search=partner.

19. Matthew 8:14–15 and Mark 1:29–31. Given that Peter's home was in Capernaum, it is likely in or near Capernaum that he heard Jesus call him from fishing (Matthew 4:18–20 and Mark 1:16–18). Much of the extended narrative at Mark 1:21–2:12 and Matthew 8:5–9:13 takes place at Capernaum, which is cited at Matthew 9:1 as "his own town." Matthew says Jesus "made his home in Capernaum" (Matthew 4:13).

20. See Philippians 2:6–8.

21. *The Book of Common Prayer* (New York: Church Publishing, 1979), 70, 124, 139.

22. E.g., 1 Corinthians 16:17–18; Philippians 1:3–11; 2:19–24; Romans 16:1–16, 21–24.

23. The saying is sometimes attributed to French existentialist philosopher Albert Camus, but with no evidence cited. Yoshitaka Franklin Ishida of the ELCA's Global Mission Unit cites it in his D.Min. thesis "Mission in Today's World: Implications of Accompaniment and *Communio* for a Lutheran Evangelism" (Chicago: Catholic Theological Union, 2001), 61, as does the brochure, "Walking Together: The Companion Diocese Program of the Episcopal Church" (New York: Episcopal Church Center, n.d.).

24. ELCA, *Global Mission in the Twenty-first Century*, 6.

25. ELCA, *Global Mission in the Twenty-first Century*, 18.

26. James Gonia, interview, October 2009.

27. Megan Bradfield, interview, October 2009.

28. Yoshitaka Franklin Ishida, "Mission in Today's World," 40–69.

29. James Gonia, interview, October 2009.

30. http://jrsusa.org/we_do_accompaniment.php.

31. http://www.anglicancommunion.org/ministry/mission/commissions/iascome/covenant/covenant_english.cfm.

32. http://www.globalministries.org/resources/mission-study/college-of-mission/who-do-you-say-that-jesus-is-i.html.

33. Portions of this chapter appeared in Titus Presler, "Companionship: An Anglican Spirituality of Mission," *The Anglican* 35, 4/36, 1 (Spring 2007), 5–13.

PART III

What Challenges Face Mission Today?

"We have this treasure in clay jars," wrote Paul to the Corinthians, "so that it may be made clear that this extraordinary power belongs to God and does not come from us" (2 Corinthians 4:7).

Our understanding of God's mission, like our understanding of the gospel itself, is bound to be partial and imperfect. Even what we celebrate in mission raises issues for the churches to address.

For instance, as mission is owned by everyone, how will particular church communions focus their work? As new resources are released for mission, how are they directed for greatest benefit? As many offer themselves for short-term engagement, how is deep and complex commitment nurtured over time?

The mission movement represented by the World Missionary Conference of 1910 in Edinburgh faced comparable issues, but in different ways. Delegates wrestled with competition among churches, and they reached for models of interchurch cooperation with a zeal that energized ecumenical progress in the succeeding century. They struggled with mission diversification represented by the rise of so-called faith missions that were unconnected to denominations, and now such missions are an accepted part of the scene. Many of the delegates in 1910 were officers of mission societies and denominational mission boards, and the continued centrality of those societies and boards was assumed.

Today's situation is different. The major concepts we have explored—democratization, sentness, difference, reconciliation and companionship—all contribute to the mission future that churches must discern and pursue. Each of them also poses particular challenges. When hundreds and even thousands of church entities are pursuing world mission, major challenges of coordination and coherence arise. More and more Christians understand that they have been sent out into mission by the God whose very nature is to send, but recent crises have forced a reevaluation of mission identity. Human difference is a major catalyst for expanded mission engagement, but today's focus on poverty challenges a full appropriation of God's invitation to cross borders of difference. Meanwhile, the internal conflict that churches are experiencing over human sexuality has challenged their witness of reconciliation in the wider world. Finally, how can a focus on true companionship—people being with people, getting to know one another, walking together amid challenges and sharing one another's burdens—coexist with the increasingly popular phenomenon of short-term mission trips? In Part III, we take up these challenges and imagine constructive responses for each.

What we imagine may enhance our participation in God's mission. Even if it does, we and our churches will still be clay jars, earthen vessels needing to be renewed yet again.

CHAPTER SEVEN

Networking for Mission:
A Challenge in Democratization

Today's mission flourishing has many upsides. People in the pews are involved, and they are contributing funds with particular enthusiasm to people and projects they personally know. Friendships are being formed that lace the world church with bonds of affection. These relationships and commitments are being brought to bear on the many wounds that need God's reconciliation—spiritual and physical, personal and communal, ethnic and national, economic and political. Truly the church is engaging God's mission.

Yet the new situation has drawbacks as well. Hunter Farrell of the World Mission office of the Presbyterian Church (U.S.A.) says the church's international companions have pointed out several:

- Mission efforts have become highly uncoordinated. For example, three congregations arrive at the same Central American community for a work trip.
- Mission outreach is less strategic. In a given year, for example, perhaps a hundred Presbyterian congregations take a mission trip to tourist-friendly Kenya, but only a few to neighboring Sudan, a poorer and less-evangelized nation with a longer history of relationship to the PC(USA).
- In some cases mission projects are less responsive to the needs as perceived by the local overseas community. U.S. congregations offer what they have, which is sometimes not what the partner needs.[1]

These are significant problems, and they are common among the denominations today. Presbyterian World Mission's strategic plan for the future contrasts the present environment with two earlier eras of Presbyterian mission. The "direct mode" of mission planted churches, schools and hospitals around the world from 1837 until after World War II. The independence movement of the 1950s and 1960s shifted the church toward working in partnership with newly autonomous churches to equip them for ministry in their own contexts. Whereas at that time Presbyterians worked through their central boards,

> . . . today there are thousands of Presbyterian "mission agencies" making mission decisions every day: the Validated Mission Support Groups and other Presbyterian mission organizations, presbytery international partnerships, congregational mission committees, congregation-to-congregation "twinning" relationships, etc. This seismic shift in the understanding and practice of mission has opened the door to direct involvement of U.S. Presbyterians at unprecedented levels.[2]

Strategic Concern

The strategic concern Farrell cites is the most important. Presumably for the God who is on mission in the world no problem is unimportant, for not one sparrow falls to the ground without God being aware of it (Matthew 10:29–31). Unlike God's, however, the churches' resources of time and attention are not infinite, and finance is likewise limited. Joining God in mission does call us to responsible stewardship of resources. Criteria of responsible stewardship are many and their application can be debated. At the very least, they must include engaging differences as well as commonalities with others; building companionship with others over time rather than temporarily; working with others for reconciliation at depth rather than on the surface; and devoting enough resources to designated settings to make a recognizable difference, rather than dabbling in a multiplicity that exceeds our ability to focus.

Strategic vision addresses not only the perennial possibilities that are relatively easy, such as companionship with Christian communities in relatively stable and free societies. A strategic approach must consider the harder urgencies of today. How are churches addressing the world of Islam, with which the "Christian West" is experiencing ever greater friction, especially since 9/11 and the ensuing wars? How can Christians contribute to reconciliation during and after such conflicts as those in Iraq, Afghanistan, Sri Lanka, Sudan, Congo and Zimbabwe? How should churches express solidarity with Christian communities beset by discrimination, persecution and totalitarianism? How should evangelization be pursued with peoples who are relatively unaware of the gospel of Christ? Is it possible for congregations and regional units to move beyond charity to justice as they reach out to the poor? How can mission build on the ease of access that globalization brings without becoming complicit in the cultural imperialism that globalization may entail?

It is from the strategic weakness of the current situation that other weaknesses follow. Duplication of effort is obvious. Among Episcopalians, for instance, so many congregations, dioceses and agencies are involved in Honduras that the question arises whether some of that relational energy should be redirected to other countries in Latin America and the Caribbean. Such redirection is difficult, however, when local groups are free—as they should be—to set their direction on the basis of locally generated vision and relationships. Drug-related violence in Colombia meant that Anglicans in that country waited years for a companion diocese relationship, raising the question of how high or low the danger bar should be set in contemporary mission relationships. If we cannot accompany in danger, what does our accompaniment mean?

Decentralization and localization, deprofessionalization, democratization and diversification—these developments in mission make local expressions of the church vulnerable to repeating the by now well identified mistakes of mission history. After all, when a congregation or regional unit picks up the mantle of world mission for the first time, it does not have the benefit of the church's history of mission learning—unless it makes a deliberate effort to access it. We celebrate the deprofessionalization of mission initiative, which now comes from the grassroots and not only from experts. Yet sometimes the results are not only deprofessionalized but unprofessional as well.

So it is not uncommon for congregations, presbyteries, dioceses, synods and conferences to rush in with money and experts to solve economic, educational and medical problems—and thereby recapitulate in six months the last three hundred years of missionaries' mistakes. Local knowledge is ignored, and the elders are insulted. Visitors' priorities take pride of place, and long-serving missionaries are not consulted. Condescension flourishes. People are defined by their needs and treated as objects rather than as companions on a journey. Results trump relationships all over again. The "simplicity" of people's poverty is romanticized. Dependence is reinforced. Resentment is renewed. And, ironically, Global North committees and teams often congratulate themselves saying, "We're not going the way the old missionaries did."

Today's problems, therefore, are not simply macroecclesial issues for leaders and managers at the churchwide level of the denominations. No, these issues should concern all congregational and regional mission committees and their members. We must ask ourselves, "Amid our global enthusiasm for God, how can we help ensure that it is God's global *mission* that we are joining? Are we just going global, or are we going global *with God?*"

Communities of Mission Practice: A Presbyterian Approach

Recentralizing mission in the headquarters of the churches is not a solution to the problems of today's democratized mission patterns. Even if it were possible to put the genie back in the bottle—which it is not—we should not wish to do so. Mission engagement at all levels is a work of the Holy Spirit through the church in our day. It fulfills the church's calling and is not a distortion. The key in today's mission environment is to work toward new patterns that celebrate and support the democratization of mission and at the same time nourish focus and coherence in mission.

"Communities of mission practice" is the approach that the General Assembly Mission Council of the Presbyterian Church (U.S.A.) adopted in early 2010 as it sought to connect the many ways Presbyterians are engaging God's mission today. This strategy, the outcome of consultations with more than nine hundred stakeholders, involves two significant shifts. Where previously the central mission board related bilaterally with what Presbyterians call partner churches in other parts of the world, the partnership is now lifted up as three-way, including the church's own members and units:

> In the last century, our church did an excellent job of including the voice of global partners in our mission reflection and action. The new context requires that, in addition to maintaining our close and mutual partnership with global partners (because we believe that God speaks with particular clarity to God's people in each place) and ecumenical partners (because of our understanding of the linkage between mission and unity), we are called to discern and engage in God's mission with U.S. Presbyterians.[3]

The remarkable fact that this church is including its own membership as a *third party* in mission consultation signals both how major the shift from centralized direction is historically and how major the mission movement in the congregations and presbyteries is believed to be. "This shift, from one highly centralized agency to thousands of highly decentralized agencies, is a massive one," said Presbyterian World Mission, as the central office is called.[4] A typical community of mission practice involves partner churches and ecumenical partners; Presbyterian World Mission, including the "mission coworkers" it sends; and mission activists of PC(USA), especially as gathered around particular initiatives in congregations and presbyteries. The plan pictures this in a diagram of three intersecting circles: Partner

Churches, World Mission, and U.S. Presbyterians. The Community of Mission Practice is located in the space that all three share.

The second shift is functional, and it is away from the equipping function that the central office exercised with partner churches in the latter part of the twentieth century, when PC(USA) played the role of older sibling or senior partner. Now the conversation is among peers. Not only have the international partners matured in their missional and organizational life, but domestic Presbyterians, along with their congregations and presbyteries, are acknowledged as flourishing in mission engagement. The central office now has as much to learn from the local initiatives and from the partner churches as it has to share with them. Though partnership language persists in the strategic plan, it is evident that the relationship being envisioned is one of companions.

How does a community of mission practice work? Here is what the Presbyterians say:

> World Mission understands a community of mission practice to be the space where Presbyterians, global partners and World Mission come together. A community of mission practice shares an identity derived from a common passion. It commits to interact regularly to learn and grow as a community and is guided and shaped by the disciplines of prayer, Bible study, reflection and worship. It includes diverse perspectives, working together toward a common purpose, sharing World Mission's core values, and developing a body of shared knowledge and practice in mission in order to increase the faithfulness and effectiveness of its participation in God's mission.[5]

The six core values of the church's world mission that are to be shared are stated clearly:

- "Dignity" in the treatment of all persons and solidarity with the marginalized
- "Empowerment" that builds capacity in long-term relationships
- "Holistic Ministry" that offers evangelism, compassion and justice
- "Partnership" in respect, trust, witness, transparency and accountability
- "Relevance to God's World" that responds to changes in the global community
- "Stewardship" that includes all resources in obedience to Christ[6]

As with virtually all other lists of mission goals, values and visions, the content and manner of mission flow into each other in this set of values. The four "critical global issues" that the church has identified for its "global discipleship" are evangelism and church nurture, women and children in poverty, reconciliation amid cultures of violence, and care for God's creation.[7]

What might a community of mission practice look like? I imagine several presbyteries and congregations in diverse parts of the United States sharing an interest in the plight of women in Sudanese refugee camps. The concept of a community of mission practice does not suggest simply a one-off telephone call about this or that logistical problem with World Mission staff or the random Sudanese Presbyterian who happens to be visiting in the United States. Rather it invites all parties to undertake a disciplined pattern of regular consultation and mutual discernment over time—Sudanese from or working in the camps, relevant PC(USA) missionaries and staff at Presbyterian World Mission, and the congregations and presbyteries involved. The time together is to be shaped by worship, scripture study, prayer and reflection. Covenanted over time, such a community would express mutual accountability—certainly for continued participation, but also for creativity, solidarity, candor, information, confession, support, admonition and thanksgiving.

The Presbyterian vision is premised on headquarters staff exercising servant leadership and "leading from within." They are to be a "bridge across places and across time, connecting the community of mission practice with mission history and with the experiences of other mission constituencies and ecumenical and interfaith partners."[8] Theoretically, initiative leadership could also come from either of the other parties in the community of mission practice, depending on gifts and interests. In any denomination it is helpful if the headquarters staff take responsibility for connecting the conversation with the church's longer history and institutional memory.

Clearly this model could be adapted by people in other churches working to coordinate the efforts of localized mission groups with both international companion churches and with churchwide staff and missionaries. Face-to-face gatherings are ideal, of course, but they are expensive, and today much of the conversation, including prayer and worship, can take place over audio and video conference calls as well as via e-mail and web-based networks. The model is workable and affordable.

In order for this pattern to be replicable with parity on all sides on a global basis, a fourth party would be added to the mix. As the stateside church expression includes both the local and churchwide impulses for mission, so the particular ministry in another part of the world would bring in that church's missional office for strategic consultation. In the Sudanese example, this would mean working with the churchwide office of the Presbyterian Church of Sudan as well as with the ministry in the camps themselves. Conversely, if several conferences and congregations of the Methodist Church in India wished to work with USAmerican Methodists on, say, poverty in Appalachia, they would bring their churchwide office into the community of mission practice, along with local United Methodists in the

U.S.A. and the relevant churchwide United Methodist office. All parties would explore possible ecumenical companions as well.

Mission Networks: An Episcopal and Anglican Approach

The democratization of mission initiative has been pushed by political and theological tensions in the churches as well as by sheer enthusiasm for world mission. For instance, in 1984 United Methodists who were critical of what they saw as the liberalism and declining missionary-sending commitment of the General Board of Global Ministries (GBGM) founded the Mission Society for United Methodists, which since then has sent more than five hundred missionaries to other parts of the world. At any one time the agency, now called simply The Mission Society, may have some two hundred missionaries deployed, close to the number deployed by the churchwide GBGM.

Such developments have further diversified world mission initiatives in the churches. This in turn complicates the efforts of mission activists, congregations and regional expressions of the churches to consult and collaborate in mission. On the one side, the diversification offers more opportunity, just as congregations' own outreach efforts diversify the range of the churches' world mission. On another side, it subjects world mission to the types of theological, ethical, social and strategic clashes that affect other aspects of the churches' work.

Mission activists should not be shocked that church politics affects the vision, mobilization and implementation of world mission. Politics has affected mission from the beginning, as we saw in Chapter Two. Jesus' efforts to mobilize his own inner circle for God's mission contended with political rivalries among the disciples, and the earliest church had political struggles over inclusion and strategy. Politics is with us to stay, so it is important that we reflect on its role in world mission.

The Episcopal Church U.S.A. offers freestanding networks as a model for how to approach the democratization and diversification of world mission. These voluntary associations are structured and persist over time. Whereas the Presbyterians' communities of mission practice focus on particular interests at particular times, networks offer their members a more diffuse but wider exposure to mission endeavor. As it happens, the network phenomenon in the Episcopal Church arose out of major theological and strategic differences about mission, and it has been further affected by the church's struggle over homosexuality. These dynamics help us understand the possibilities and limitations of networks. Exploring them helps us recognize and accept the inevitability of competitive and adversarial currents in the politics of world mission.

Attention to the urban and racial crises of the United States in the 1960s resulted in drastically reduced funding for Episcopal missionaries, with numbers sinking from about 260 in 1968 to about 70 in 1974. This upset Episcopalians committed to world mission, and they wondered whether their centralized agency, the Domestic and Foreign Missionary Society (DFMS), would ultimately abandon missionary-sending altogether. So during the 1970s and beyond, various Episcopalians founded mission societies on the voluntary principle of the Church of England: the Episcopal Church Missionary Community (now the New Wineskins Missionary Network), the South American Missionary Society–U.S.A. (now the Society of Anglican Missionaries and Senders), Episcopal World Mission (now Global Teams), Sharing of Ministries Abroad–U.S.A., Anglican Frontier Missions and other groups.

This development prompted tension and even animosity between the new groups and agencies of the Episcopal Church Center in New York City. The new groups felt DFMS had abandoned its historic commitment to mission and missionaries in favor of a liberal development agenda. DFMS units felt the new groups were alien to the mission ethos of the Episcopal Church and that they were intruding on work assigned to the DFMS since 1835.

Earnest striving for rapprochement resulted in the founding in 1990 of the Episcopal Council for Global Mission (ECGM). Despite the conciliar name, the group was never designed to direct, legislate or adjudicate. Instead, it was a network through which mission organizations were invited to consult and collaborate rather than compete, working within a framework of four covenants: share information, work in partnership, explore theological diversity and affirm reaching underevangelized peoples. Initially it embraced about twenty-five agencies, which included voluntary societies, congregations, dioceses, seminaries and DFMS units.

The network was structured specifically to curb the politics of personal ambition and party competition. This reflected an environment of differing emphases on evangelism, church-planting, underevangelized peoples, and infrastructure development, and differing views on social issues, especially the status of lesbian, gay, bisexual and transgender people in the church. Decisions could be made only by consensus, not voting, and the steering committee was chosen by literally drawing names from a hat—measures also promoted as nurturing openness to the Holy Spirit's guidance. For similar reasons the network did not appoint an executive director, preferring instead an administrator who implemented decisions of the annual meeting and the steering committee.

Through the council, trust increased to a remarkable extent among individuals and groups who previously had viewed each other with suspicion. Evangelicals and liberals, traditionalists and progressives began to consult, learn from one another and recognize shared commitments in mission. The network undertook major initiatives such as conferences on underevangelized peoples, persecuted Christians and suffering children, and a mission exposure program in Central America.

Equally important, the mission office at headquarters, called Anglican and Global Relations at the time, endorsed the newly decentralized flourishing of mission. Much as Methodists and Presbyterians today are reorganizing to support localized mission efforts, the Episcopal mission office took the even more radical step in 1994 of proposing that the DFMS cease sending missionaries as a normative practice:

> Instead, national staff will collaborate with interested dioceses, congregations and institutions—especially those gathered under the umbrella of the Episcopal Council on [sic] Global Mission—to see that qualified persons continue to participate in cross-cultural and overseas mission. Funding for such mission will come from local sources, with the Executive Council using certain monies restricted to the Volunteers for Mission program to assist, in ways yet to be determined.

The rationale for the proposal was stated clearly:

> Why this change in direction from a national program to one more broadly based? One of the results of the Executive Council's conversations with the Church is a conscious decision not to carry out on a purely national level program and activities that can better be delegated to other interested sectors of the community.[9]

A more complete reversal of mission centralization was hard to imagine. Nevertheless, the proposal prompted consternation in many parts of the church, including virtually all the organizations of the Episcopal Council for Global Mission. Many felt that the DFMS would be abandoning the function for which it was established and that missionary work was so integral to the church's nature that missionaries should continue to be sent on a churchwide basis. The proposal's openness to institutional diversification was read, instead, as abdication from world mission.

One group of mission activists began to envision another network that could step into the breach. They reasoned that if the DFMS would not be sending missionaries, it was ecclesially logical to turn to the next canonical structure of the church, namely, the dioceses and their bishops. Thus the Global Episcopal Mission Network (GEM Network) was formed to connect dioceses in supporting world mission, possibly to the extent of sending missionaries on the kind of collaborative model that the original proposal suggested.

Ultimately, the missionary termination proposal was rejected by the 1994 General Convention, and the DFMS continued to send missionaries internationally. The Episcopal Council for Global Mission continued as a network, now alongside the new GEM Network, which organized to encourage dioceses. It also networked with the Partnership for World Mission, a newly formed loose association of the historic mission societies of the Church of England. The controversy continues to be important in today's developments throughout the denominations, because it pushes us to ask important questions: What is the continuing role of central mission offices in the churches? Are there limits to decentralization, beyond which a church's international work loses coherence? Are there some mission functions that should always have a churchwide expression?

The politics of mission inclusion continued to be unsettled as missionaries sent by the voluntary societies were not recognized as "official" missionaries of the Episcopal Church, as were those sent by the DFMS. A reorganization of the council to bring it into closer relationship with the church's central structures and to develop mutually agreed standards for the sending and churchwide endorsement of missionaries gave birth to the Episcopal Partnership for Global Mission (EPGM) in 2000. Networking flourished even more than before, and the partnership grew to include more than sixty societies, congregations, dioceses and central units, while the GEM Network drew forty to fifty dioceses.

Politics intervened yet again, this time through the theological ramifications of clashing views about homosexuality. Some in the mission community were profoundly disturbed by the confirmation and consecration of an openly gay and partnered priest to be bishop of New Hampshire in 2003, a controversy that continues to roil the Anglican Communion today. A number of traditionalist organizations in the Episcopal Partnership for Global Mission reconsidered their collaboration within the group. Earlier the voluntary societies had sought recognition from the church's central structures, but now many viewed that link as tainted. Practically, the societies were concerned that their work with Anglican dioceses and provinces upset by the Episcopal Church's decisions would be jeopardized by association with its central structures. Beginning in 2004, traditionalist groups began to withdraw from the partnership and form yet another mission network, Anglican Global Mission Partners (AGMP), and today some of its organizations no longer identify themselves as Episcopal.

This was a major blow to the international mission work of the Episcopal Church. Engaging difference within the mission community had enhanced organizations' vision for engaging difference abroad. Participants had learned both from kindred spirits and from those who differed with them theologically and strategically. Each separate network now has twenty to thirty member organizations, and there is little contact between organizations on opposite sides of the sexuality divide. The church's mission vision and work are poorer for the split.

A strategic ramification of the fracture of EPGM is that if the missionary termination proposal of the mid-1990s had been approved, the Episcopal Church today would have few, if any, missionaries who could be said to be sent by the whole church, for the new agencies that actually sent missionaries—the point at issue in 1994—are all now affiliated with Anglican Global Mission Partners. A lesson for congregations, regional groupings and central offices of the denominations is that world mission engagement is important at all levels of a church. Just as we rejoice in today's wide sharing of mission initiative at the grassroots, we should steward well the continuing involvement of churchwide structures.[10]

The essential gift of the Episcopal story for mission activists is that the networking of groups involved in mission offers vital opportunities for collaboration. Congregations, agencies, regional groupings, seminaries and central offices of whatever denomination can all compare notes and learn from one another both at periodic gatherings and on an ongoing basis. Networks celebrate the diversification and democratization of world mission, yet help to bring the many dispersed parties into communication and collaboration with one another. Yes, the Episcopal story includes the sadness of alienation and fragmentation. At least, however, people have been free to align themselves as they feel moved, and arguments about mission have been open rather than under the table. Perhaps the impulse to reconcile in the encounter with difference, an impulse that we have seen is at the heart of mission, will yet bring disparate mission activists together again.

Mission Conferences and Ecumenical Networks

Mission conferences have been a staple of mission strategy and inspiration since the mid-nineteenth century, both in the Global North and in the Global South, the latter initially drawing together missionaries in the field and now organized by churches in the Two-Thirds World. The many publications and global events celebrating the centennial of the 1910 World Missionary Conference in Edinburgh testify to how that conference energized important movements in mission and ecumenism over the twentieth century. There have been many world and regional conferences before and since. Those of the International Missionary Council continue under the auspices of the Commission on World Mission and Evangelism of the World Council of Churches, and many evangelical groups gather in conferences organized by the Lausanne Movement for world evangelization. The websites and publications of these initiatives are well worth following.

More accessible to congregations and mid-level regional units of the churches are the network and churchwide mission conferences that are now becoming more active. Since 1975, the ELCA has held sixty-five "Global Mission Events," some of them involving thousands of people, including long-term missionaries, young adult volunteers, central staff, and many activists from congregations and synods. Altogether, thirty-eight thousand people are said to have attended so far to "celebrate, challenge, share stories, and [be sent] out inspired to serve the other." Under the theme of "connecting the global and local," a number of regional events are held annually that provide basic orientation to mission action and support, including how to "travel internationally in a way that is effective, sustainable, respectful, and cross-culturally sensitive."[11]

Presbyterians began holding a biennial Mission Celebration in 2007, the first being organized by the central office. The 2009 version drew about seven hundred people to Cincinnati, Ohio, and was organized by a wide range of Presbyterian mission groups. Large churchwide gatherings among United Methodists are longstanding. Lutherans, Presbyterians and Methodists have established extensive infrastructures of information and education, including regularly published mission magazines and study materials, all of which are easily accessed on the web.

Evangelical Episcopal mission activists began a triennial mission conference, New Wineskins for Global Mission, in 1994, and in 2008 a more centrist triennial mission conference, Everyone Everywhere, was inaugurated and drew about three hundred people. Meanwhile, the three networks with roots in the Episcopal Church each hold conferences annually, and these smaller gatherings offer opportunity for intensive mutual learning and consultation.

At the same time, mission activists concerned with particular peoples and issues around the world are increasingly networking with others in their own churches and beyond to coordinate efforts. The many area networks among Presbyterians are an outstanding example of this trend as activists communicate regularly with each other, even keeping minutes of their face-to face gatherings and electronic conferencing. Christian Connections for International Health offers networking to 125 member organizations committed to medical mission and includes 33 international affiliates.

"The inter-Methodist and intra-board work that is coalescing around Haiti is a significant step in our mission strategy," said Thomas Kemper, general secretary of Global Ministries for the United Methodist Church following a consultation that drew together a number of Methodist and other organizations a few months after Haiti's 2010 earthquake. Kemper advocated a "roundtable approach" in mission planning and implementation.[12] Similar networks have been formalized among Episcopalians. The Haiti

Connection, for instance, draws scores of congregations, agencies and regional church units to an annual conference to coordinate efforts with the Diocese of Haiti. Groups named "friends of . . ." have been formed to support Anglican churches in such places as Sudan, Honduras and Peshawar, Pakistan.

The era of mission democratization and diversification could be one of fragmentation and incoherence, but it need not be. As mission activists seek companionship with communities in other parts of the world, we should likewise nourish companionship with one another for the flourishing of God's mission.

Notes

1. Hunter Farrell, "We're Better Together," *Presbyterians Today*, May 2010, 14.

2. Presbyterian World Mission, "Community of Mission Practice Concept Paper," February 2010, 1, accessible at http://missional.info/archives/125.

3. Presbyterian World Mission, "Community of Mission Practice Concept Paper," 1–2.

4. Presbyterian World Mission, "Community of Mission Practice Concept Paper," 1.

5. Presbyterian World Mission, "Community of Mission Practice Concept Paper," 2.

6. "Presbyterian World Mission Strategic Direction," 1–2, accessible at http://missional.info/archives/125.

7. Presbyterian World Mission, "Global Discipleship: Four Critical Global Issues for Global Mission's Strategic Focus," memorandum, April 16, 2010, 1–2; Hunter Farrell, personal correspondence.

8. Presbyterian World Mission, "Community of Mission Practice Concept Paper," 2.

9. Memorandum, "Appointed Missionaries and Volunteers for Mission: A New Vision," on Episcopal Church Center stationery, undated (1994).

10. For a more complete account and documentation of the material in this section, see Titus Presler, "Episcopal Networking for God's Mission: A History of the Episcopal Partnership for Global Mission," in preparation for publication, a shorter version of which appears at the EPGM website, www.epgm.org. See also www.gemn.org and www.agmp-na.org.

11. http://www.elca.org/Who-We-Are/Our-Three-Expressions/Churchwide-Organization/Global-Mission/Engage-in-Global-Mission/Global-Events/Global-Mission-Events.aspx.

12. http://gbgm-umc.org/global_news/full_article.cfm?articleid=5746.

CHAPTER EIGHT

Missionary Calling and Identity:
A Challenge in Being Sent

Reconciling mission in a world of difference—this is what God is up to. God's mission is to reconcile a world that has turned difference into a reason for dealing death. Reconciling difference is God's vision for the human and cosmic community.

Reconciling mission in a world of difference—the phrase also highlights an internal struggle for many Christians: reconciling themselves to the very concept of mission and to the notion that they are integral to the mission of God in the world.

While excited about being sent by churches to participate in God's work in the world, some outgoing personnel initially prefer not to see themselves as "missionaries" or their ministry as "mission." Even as churches use the word "mission" more than ever before, they have, paradoxically, been ambivalent about using the term for their international and cross-cultural work. Similarly, talk of missionaries and Christian mission as a category often prompts skepticism and criticism, whether in ordinary conversation or public discourse.

Five Crises of Mission Awareness

Such reservations about mission in the twenty-first century express the continuing impact of five crises of awareness that dramatically affected mission thinking in the last century, what I refer to as mission's Century of Self-

Criticism. Events in the world prompted intellectual and theological shifts that were experienced as so major, even traumatic, that mission leaders and ordinary Christians in the historic Protestant mainline churches felt that their worldview was in crisis.

Crisis 1: A universal gospel?

First, a crisis of confidence in the universal validity of the Christian gospel prompted skepticism in mainline churches about evangelism, conversion and church planting. In the first centuries after Christ, Christianity grew as one of many options in a multireligious environment, but to twentieth-century Western Christians witnessing the collapse of monolithic Christendom, religious diversity felt like a brand-new situation. They needed to step back and take their bearings. If mission meant mainly "converting people," they were no longer so sure about mission. Dialogue with people of other religions, not proclamation, was seen as the urgent need.

Crisis 2: Toxic mission?

Second, a crisis of guilt and repentance for political colonialism and cultural imperialism prompted Christians in the Global North to fear that mission was just meddling, what a student of mine called "toxic mission." Doubt deepened when supposedly Christian nations ignited two world wars, allowed the Holocaust and continued to monopolize the world's resources while polluting the earth. If mission meant mainly spreading Western culture, many were no longer so sure about mission. The globalizing power of European and North American finance, technology and culture made many fear that mission from the North would repeat the colonial past. In the 1970s, church leaders in the Global South called briefly for a moratorium on missionaries. While it was never implemented, European and North American mission agencies took the concerns seriously, and the number of missionaries across the mainline denominations decreased radically.

Crisis 3: What about our backyard?

Third, the 1960s brought a crisis of responsibility to Western churches as they recognized the interlocking realities of poverty, racism and injustice in their own societies. "Why send missionaries abroad," many asked, "when we've got so many problems unsolved at home?" Although numerous African Americans served as missionaries in the Western mission enterprise, the predominant association of mission with initiatives by white people toward people of color linked mission with racism in the minds of many. International mission was viewed as expressing simultaneously a know-it-all arrogance about other people's problems abroad and a stubborn denial of problems at home that the churches had long ignored.

Crisis 4: Through institutions?

These shifts prompted a fourth, a crisis of confidence in institutions. The institutional networks regarded as most sinister were the "military-industrial complex" and "corporate America," but educational, social and commercial institutions of all kinds became suspect. Individualized, spontaneous and grassroots expressions in many areas of life came to be preferred over institutional, impersonal and corporate expressions. Many Global North Christians felt reluctant to support missionaries who would represent anything so fallible as an institutional church. They realized that injustice was nourished not only by personal sin but also by the complicity of institutions, including churches. Lacking congregational support, world mission shared the general malaise of the institutional church.

Crisis 5: Game over?

Ironically, success brought its own crisis. It was mission, after all, that founded and nurtured churches in villages, towns and cities around the world over several hundred years and established the myriad educational, medical and other empowerment institutions that ministered to communities in the host societies. By 2000, Christians numbered 2 billion, the clear majority of them now in the Two-Thirds World, and they were the most populous and widely distributed religious affiliation on earth. The mission movement had always expected missionaries to work themselves out of their jobs. Westerners made way for indigenous pastors, doctors, nurses, teachers and theologians, and Christianity in the Global South multiplied and diversified in spectacular ways. In this changed environment, Global North churches wondered what direction their global outreach should take, and even if they should have one.

   This questioning has affected even the names that churches give to their global engagement. The Board of Missions of the United Methodist Church became the General Board of Global Ministries in 1972, the name still used today. Successive reorganizations of the Episcopal Church's global work retained the word "mission" until 1991, when "partnerships" became the operative word, followed by Anglican and Global Relations as the departmental name in 1994, which then was split in 2008 between a Partnerships Center and a Networking Center. By contrast, Global Mission has been the departmental name in the ELCA since the church's formation in 1988, before which the predecessor churches used "world missions" in combination with "interchurch cooperation" and "ecumenism." Presbyterian World Mission is forthright about mission but prefers to call the people sent abroad "mission coworkers" rather than "missionaries." Lutherans, Episcopalians and Methodists continue to use the traditional term "missionary" for their personnel, though there has been advocacy for the term "mission partner." In England, the Church Mission Society calls its personnel "mission partners" and USPG calls its workers "mission companions."

Clearly, reconciling ourselves to mission continues to be a struggle even amid the positive directions that mission has taken over the last half century. "Isn't there another word that we could use instead of 'mission'?" I am often asked in discussions and classes, with questioners going on to say something like, "It seems like 'mission' has so many negative connotations that it gets in the way." The association that mission has in many people's minds with condescension, arrogance and imposition certainly poses obstacles to understanding. The difficulty is that no viable substitute term has emerged from the extensive missiological reflection taking place worldwide, in the Global South as well as in the North. Despite the negative connotations, "mission" uniquely encapsulates in one word the quality of being sent beyond the boundaries of home, the encounter with difference that is inherent in going out and the rich history of an enterprise that has been pursued in many diverse ways for two thousand years.

The response I suggest to the problematic associations is not to discard the term "mission" but to rehabilitate it. This takes many forms. Considerable renovation has already taken place as churches today designate a wide range of activities as mission. People now recognize that mission includes social service as well as evangelism, work nearby as well as work far away. As we have seen, this usage is appropriate so long as mission is understood as ministry that reaches out to difference. On the question of home versus abroad, more people today recognize that "problems" should no longer be the primary focus of international mission and, conversely, that stubborn problems at home do not invalidate mission abroad. Indeed, cross-cultural encounters shed light on issues at home and vice versa. Another way to rehabilitate mission is to help people understand the history more fully and fairly. While some missionaries' attitudes were condescending and colonial, other missionaries worked in humility and servanthood. While some programs alienated people from their cultures, other initiatives listened deeply and empowered local cultures. As with any historical phenomenon, the record is not uniform but mixed.

Churches' Priorities for Twenty-First-Century Mission

Knowledge of what today's churches mean and intend by mission can help people who are interested in global engagement as Christians but cautious on account of their rough impressions of mission history. It can help to reconcile us to the notion of mission. Further, as mission activists in the congregations and mid-level units of the churches pray and plan mission initiatives, it is important to be aware of the overall vision of their churches and of how that vision relates to a wider ecumenical consensus. Such awareness helps faster coordination among the many entities pursuing mission and nurture reconciled relationship within mission communities.

This consideration is focused by examining and comparing the goal statements for mission that have been put forward by the four North American mainline churches that have been reference points in this book: the Evangelical Lutheran Church in America (ELCA), the United Methodist Church (UMC), the Presbyterian Church (U.S.A.) or PC(USA), and the Episcopal Church U.S.A. or ECUSA.

Unlike more extended lists of qualities or criteria of mission service that the churches have suggested, the lists of goals are all relatively succinct. Methodists, Presbyterians and Lutherans have each suggested four goals or priorities, and the Anglican Communion, of which the Episcopal Church is a member province, has set forth Five Marks of Mission.[1]

There is a striking consensus among the churches that the first priority is gospel witness and proclamation. The Lutherans' first goal for the twenty-first century is to "Share the good news of Jesus Christ with those who acknowledge no faith, people of other faiths and adherents of various ideologies, and of those who have become inactive in or have abandoned their Christian faith." In addition, the church's first criterion of accompaniment is "witness in word and deed." Lutherans are forthright about having evangelism in mind.

Similarly, Presbyterian World Mission lists "Be My Witnesses" as the first of its "four critical global issues for strategic focus." In explanation, the church mentions places where "people have not yet heard the good news and we are compelled to answer God's call to share the gospel." "Make Disciples of Jesus Christ" is the top priority of the General Board of Global Ministries of the United Methodist Church, which goes on to say, "We will witness by word and deed among those who haven't heard or heeded the Gospel of Jesus Christ." The first Anglican mark of mission is "To proclaim the Good News of the Kingdom," a mark that has been widely interpreted to endorse evangelism.

This concurrence on the priority of gospel proclamation represents an important shift from the skepticism that pervaded mainline denominations in the latter part of the twentieth century, when forthright gospel proclamation was pushed aside in favor of the priority of interreligious dialogue. In relating to other religions, churches and mission agencies today realize that witness means listening and learning as well as proclaiming. Interreligious encounters need people who will live in the interface between religions, and missionaries are generally the people willing to do that. Likewise the churches recognize anew that in the global religious dialogue, Jesus' gospel is a gift that needs sharing, especially among the many who have never heard it.

Growing in understanding with people of other religions continues to be a priority of the four churches, although it is not listed among the top goals. For the Lutherans, "interfaith witness and dialogue" is the third criterion of accompaniment as they say, "The ELCA is committed to include interfaith witness and conversation in its programs in order that there might be mutual understanding and respect between the ELCA and people of diverse faiths." A list of Ten Marks of Anglican Mission proposed in 2001 included "cooperation with people of other faiths" as the ninth mark.[2]

Methodists and Anglicans join in listing as their second priority the nurture of communities of faith. "Strengthen, Develop and Renew Christian Congregations and Communities" is the second Methodist goal. "We will work mutually with mission partners in common growth and development of spiritual life, worship, witness and service," the church explains. The Anglicans' second mark is "To teach, baptize and nurture new believers," widely interpreted to include planting new churches as well. Presbyterians include concern for the church in the subtitle of their top priority of witness: "Strengthening the church's capacity to survive, to thrive and to witness to the good news in Jesus Christ." They explain that "global discipleship promotes an awareness of the health and vitality of the church throughout the world; stands in solidarity with persecuted churches; assists in developing leadership for growing and new churches," and the like.

For Lutherans, concern for the church is diffused between their third and fourth major goals. The third is to "Accompany churches around the world and invite them to accompany this church in expressing the unity of the Body of Christ and in cooperating in the mission of the Triune God," which includes activities like leadership development, education and ecumenism. The fourth is to "Work with the ELCA in developing our gifts as a church and embracing the gifts of others as we walk together in global mission," specified as global education, global relationships, stewardship and prayer. Here it appears that Lutheran goal-setting essentially fused method with content.

"Alleviate Human Suffering" is the third goal of Methodists, who explain, "We will help to initiate, strengthen and support ministries to the spiritual, physical, emotional and social needs of people." In a similar vein, the third Anglican mark of mission is "To respond to human need by loving service." The second Lutheran goal is similar, but it is articulated in terms more in line with contemporary missiology: "Be in solidarity with and advocate for people who are oppressed, poor and suffering, and share our resources to meet human need."

Presbyterians narrow their focus to "Women and Children First: Addressing the negative effects of economic globalization on the poorest and most vulnerable in every society, women and children." In addition to highlighting Jesus' phrase "the least of these," this focus may represent an assessment that limited resources are most effective if they are more narrowly targeted than when they are dispersed to address the entirety of global poverty and suffering.

The Methodists' fourth and final goal returns to the broad-brush approach: "Seek Justice, Freedom and Peace," and they explain, "We will participate with people oppressed by unjust economic, political and social systems and programs that seek to build just, free and peaceful societies." The Anglicans' fourth mark of mission is similar: "To seek to transform unjust structures of society."

It is only the Presbyterians who cite reconciliation explicitly, in the third of their critical global issues: "Living God's *Shalom*: Engaging in reconciliation amidst cultures of violence." They name interethnic, interreligious and domestic violence and include poverty as a type of violence: "The violence of poverty results in many daily indignities, sorrows, and harm." They highlight peacemaking and nonviolent conflict resolution as approaches to reconciliation. As though seeking to remedy an omission, the Anglican Consultative Council in 2009 endorsed a Canadian suggestion to add a sixth mark to the Anglican five that would relate to "peace, conflict transformation and reconciliation"[3] and the proposal is currently being studied.

Ecological mission is a priority for Presbyterians and Anglicans. "Restoring and Caring for God's Good Creation: Responsible and respectful care of the environment and its nonhuman inhabitants" is the fourth and final critical issue for Presbyterians. The Anglicans fifth and final mark of mission is "To strive to safeguard the integrity of creation and sustain and renew the life of the earth." Although Lutherans do not include ecology as one of their four major goals, they cite "Justice, Peace and Integrity of Creation," the classic World Council of Churches formulation, among their twelve criteria of accompaniment.

This comparison and contrast offers a number of messages for mission activists, mission committees and denominational mission offices: The ecumenical consensus about mission is not vague and abstract but strikingly specific. Your own church's emphases are not idiosyncratic but arise out of broadly based ecumenical reflection. Churches have worked out their mission vision in considerable detail, and it is worthwhile to go to the respective websites and study them. Finally, as you undertake mission, you need not be tongue-tied about what your church means by mission. Excellent resources are available to diversify and strengthen your discourse about God's mission in the world.

Mission Begins with God

The crucial way to reconcile ourselves to mission—and, as a side benefit, to renovate the term "mission"—is to develop and live into a missional ethos that draws us and others to join joyfully what God is up to in the world. What we need is an ethos of mission to which people will respond not by shrugging their shoulders or turning away, but with intrigued curiosity, saying, "Ah, if *that's* what mission is, I'd like to explore it—and I can even see myself being a part of it."

An ethos for mission highlights not so much the *what* of mission as the *how* of mission—the mode, the approach, the orientation with which mission is undertaken. We have identified this mode as companionship and accompaniment. Earlier we explored its outworking in some detail, and it is time now to elaborate its source in God's story with us.

While the fruit of mission companionship is expressed in relationships among Christians and churches in different parts of the world, its root lies in the relationship between God and ourselves. Emmanuel, "God with us," the name cited for Jesus in Matthew's gospel, expresses God's solidarity with us as a companion in the joys and griefs of what it means to be human. Thus the incarnation, the very heart of our faith, enacts companionship, God accompanying us in the human journey. Yet true companionship is mutual, not simply the service of one side to the other. We have seen how Jesus needed the companionship of his friends. The gospels depict vividly both how they courageously accompanied him and how in the final crisis they abandoned him and betrayed the companionship. Even as the one who images God's companionship with us, Jesus in his humanity images our own need for companionship with God and with one another.

This companionship plays out in the mission that Jesus gave to his disciples. As we read the gospels, we tend to focus on the gravity and privilege of the task that Jesus conferred in sending them out. Equally important, though, is the manifest reality that he *needed* them in order for his work to continue. In calling them together, he created a community that could observe him closely and then replicate his ministry. In sending out the twelve and then the seventy, the work he gave them to do was precisely the work he himself had been doing in proclaiming and enacting the reign of God. In his final instructions he turned over to them the fullness of his own mission. Added to the personal companionship he needed from them, therefore, was the companionship in mission that he would need with them beyond his earthly ministry. Echoing the Emmanuel theme at his gospel's opening, Matthew quotes Jesus as promising a reciprocal companionship in the Great Commission with which his gospel closes: "And remember, I am with you always, to the end of the age" (Matthew 28:20). "*With* you."

As with the gospels, so with Pentecost we tend to emphasize the great gift and privilege conferred on the disciples as God sent them the Holy Spirit to fill and equip them. Equally important, this gift empowered the disciples to continue in the mission companionship that Jesus had inaugurated with them and which now needed fulfillment. God *needed* that company of disciples for the mission to continue, and as they proclaimed the gospel in word and deed they were enacting a mission companionship with God.

In the long prayer John depicts Jesus as offering on his last night, Jesus pictures our companionship with him as a mutual indwelling and declares that it is for the sake of mission: "As you, Father, are in me and I am in you, may they also be in us, so that the world may believe that you have sent me" (John 17:21). This enmeshed companionship in mission is sustained by the eucharistic reality that Paul celebrates with the Corinthians when he asks, "The cup of blessing that we bless, is it not a sharing in the blood of Christ? The bread that we break, is it not a sharing in the body of Christ?" (1 Corinthians 10:16). The Greek word for sharing here is *koinonia*, which also means community, itself premised on companionship. Paul's image of the church as the body of Christ (1 Corinthians 12) depends on such eucharistic and mystical intuitions of the mutual companionship between God and the community that continues God's mission in the world. The body image continues the incarnational dynamic of Jesus the Word made flesh, but now on a sacramental level wherein the church is the continuing presence of Christ in the world.

The bottom line is this: As we join what God is up to in the world, we are offering companionship to God in God's own mission. As we join that movement, God offers us a sustaining companionship. As we go global with God, God goes global with us. Both sides need. Both sides offer. Such genuine and mutual companionship may not only reconcile us to mission but immerse us in mission, for it is the current of God's life in the world.

Notes

1. For the ELCA's mission goals, see ELCA, *Global Mission in the Twenty-first Century* (Chicago: Evangelical Lutheran Church in America, 1999, reprinted 2007), esp. 24–34. For those of PC(USA), see Presbyterian World Mission, "Global Discipleship: Four Critical Global Issues for Global Mission's Strategic Focus," memorandum, April 16, 2010, 1–2. For the UMC's goals, see http://new.gbgm-umc.org/work/goals/. For Anglicanism's Five Marks of Mission, see http://www.anglicancommunion.org/ministry/mission/fivemarks.cfm.

2. Titus Presler, *Horizons of Mission* (Boston: Cowley, 2001), 173–75.

3. Resolution 14.05: "Sixth Mark of Mission (Mission)," May 11, 2009, at fourteenth meeting of the Anglican Consultative Council; http://www.anglicancommunion.org/acns/news.cfm/2009/5/12/ACNS4630.

CHAPTER NINE

Poverty and Wholistic Mission:
A Challenge in Difference

W e have seen how poverty and its many attendant ills—social, educational, medical—are embraced by the urgency of God's reconciling vision. We have seen how systemic poverty is built by using human
differences as pretexts for avarice for one's own group and the exclusion
of others.

Over the last several decades and certainly in the first decade of the
twenty-first century, a number of factors have coalesced to make poverty and
its effects the primary focus of mission for many churches in the Global
North and in other parts of the world. This focus, however, may actually
smuggle in assumptions contrary to authentic mission, and therefore it must
be examined. This may seem a startling turn in the discussion, given the
centrality of difference and reconciliation. Yet the focus on poverty today is
so prominent that it merits special attention as a challenge to our mission
thinking and practice in relation to difference.

A Critique from the Global South

Mano Rumalshah has what he calls "a deep pain" in his heart. "When we
are reaching 'down' to people who are poor, who are of a lower class and
who have little social influence," he says, "we call it 'mission.' When we go
to people of our own status and class, or who are above us in economic and

social status, we call it something else—'friendship evangelism,' 'inter-church relations, 'fraternal work,' or something like that."

Rumalshah's critique is striking, especially considering how much of his life's work has been focused on the needs of a church that is truly down-trodden in the classic biblical sense. He is bishop emeritus of the Diocese of Peshawar in Pakistan and was the first person from the Two-Thirds World to be general secretary of the United Society for the Propagation of the Gospel, Anglicanism's oldest mission society. Although the largest religious minor-ity in Pakistan, the 3.9 million Christians are a small minority of 2.5 percent among the overwhelming Muslim majority in the country of 153 million people. The Church of Pakistan, of which Rumalshah is a bishop, is a unit-ing church that brought together Presbyterians, Anglicans, Baptists. Methodists and Lutherans in 1970, now with well over a million members. Christians are marginalized by being excluded from the many ordinary edu-cational and professional opportunities that are reserved for Muslims. Per-secution in the form of beatings, church burnings and killings occurs sporadically, especially as Pakistani Islam has taken a fundamentalist turn under the influence of the Taliban.

"In Pakistan we are not only the church *for* the poor," says Rumalshah, "we are the church *of* the poor." Many Christians are sweepers and cleaners, doing the lowliest jobs, which in the predominantly Hindu society of neigh-boring India are done only by outcastes. Since Pakistan and India before 1947 were one society, caste consciousness affected Muslims as well, so that today Pakistan's outcastes are its Christians. Shoring up institutions that edu-cate Christians and prepare them for professional careers has been a major emphasis of the church, as has been the support of women's economic coop-eratives in the *bastis*, or slums, where Christians live.

For years Rumalshah encouraged financial support from abroad for the church in Pakistan, and he continues to do so in assisting the efforts of his successor Humphrey Salfaraz Peters. Much of the financial support helps the many church institutions that communicate Christ's compassion and signify the Christian community's concern for the poor, sick and marginal-ized of Pakistan through schools, clinics, hospitals and vocational centers. What Rumalshah calls the *diakonia*, or service, of these institutions is eco-nomically accessible mainly to the country's Muslim majority.

With this lifetime commitment to ministry to the poor in his own coun-try, Rumalshah's critique of Christian mission's link with poverty today has special force. What is he saying? He is identifying a silent bias in contempo-rary Christian mission thinking, an assumption so common and so basic that many are unaware of routinely expressing it in words and actions. The assumption is that mission mainly means reaching out to the poor. Rumal-shah is questioning that assumption. He is asking whether reaching the poor describes completely the content of Christian mission. What assumptions does the poverty bias carry about class and social location? Does it enter into the fullness of God's mission?

Mission's Association with Poverty

Many Christians around the world, and certainly in the Global North, understand mission primarily as reaching out to people who are in some kind of need. The need may be religious, as when a church or agency feels that a particular people group needs to hear the good news of Christ, or when churches send pastors to minister with congregations in parts of the world where there are few clergy. Historically from the time of Jesus on, the outward thrust of the Christian movement has had a strongly religious tone: Christians had good news to share about what God was up to in Christ Jesus, and they were eager to share it. This evangelistic fervor accounts for the fact that there are now more Christians in the world than adherents of any other religious worldview.[1]

Today in the mainline churches of the Global North, however, mission is more often seen in terms of economic, medical or educational need. Congregations, regional judicatories and entire churches reach out to such need in a variety of ways. Relief teams fly quickly to the aftermath of earthquakes, floods, fires and tsunamis. Economic missioners nurture microenterprise projects and manage sustainable development programs to alleviate poverty. Doctors, nurses and administrators staff clinics, hospitals and specific health initiatives in HIV/AIDS, malaria and tuberculosis. Teachers go to work in schools, colleges and adult literacy programs. The vocabulary associated with this kind of ministry is familiar and ubiquitous. Christians speak of reaching out to "the poor," "the needy," "the marginalized" and "those less fortunate than ourselves."

This approach is often lifted up as an up-to-date form of mission, more appropriate than the historic evangelization that is often viewed as imperialistic "Bible-thumping" that "shoved the gospel down people's throats." Better-informed policymakers in Global North churches recognize evangelization as a continuing task but often feel it is now the responsibility of indigenous churches rather than their international companions. The mainline churches take up mission in the material dimension, which is seen as outreach to the poor.

The human need highlighted by poverty tends to be the exclusive focus of short-term mission trips, which today are how most people in Global North churches experience mission, whether within their own countries or in other societies and cultures. The major domestic destinations of teams from USAmerican congregations are Appalachia, New Orleans since Hurricane Katrina, and Native American reservations, chosen because the people living there are understood to be especially poor and needy. Teams do not typically go to affluent sites such as the lakeside towns north of Chicago, the upper east side of Manhattan or La Jolla, California, although there may be significant dimensions of difference in those areas. What would there be to do there? No, it is thought, mission concerns the needy. Similarly, teams going abroad typically visit a barrio in Honduras or a township in South Africa, not a posh area of London or Tokyo. Whether at home or abroad, teams carry out tasks that are often needed in poor communities. They build homes, paint schools and help with feeding and daycare programs for children and the elderly. We understand ourselves to be on mission when we reach out to the especially poor in societies that we understand to be more generally needy than our own.

The association of mission with the human needs concentrated in the geography of global poverty also affects theological formation for mission. The grants program of the Seminary Consultation on Mission, a cooperative venture among Episcopal seminaries, funds students for internships in all parts of the world outside the United States—except Europe. One aspect of this policy decision—in which I myself participated—was a concern that seminarians experience a degree of cultural difference greater than was thought to be available in Western countries. Also influencing the policy was, again, the association of mission with poverty.

Missionary assignments made by central mission offices of the mainline churches are broader, for there are Methodist, Presbyterian, Lutheran and Episcopal missionaries across Europe, with Lutheran missionaries especially numerous in eastern Europe. At missionary orientations, though, trainees sometimes joke among themselves about assignments in western Europe: "Oh yeah, Paris, *that's* a hardship post!" This reflects an underlying assumption that *real* mission work is among the needy in places that involve deprivation as missionaries rough it alongside the poor.

Globalization is now well known to be a phenomenon with mixed effects. Travel and communication have been made more accessible to millions, and many have benefited from the spread of a global market economy. On the other hand, that same economy has made the livelihoods of many people subject to the market whims of global economic elites and distant consumer populations. Multitudes labor for low wages in difficult factory conditions to make ephemeral goods they themselves will never wear, play or work with. The near collapse of the global economic system as a result of a USAmerican housing bubble in 2008 illustrated the dynamics on a catastrophic scale. Although much mission outreach to the poor today is not designed to challenge these dynamics in any fundamental way, the effects of globalization make many Christians passionate about ameliorating its effects.

Agencies devoted to the material dimensions of human need have developed verbal catchlines that encapsulate the churches' concern for the poor. "Building a better world for children" is the motto of World Vision, which describes itself as "a Christian humanitarian organization dedicated to working with children, families and their communities worldwide to reach their full potential by tackling the causes of poverty and injustice."[2] Amid all the world's needs, the welfare of children is put foremost as the group wrestles with what it perceives as the two major obstacles: poverty and injustice. Lutheran World Relief's self-description is similar in naming its principal concerns in addressing human need: "Affirming God's love for all people, we work with Lutherans and partners around the world to end poverty, injustice and human suffering."[3]

"Healing a hurting world" is the intriguing catchline of Episcopal Relief and Development, which organizes its work toward fulfilling the Millennium Development Goals, the United Nations' ambitious 2015 objectives for poverty, hunger, health, education, women and the environment.[4] The motto is both emotive and theological. The world's ills are encompassed in the experience of pain that they bring to sufferers, whether the pain is economic, social or physical. The many remedies are summed up in healing, a straightforward empirical category that is also open to being interpreted theologically as a participation in the healing work of God in the cosmos. Interestingly, "a hurting world" can be seen as a world that *inflicts* pain as well as suffers pain, and this could suggest an agenda of confronting the hurting powers, as well as ministering to those they hurt.

Poverty in Scripture, Christian History and Theology

Where did the association of mission with poverty come from? The Bible, or a certain way of reading the Bible, is one important source. The assumption that our participation in God's mission is or should be a response to human need has solid biblical foundation, especially in the New Testament's depiction of the ministry of Jesus. In Luke's account, Jesus began his ministry by declaring in the synagogue at Nazareth that he in his person and work was a pivotal fulfillment of Isaiah's prophecy: "He unrolled the scroll and found the place where it was written, 'The Spirit of the Lord is upon me, because he has anointed me to bring good news to the poor. He has sent me to proclaim release to the captives and recovery of sight to the blind, to let the oppressed go free, to proclaim the year of the Lord's favor'" (Luke 4:17–19).

Following up on this declaration, Jesus declared blessing for the poor and hungry in his beatitudes, and he fulfilled that blessing as he declared jubilee liberation for the oppressed and fed thousands from a few loaves and fish. Outraged by injustice, he excoriated scribes who "devour widows'

houses," that is, appropriated the resources of the most vulnerable and economically powerless in society (Luke 20:47). Jesus viewed excessive wealth as
itself a sign of unjust and oppressive economic behavior that would be pun-
ished at the time of judgment: "But woe to you who are rich, for you have
received your consolation. Woe to you who are full now, for you will be hungry" (Luke 6:24–25).

To the blind, deaf, lame and leprous, Jesus brought healing that restored
them to able-bodied wholeness. This transformed their lives economically as
well as emotionally and socially, for those afflictions were not only personal
disabilities but livelihood handicaps in a hard-pressed agrarian society stag-
gering under an occupying army. So it was that Jesus was often found on the
margins of society, reaching out to those whose situations left them outside
the mainstream.

It is the compassion of Jesus that we often find most exemplary and
instructive in his reaching out to need. Jesus professed compassion in Mark's
account of the feeding of four thousand people: "I have compassion for the
crowd, because they have been with me now for three days and have nothing to eat" (Mark 8:2). The verb for "have compassion" in the original Greek
is a vivid one just to pronounce: *splanknidzomai.* Its root is equally vivid, for
it suggests a feeling so deep and intense that it splits the gut. It connotes
empathy, the response of feeling with another, hence the term "compassion," the Latin root of which denotes suffering *with,* sharing the suffering
of another.

"When [Jesus] saw the crowds," Matthew tells us, "he had compassion for
them, because they were harassed and helpless, like sheep without a shep-
herd" (Matthew 9:36). Expressed through the same verb, Jesus' compassion
arose from his experience of traveling among cities and villages, "teaching in
their synagogues, and proclaiming the good news of the kingdom, and curing every disease and every sickness" (9:35). Spiritual and physical needs were
at issue, and Jesus met both through his preaching and healing.

Into that "plentiful harvest" Jesus sent his disciples to proclaim, "The
kingdom of heaven has come near" and to "cure the sick, raise the dead,
cleanse the lepers, cast out demons" (Matthew 10:7–8). So there was a direct
connection between Jesus' ministry and the disciples' ministry—and, by
extension, with our ministry, for we typically hear ourselves being sent along
with Jesus' disciples. We would like to be found alongside the Good Samaritan who in Jesus' parable "had compassion" (Revised Standard Version)—
again the same verb, but rendered by the New Revised Standard Version as
"moved with pity"—in reaching out to the man who was mugged and left for
dead between Jerusalem and Jericho (Luke 10:33). We hear ourselves
addressed alongside the disciples in Jesus' postresurrection declaration, "As
the Father has sent me, so I send you" (John 20:21). Sent as Jesus was sent,

we feel called to share the compassion with which he ministered, drawn into the orbit of that embrace of the world through which he shared and continues to share its suffering.

This has been a common theme in Christian history. Francis of Assisi, an especially popular saint, felt called to give up his inherited wealth and live as one of the poor, and he encouraged his brothers in the mendicant way of proclaiming Christ as they literally begged their next meal in the streets. More recently, the so-called Martyrs of Memphis are a striking instance of identification with suffering. During the 1878 yellow fever epidemic that killed more than five thousand people in the Tennessee city, Episcopal Sisters of St. Mary and several clergy ministered so constantly and closely with the sick that they themselves fell ill, and some died. The Belgian Roman Catholic missionary Damien Veuster, better known simply as Brother Damien, lived and worked with lepers on the Hawaiian island of Molokai, contracted the disease himself and died in 1889. Mother Teresa, the most renowned missionary of the twentieth century, established the Missionaries of Charity in India after she held a dying man in her arms on a Kolkota street and there beheld the face of Jesus. Sacrificial solidarity with the poor is what made her witness compelling worldwide. Today thousands of Missionaries of Charity work among the poor in cities throughout the world.

Moving beyond the theme of charity is the movement of liberation theology that took hold beginning with the 1971 publication of Peruvian theologian Gustavo Gutiérrez's *Theology of Liberation*.[5] Several themes and developments characterized a movement that has produced powerful grassroots organizations, many publications and considerable controversy. One is a conviction that systemic poverty results from systemic injustice. Situations of oppression can be changed only when unjust powers are confronted and new models are introduced into the system to overcome old patterns. Another theme is the conviction that the situation of the poor cannot be alleviated from outside but only by the poor themselves as they appropriate the power they already have. This is grasped through the liberating gospel of Christ as people develop the vision and strategy that enable them to take power over their community situations and overcome the powers that oppress them. This conviction gave rise to the proliferation of Base Ecclesial Communities, especially in Latin America. Small groups of Christians gathered to reflect on their situations in light of scripture and their experience of Christ and then organized their communities for resistance and creative action.

Foundational in liberation theology has been the concept of God's preferential option for the poor, the conviction that God is concerned especially for the poor. The poor are the vulnerable, their humanity exposed to being wounded by the limitations endemic in poverty and by its disproportionate share of disease, displacement, despair and death. Because God wants all people to flourish fully, the perennial withering of the hopes of the poor evokes God's particular concern. How the poor fare becomes a test of human faithfulness to God, for all are created in God's image.

Correlatively, the vulnerability of the poor offers them particular access to the reality and nature of God, according to many liberation theologians. The God who in scripture expresses concern *for* the poor is experienced with particular authenticity *by* the poor, for they do not participate in the God-alienating lies and oppression that are inherent in unjust structures. From the standpoint of liberation theology, ways in which the poor pray and read scripture have at least the potential of offering uniquely valuable insight into how God may be experienced and what God is saying. That is why Ernesto Cardenal, a Roman Catholic priest and sometime member of the Sandinista government in Nicaragua, captured and transcribed the dialogues that community members had about scripture readings where he lived for ten years on the Solentiname Islands.[6]

One of the most stirring pieces of Christian song I have experienced is a chorus I was introduced to late one night at the home of Edward and Beatrice Mangwanda, friends in the village of Chirarwe in Zimbabwe. I was visiting there in 2000, years after working as a rural pastor with Edward, who was catechist of St. Gabriel's Church. They had gathered a number of peasant farmer friends for a late night of singing, preaching and praying. The country was in economic chaos, people's livelihoods were fragile and political coercion was a constant threat. *"Kunyange zvorema, kunyange zvorema,"* the group of fifteen or so sang at high volume, brought to their feet with drums and rattles—"Though things are hard, though things are hard"—*"Daidzai Jesu, ndiye mutungamiriri wakanaka!"*—"Call upon Jesus, he is a good leader!"

By themselves the words sound like pat cliché, but the lilt of the tune, the passion of the singing and the context transformed them into pure gospel. Part of the wider context was the testimony offered by a teenage girl who was working in the home of one of the attendees, taken in because she had been abused and cast out by her distant relatives. She spoke haltingly and with tears about how real Jesus was to her in the experience of poverty and oppression, bringing the group again to its feet—*"Kunyange zvorema . . ."*—"Though things are hard . . ." As on that night, innumerable other experiences of Bible study with Zimbabwean Christians and listening to them preach and pray have been revelatory for me, suffused with a sense of clear access to God.

Whether they are familiar with liberation theology or not, many contemporary missionaries, both short-term and long-term, know the experience of discovering new depths of Christ's gospel through the insights of the poor. In sum, it is clear that Christian mission's concern with the poor has solid and indeed compelling foundation in scripture, theology and the history of Christian practice.

Reconciliation, Poverty and Mission

Given the scriptural and theological grounds for associating poverty and its many attendant ills with God's concern, is there a problem with our participation in God's mission having a focus on the poor? Why is Mano Rumal-shah, a consistent and passionate advocate for the poor and one who lives in a church *of* the poor, uneasy with Christian mission being so widely and sometimes exclusively associated with outreach to the poor?

Your God Is Too Small was the proclamation of theologian J. B. Phillips in his 1952 book of that title. Phillips discussed a number of inadequate conceptions of God such as Resident Policeman, Parental Hangover, Absolute Perfection, Heavenly Bosom and Managing Director. Some of our conceptions of God in mission may likewise be subject to Phillips's dictum, "Your God is too small," and to a similar dictum, "Your mission is too small."

Eradicating poverty, curing disease, eliminating illiteracy and purging violence against women are crucial tasks in fulfilling God's vision for human flourishing. Their scope is enormous, as are the resources and time needed to achieve them. Nevertheless, defining mission in terms of those tasks alone makes mission too small. Defining *God's* mission only in those terms makes *God* too small, for it reduces God to two other attractive but ultimately inadequate roles, World Problem-Solver and Global Development Director.

What is God up to? I have asked in this book. We have seen that the most compelling and comprehensive response to that question is the summary Paul offers: "In Christ God was reconciling the world to himself . . . and entrusting the message of reconciliation to us" (2 Corinthians 5:19). We have seen that far from being an inoffensive and convenient avoidance of hard issues, the paradigm of reconciliation pushes expressions of mission to a radical edge, where the missional church insists both that justice be done and that people and communities be actually reconciled.

It is within the framework of reconciliation that the role of poverty in mission becomes clearer. Systemic injustice, poverty and violence are among the results of humanity's distorted relationship with God. Other results are often related to economic issues but can also stand alone, such as hatred between ethnic groups, discrimination based on gender and sexual orientation, class conflict and the will to power that incites wars. Of equal importance are hostility to the concept of God, resistance to relationship with God and dismissal of Christ's offer of love. All these conditions call equally for reconciliation. All are equally on the agenda of God's mission in the world.

Tying mission to poverty prompts a startling contrary realization: The gospel cannot be reliant on the existence of poverty for its continuing validity. What would the urgency of the gospel be if extreme poverty and hunger were halved by the year 2015, the deadline cited by the Millennium Development Goals, and eradicated sometime later, and if the related goals of adequate primary healthcare, universal children's education, women's empowerment, environmental sustainability and global partnership in development were all achieved? This thought experiment challenges us to wrestle with what we understand God's mission in the world to be. The centrality of reconciliation means that God's mission would be equally urgent even if poverty and the related ills were solved and healed.

Tying mission to economic status imprisons it within the economic relations of particular historical situations and periods. Further, if mission is confined to relationships of beneficence, the work that is held up as an expression of our gospel faithfulness can quickly become a vehicle of self-congratulation. Worse, it can operate subtly as a way to reinforce inequity and injustice. "Mission to the poor" becomes a way of expressing the material abundance and imagined omni-competence of the missioner and impressing on the missionized poor how little they have and know, and how dependent they are on the wealth and knowledge of the sending community. If this self-perception takes hold among the poor, as it sometimes does, it saps the confidence and creativity that could develop homegrown approaches to the challenges people face.

Two weeks after the 2010 earthquake in Haiti, medical workers flooded in from many parts of the world to offer healthcare in a medically catastrophic situation. As National Public Radio reporter Ray Suarez toured Port-au-Prince's L'Hôpital Général with director Dr. Alix Lassègue, the extent of the disaster was clear. Injured people were everywhere, many being cared for in tents they refused to leave for fear of being caught inside collapsing buildings again. One hundred thirty staff nurses lay buried beneath the rubble of one hospital building, and the smell of decomposition was heavy in the air. "We need help," Dr. Lassègue said as he expressed gratitude for the outpouring of international medical aid. Yet he had a caution: "We do not want people telling us how to do it. This is *our* job. This is *my* country."[7]

The doctor was identifying how the familiar offer, "We want to help," in needy situations often shifts to, "Move aside: we're taking over because we know better how to get this job done." The aid-givers present themselves as the all-knowing analysts of the situation, fully equipped with the supplies and logistics that they think they know the needy need. The poor become a fixed category in their thinking, incapable of moving out of a generalized status that bleaches them of individual gifts and possibilities. They are not thought *philosophically* to be incapable, of course, but in the situation at hand they are treated *practically* as incapable. Put this way, it becomes clear that the needy are being treated as less than fully human.

Individuals, committees and agencies considering mission must realize that there are many kinds of difference to be engaged in mission. Restricting the sphere of mission activity not only to the dimension of economic difference but to relationships where the missioner is more affluent than the missionized constructs a paradigm in which the missioner is always more powerful, more mobile and better educated than the missionized. It is inevitable that presumption and manipulation develop in those caught in this paradigm, as the history of mission in the modern period demonstrates.

Instead, mission planners are called to ensure that their outreach embraces a broad range of differences and that, in particular, the people engaged represent a broad range of economic strata. The mission personnel offices of USAmerican denominations typically do send people to work in a range of settings, some of which are economically peer settings, as in western Europe or Japan, where missionaries are engaging difference in major ways yet working with people considerably more affluent than themselves. Missionaries gathered from diverse settings periodically for fellowship, therefore, can share experiences that challenge the common assumption that mission is from rich to poor, from the more powerful to the less powerful.

This diversity of perspective is harder to develop in the mission outreach of congregations and mid-level judicatories. It is there, where the short-term mission phenomenon flourishes, that the exclusive association of mission with poverty is strongest. Financial resources at those levels of the church may be considered too limited to fund mission in more affluent settings. However, perspective can be broadened by intentional efforts that, for instance, engage speakers to come and share from mission experience in such situations. It is through relating missionally with the full range of class and affluence that the mission-sending community becomes able to nurture relationships of authentic companionship with all—offering and receiving, learning and teaching, traveling together and sharing one another's burdens on the road.

Mission Horizontal and Upward in Scripture and Christian History

Only recently in Christian history has mission been typecast as outreach from the affluent to the poor, from the privileged to the underprivileged. The sixteenth-century Spanish and Portuguese Roman Catholic missions in the Caribbean and in Central and South America opened the new era atrociously with their coercive methods, applied alongside brutal patterns of forced labor in mines and on plantations. With the later Protestant and

Roman Catholic missions from Europe and North America, global mission came to be associated with the evangelistic and "civilizing" or "development" efforts of Euro-American peoples among the poorer peoples of Africa, Asia and Latin America. The charges of religious and cultural imperialism frequently leveled against these efforts—sometimes with good reason and sometimes not—have further cemented mission's association with outreach from the affluent to the poor.

Examining mission history from the standpoint of economic status and social class shows that much mission has been carried out among people of the missioners' own status and among those of higher status. The mission of Israel in the Old Testament emphasized not going out to proclaim but rather being a light to which the nations of the world would come. Within that framework, Israel's witness to Yahweh was to nations that generally were wealthier and more powerful, such as Egypt, Lebanon and Syria. During the conquest of Canaan—and however one feels about that conquest—it is clear that Israel was among peers: battles were hard fought, and Israel did not always win. There are many instances in which the chosen people witnessed to the more powerful. Abraham, Sarah and their immediate descendants were tenting immigrants from a far land. Joseph bore witness in Egypt as a slave, and Moses prophesied to Pharaoh on behalf of a slave nation. The story of the healing of leprous Naaman the Syrian begins with the touching witness of a Hebrew slave girl in his household. Naaman's initial indignation at being asked to bathe in the Jordan expressed the contempt with which he regarded Israel as a nation. Likewise the witness of Daniel and his companions in the court of Babylon was the testimony of captives. Jonah resisted being sent to Ninevah partly because he felt intimidated by the prospect of prophesying to such a great city.

Mercy and generosity to the poor is a mandate throughout the Old Testament. The sabbatical year as set forth in Deuteronomy 15 and the jubilee year as proclaimed in Leviticus 25, both for the canceling of debts, convey remarkable visions of economic justice, even if there is little evidence of their ever being implemented. King David's arrangement of Uriah's murder in order to secure Bathsheba for himself was depicted by Nathan the prophet as predatory behavior by the rich and powerful. Prophets such as Amos inveighed against the systemic oppression of the poor by the rich, and Micah insisted, "What does the Lord require of you but to do justice, and to love kindness, and to walk humbly with your God?" (6:8). These mandates on behalf of the poor, however, were not primarily missional mandates in the sense of shaping Israel's witness in the dimension of difference. Rather, they were mandates of justice within Israel's own life as God's covenant community.

In his teaching, Jesus continued the prophetic tradition of defending the poor against exploitation and oppression by the rich. The parable of

Lazarus and the rich man is startlingly vivid. On earth, the rich man has only callous disregard for Lazarus' sore-ridden degradation, but after death, the rich man suffers torment in hell while Lazarus rests in the bosom of Abraham (Luke 16:19–31). The famous parable of the sheep and the goats is striking for how Jesus communicates not only solidarity with the hungry, thirsty, strange, naked, sick and imprisoned but a sacramental union with them, such that at the judgment he can say "*I* was hungry and you gave me food . . . *I* was thirsty and you gave me nothing to drink" (Matthew 25:31–46; italics added). These teachings and others like them highlight one particular dimension of difference, the economic, and they have helped steer many Christians toward identifying real mission with outreach to the poor.

Yet it is important to observe and learn from Jesus' practice as well. Jesus came from an artisan family of modest means, and he claimed that in ministry he had "nowhere to lay his head." The generosity of affluent patrons, many of them women "who provided for [him] out of their resources" (Luke 8:3), meant that he was economically in a separate category as a wandering rabbi—not a farmer with farmers, nor a fisherman among fishermen. Yet no one would have seen him as affluent. He was a peasant alongside peasants, not a benefactor sharing from his means. Thus in much of his preaching and healing and feeding Jesus was not reaching down to people below himself economically, but reaching out alongside, horizontally to those in a stratum similar to his own.

Jesus also reached up to people at economic levels above his own. In the home of Simon the Pharisee, Jesus was dining with a person of means. The woman "sinner" who anointed him with ointment did so from a costly jar. Jesus not only accepted the anointing but dramatized her devotion with a parable based on levels of financial debt forgiveness, indicating he was aware of her affluence as he defended her. In ministering to the centurion whose daughter was sick and to Nicodemus who came by night, Jesus was likewise reaching up in mission to those above himself economically and socially.

We often interpret marginalization in economic terms only and situate mission exclusively on that margin. Yet when Jesus socialized with tax collectors—something he was notorious for doing—he was reaching up economically, as illustrated by Zaccheus, who promptly resolved to divest himself of his ill-gotten gains and give them to the poor. Zaccheus was not on an economic margin at all, but he had put himself out on a social and moral margin by collaborating with the taxation system of the occupying Romans and thereby becoming rich. People in our own time comparable to Zaccheus might be the bankers and mortgage lenders of Wall Street and Fleet Street who brought the world economic system to the brink of collapse in 2008 and who still reaped millions in contractual bonuses. Reaching up to them would be a challenge for any of us, for we might not wish to be seen with them in that particular dimension of difference. Yet we would have Jesus as our example in doing so.

When Jesus sent disciples out on mission intended to replicate his own—preaching the kingdom, healing the sick, casting out demons—he was sending them into a dimension of difference, for he was sending them beyond the discipleship community to proclaim God's reign to strangers who might be hostile to the proclamation. He was not sending them to a separate economic universe, however, for many in their audience were people like themselves economically: fisherfolk, farmers, artisans, clerks. Similarly, Jesus' missional directives at the ends of the gospels and at the start of Acts have no socioeconomic reference but rather send the disciples to all people over the full extent of the known world. The mission of the earliest church fulfilled that commission, as three thousand people joined the movement at Pentecost, and its lifestyle was one of people sharing all things in common, those who had more and those who had less.

Lest we slip into thinking that the disciples were a privileged lot by virtue of their understanding of the gospel, it is helpful to recall the assessment of the priestly council in Jerusalem after the healing of a crippled beggar: "Now when they saw the boldness of Peter and John and realized that they were uneducated and ordinary men, they were amazed and recognized them as companions of Jesus" (Acts 4:13). It was the disciples' uncouth scruffiness that confirmed their connection with Jesus. Ordinary and uneducated, they were socioeconomically closer to the person they had healed than the priests were to them. The churches Paul and others established around the Mediterranean world—in Antioch, Philippi, Macedonia, Corinth, Galatia—were churches of neither the poor nor the rich, but communities of artisans and laborers, those who made up by far the majority of the population. The missionaries were themselves of that class, so they were generally reaching out to their economic peers, though their audiences embodied cultural, religious and sometimes linguistic dimensions of difference.[8]

The collection Paul took up among these churches for the Christians of Jerusalem was an outreach to the poor, which he justified on many grounds, including the generosity of Jesus, who "though he was rich, yet for your sakes he became poor, so that by his poverty you might become rich" (2 Corinthians 8:9). The same collection also demonstrated the oneness of the body of Christ, which included both Gentile Christians, from whom Paul solicited funds, and Jewish Christians, who were suffering economically and might be questioning the legitimacy of Gentile Christians. The mission in Paul's view was proclamation and reconciliation, and the collection was designed to strengthen that mission.

Peer proclamation was the pattern that contributed to most of the Mediterranean world becoming aware of the gospel of Christ by the year

300 and a large percentage making Christian profession, well before the conversion of the emperor Constantine in 312.[9] The mission of God through which much of that world became Christian was not outreach by the privileged to the underprivileged, but outreach by all to all, mainly by artisans, laborers, soldiers and bureaucrats to those like themselves. The alliance between church and state that Constantine forged introduced the fundamentally distorting element of state coercion into Christian life and mission in the Roman Empire and in the later Holy Roman Empire of Charlemagne and his successors. Yet in his conversion Constantine was not embracing a tiny fringe element. Rather, he became a Christian substantially because it appeared that much of his world was already becoming Christian, and this was happening through a mass movement of ordinary people witnessing to ordinary people.

The prominence of the monastic orders in Christian mission from the sixth century through the High Middle Ages is sociologically complex. In taking vows of poverty, monks and nuns were poor in name alongside the poor villagers they evangelized throughout western Europe and later on other continents. They were members of what became wealthy religious orders, however, so they did not share the vulnerable and grinding poverty of the truly poor, and often they lived rather too well as they, like the nobility, held peasants in serfdom on their farms. Yet in times of particular stress, the poor looked to the monasteries and convents for assistance, and the religious orders often responded with alms and food, beginning the pattern of beneficence in mission. As custodians of learning, the orders later began establishing schools in which many people, whether in Europe, Africa, Asia or Latin America, became literate for the first time. Hospitals followed, and so developed the classic and wholistic missional pattern of church, school and hospital that Anglican and Protestant mission work later replicated. Historically, missionaries and mission agencies sometimes extended this wholism to confront systemic injustice as well, such as with the trans-Atlantic slave trade, commercial exploitation of west Africans by liquor distillers, the binding of women's feet in China and the burning of widows in India.

Recalibrating the Place of Poverty in Wholistic Mission

Where does this discussion of mission, poverty and difference take us? It may seem that a current understanding of mission is being challenged, and also that the common understanding has more than a grain of continuing truth to it. If so, that is true.

Christian mission in the modern era has been critiqued consistently for a tone and attitude of condescension. Bounty of various kinds—spiritual, religious, material, agricultural, medical and educational—was being bestowed on populations that missionaries and their supporters regarded variously as uncivilized and underprivileged, empty vessels who needed filling. Sometimes missionaries thought this way and sometimes they did not, but such is the stereotype of their tone and attitude.

The main danger in contemporary Christianity's sometimes exclusive association of mission with poverty is that, despite all the best intentions to the contrary, such condescension carries over into today's outreach, not only from the West to the Two-Thirds World but also from elites in the Global South to poor communities in their midst. We cringe at the past association of the word "civilization" with Christian mission, because we rightly believe it disparaged cultures that had depth and value even if they did not have, say, telegraphs and pianos. Many people today, however, enthusiastically link "development" with mission and fail to discern the ways in which development initiatives sometimes smuggle in assumptions similar to the "civilizing" initiatives of the past: that other cultures are backward or regressive, that Euro-American patterns of life are best for full human thriving, that Westernization is inevitable. This reflex flourishes when people of the North Atlantic countries think of mission primarily in terms of the poor, because it puts them firmly in the situation of being the givers, the bestowers, the experts, the developers, their visions and actions playing out over the poverty-ridden lifescape of the world.

The now common phrase "reverse mission" alerts us to some of these assumptions. It is used by Global North Christians, often with hints of amazement and humor, to refer to mission initiatives from the Global South to communities in Europe and North America. The phrase may be unobjectionable if it is clear that what is being reversed is the historic movement of missionaries from the West to the Two-Thirds World and the view that it was only in the latter that there was mission to be done. Often, however, there is also the sense that real mission *continues* to be from the affluent to the poor and that "reverse mission" from the poor to the affluent, while intriguing, is quixotic and faintly amusing. Nothing could be further from the truth.

The access key to the whole of God's mission is reconciliation, the healing of relationship between God and humanity and within the human community. Poverty and its associated ills are prominent results of the alienation and estrangement in these relationships. God does have special concern for the poor, because the effects of poverty are especially blunt in threatening people's ability to live out the image of God within them. At the same time God's mission is not captive to any particular economic differential, for it comprehends *all* the effects of our estrangement and seeks reconciliation in them all.

The phrase "wholistic mission" is often used to emphasize that our participation in God's mission must address people's physical and economic needs and not only their spiritual and religious needs. "It's no good preaching to someone who has an empty stomach," is a common expression of this conviction. Since the 1970s evangelical Christians, who used to be thought in need of such a corrective admonition, have through the Lausanne Covenant Movement embraced wholeheartedly the importance of ministering to the whole person, and not simply the soul. Alongside their historic commitments to evangelism and church-planting, evangelicals have undertaken important initiatives in social justice as well.

Today it may be the historic mainline churches that need the correction of wholism, but now in the direction of embracing the fullness of reconciliation to which God may be calling them in mission. That includes poverty and its effects. It includes the classic "isms" of our time—racism, sexism, classism, homophobia, consumerism, militarism, ethnocentrism—all of which call for discerning and systemic work in reconciliation. It includes alienation from God, which calls for sharing the gospel in ways that heal and restore people to friendship with God in the full range of evangelism and establishing worshiping communities.

These are horizons of mission that draw us across all boundaries of difference and in all social, economic and political directions, and not only in those directions that help us feel competent, knowledgeable and powerful. In those directions we learn as well as teach, receive as well as give.

Notes

1. In 2010, Christians numbered about 2.3 billion and constituted 33.2 percent of the world's people. Muslims were the next largest group at 1.5 billion, 22.4 percent of the global population. Todd M. Johnson and Kenneth R. Ross, eds., *Atlas of Global Christianity, 1910–2010* (Edinburgh: Edinburgh University Press, 2009), 7.

2. http://www.wvi.org/wvi/wviweb.nsf/maindocs/3F50B250D66B7629882573640 0663F21?opendocument.

3. http://www.lwr.org.

4. http://www.er-d.org.

5. Gustavo Gutiérrez, *Theology of Liberation: History, Politics, and Salvation*, rev. ed., trans. Caridad Inda and John Eagleson (Maryknoll, NY: Orbis, 1988).

6. Ernesto Cardenal, *The Gospel in Solentiname*, trans. Donald D. Walsh (Maryknoll, NY: Orbis, 1976).

7. "The News Hour," Public Broadcasting Service, January 26, 2010.

8. See Wayne A. Meeks, *The First Urban Christians: The Social World of the Apostle Paul*, 2nd ed. (New Haven, CT: Yale University Press, 2003); and Abraham J. Malherbe, *Social Aspects of Early Christianity*, 2nd ed. (Eugene, OR: Wipf and Stock, 2003).

9. David Barrett, ed., *World Christian Encyclopedia* (Nairobi: Oxford University Press, 1982), 24.

CHAPTER TEN

Churches in Turmoil:
A Challenge
in Reconciliation

"I'd like us to explore having another companion diocese relationship," a participant at a 2010 Episcopal diocesan mission conference said during a workshop. "I would too," responded another person with years of experience in inter-Anglican relations, "but do you think anyone would want to develop a relationship with us, in the present state of the Anglican Communion?" Pessimism like this indicates the impact of internal church strife on people's hopes to go global with God.

Given that reconciliation is the direction of God's mission, it is ironic when the church as the body of Christ in the world is profoundly unreconciled within itself. Today the controversy surrounding human sexuality has become an extended crisis in a number of church communions, and it poses a major challenge for internal reconciliation.

"When you are offering your gift at the altar," said Jesus, "if you remember that your brother or sister has something against you, leave your gift there before the altar and go; first be reconciled to your brother or sister, and then come and offer your gift" (Matthew 5:23–24). Jesus' counsel was partly prudential, but at a deeper level he was saying that one cannot fully appropriate the grace of God's reconciliation without at the same time being open to such reconciliation with the estranged neighbor.

John stressed that love of neighbor is a corollary of love of God: "Those who say, 'I love God,' and hate their brothers or sisters, are liars; for those who do not love a brother or sister whom they have seen, cannot love God whom they have not seen" (1 John 4:20). Wrestling with the scandal of lawsuits among the Corinthian Christians, Paul insisted that they should be able to sort out their disputes among themselves rather than resorting to the courts (1 Corinthians 6:1–8).

These are painful admonitions for churches that today are experiencing their community life and shared mission being torn by controversy over the ethical status of homosexuality and its place in the life and leadership of the churches. The churches are called to share in God's mission of reconciliation in the world, but their own communions are experiencing enmity that stretches many relationships to the breaking point, legal strife that constitutes public scandal, and stress that threatens the companionship in mission that has taken decades to develop. Turmoil about sexuality is affecting not only the North American mainline denominations, which have tended toward greater inclusion, but evangelical groups as well. Church conflict is as old as the church itself, of course, but that does not make its recurrence any less painful or any less damaging to its witness.

Conflict within Churches

The blessing of same-sex unions and the ordination of lesbians, gay men, bisexual and transgendered (or LGBT) people have become matters of Christian faithfulness for members of numerous church traditions. Opponents perceive these issues as a test of whether churches will be faithful to what they believe is God's vision for the sexual complementarity of men and women as indicated in scripture. Proponents perceive a test of whether the churches will be faithful to what they believe is God's vision for the relationships and ministries of LGBT people, on analogy with church struggles over racial and gender inclusion.

Churches are at different stages of turmoil, and quarreling is most advanced among Anglicans. Tension about the place of homosexuality in the Episcopal Church began to build during the 1970s with initiatives at diocesan and churchwide assemblies. The issue was center-stage for global Anglicanism at the 1998 Lambeth Conference, when a majority of bishops at the once-a-decade gathering passed a resolution rejecting same-sex blessings and gay ordination. The flashpoint came with the 2003 Episcopal Church General Convention's consent to the election of a partnered gay man as the Episcopal bishop of New Hampshire. Conflict escalated with some Anglican provinces breaking relationship with the Episcopal Church and the Anglican Church of Canada, which has also moved in a more inclusive direction. Some Anglican provinces have grouped themselves into associations that appear to compete with central Anglican structures.[1] A proposed Anglican Covenant currently being reviewed by all provinces could, if approved, be used to downgrade the membership of some provinces in the communion.[2]

In 2009 the Churchwide Assembly of the Evangelical Lutheran Church in America opened the door to rostering partnered homosexual persons in the ordained ministry of that church. As of this writing, that shift has disturbed a few relationships with companion churches in the Lutheran World Federation, but thus far the disruption has not been major. Controversy continues within the ELCA, however, and it is not likely to subside soon. Methodists and Presbyterians have experienced a great deal of internal controversy, but so far their policies have not shifted radically in a more inclusive direction.

Renewed Awareness of the World Church

These struggles have affected shared mission with church companions around the world, particularly among Anglicans. The positive and negative aspects of their turmoil anticipate what members of other communions may experience as the process unfolds in their life.

On a positive note, many Episcopalians have become aware for the first time that they are Anglicans as well as Episcopalians, and that they are members of a worldwide communion of 80 million Christians. It was disconcerting that this realization coincided with news that some other Anglicans questioned whether the Episcopal Church should even be a member of the Anglican Communion. Nevertheless, the wider church awareness has made many Episcopalians' sense of church less limited to their local context and more catholic as they have begun to understand the cross-cultural diversity of the Anglican Communion and world Christianity.

Newly aware of the world church, many North American mainline Christians have asked important questions: "What is this turmoil doing to our relationships with Christians in other parts of the world? Don't we need to work together with them on today's pressing problems, like poverty, hunger, AIDS and violence? So how do these issues affect our common mission?" This sharpened sensitivity to the mission imperative is a positive effect of the controversy, as is the realization that mission elsewhere must be undertaken in companionship *with* other churches rather than *for* them.

Likewise, even as mission relationships have suffered in some quarters, in others they have flourished. Realizing how fragile their international links with other churches can be, Episcopalians have been moved to celebrate and tend their relationships instead of taking them for granted. They understand now that mission typically is their major point of contact with the wider Anglican world.

The potential threat to the churches' shared response to pressing human crises has prompted some to cherish mission anew as a central criterion of Christian faithfulness. This in turn has adjusted people's understanding of the relationship between unity and mission in the church. As unity becomes tenuous, people have asked why it is important, and the answer has been obvious: unity is important for the sake of mission, for the sake of God's work in the world. Thus the church's unity has taken its proper place in service to the church's pursuit of God's mission.

Impaired Communion and the Threat to Mission

Alongside these positive developments, there have been damaging ones as well. Fear is one, for apprehension that mission is threatened has been strong among many Anglicans. For instance, in its Windsor Report of 2004, the Lambeth Commission on Communion said that the distrust that had developed among adversaries in the controversy is "catastrophic in terms of our mission which . . . includes the call to model before the watching world the new mode of being human which has been unveiled in Christ."[3] The varying degrees of impaired communion declared by some provinces were said to be "detrimental to our common mission and witness."[4] During the 2008 Lambeth Conference, the Windsor Continuation Group detailed "the severity of the situation" in its "Preliminary Observations" and then echoed the widespread view of mission as threatened: "All this amounts to a diminishing sense of Communion and impoverishing [of] our witness to Christ . . ."[5]

Even as mission has been lifted up as central by many Anglicans, it has also become a point of mutual accusation, each side blaming the other for acts that threaten mission or break links between churches. Traditionalists and progressives alike accuse each other of being obsessed with sex—whether through culture-bound permissiveness or through culture-bound homophobia—and inattentive to mission imperatives. Antagonists have found it difficult to hear one another's concern, and so they talk past each other.

Mission companionship has suffered in the turmoil. Some missionaries felt pressure to repudiate their sponsorship by the Episcopal Church's Domestic and Foreign Missionary Society and to affiliate instead with free-standing mission agencies. There were seven such instances soon after 2003, and while this is not a large number, it is sizable proportionately when the total number of Episcopal Church–sponsored missionaries hovers around only seventy. While most mission companionships have continued, even between dioceses and provinces that disagree about the central issue, a few have had to be discontinued, including longstanding diocesan links and work funded by Episcopal granting organizations. Some of the congregations and dioceses that have left the Episcopal Church to affiliate with other Anglican provinces or the newly formed Anglican Church of North America had major engagements in world mission, so their departure diminished the global work of ECUSA. The fracturing of the church's major mission network has been another blow to shared mission, as we saw in Chapter Seven.

Traditionalist bishops from various parts of the Anglican Communion have not only broken ties with the Episcopal Church but have ordained bishops for ministry in the United States and undertaken other actions within Episcopal dioceses. Such interventions have been taken in the name of mission, that is, the mission of proclaiming an uncorrupted gospel and ministering to traditionalist Christians who feel marginalized in a more liberal church. This clouds the reputation of mission by recapitulating the open competition between churches that characterized some earlier eras of Christian mission. Oversight Anglican bodies censured such actions as well as the ordination of gay bishops, and the Archbishop of Canterbury has called for the resignation from inter-Anglican commissions by representatives of churches deemed to have contravened Anglican norms.[6]

Open conflict is occurring not only between Global North and Global South and within North Atlantic churches. Anglicanism in Zimbabwe is more conflicted than anywhere else in the world. Two dioceses are riven by conflict that stemmed, in each case, from a bishop declaring that he was taking his diocese out of the Province of Central Africa because it was not taking a hard enough line against homosexuality. Each diocese has rival bishops, one endorsed by the communion and the other holding onto diocesan property and finances. Managing a conflict that frequently takes the form of physical confrontation continues to drain missional energy from those dioceses and from the province as a whole.[7]

The discord has very local effects on mission as well. In one instance, an Episcopal congregation with a substantial number of gay members had built close and extensive contacts with an African diocese, despite differences around sexuality. However, when the archbishop of the pertinent African province made international headlines with strong comments against Christian acceptance of homosexuality, gay parishioners began to raise questions whether the relationship was viable. Likewise, a split in a large Episcopal parish complicated the management and future work of a separate non-profit organization for children that had been spun off from the parish's longstanding relationship with an African diocese. When departing traditionalists withdrew from the nonprofit's board, the bishop of the African diocese was hesitant to associate with the continuing agency.[8]

Addressing Conflict through Accompaniment in Mission

How can churches pursue international mission faithfully amid the current controversy? How can communities so at odds with one another over human sexuality come to deeper mutual understanding? How can all sides embrace God's reconciling mission, and thus bear the fruit of reconciliation within the churches as well as in the world? These are urgent issues in this time of anguish.

The emerging ethos of accompaniment and companionship offers a mode of mission that is ideally suited to the current situation. Indeed, we can see it as a providential blessing. The ethos of partnership that took hold from the 1970s cultivated mutuality and interdependence and broke with earlier patterns of imposition. But partnership emphasized formal, business-like commitments, responsibilities and projects—precisely a weight that suddenly fragile relationships have difficulty bearing.

In today's tensions, the ethos of accompaniment, by contrast, makes available to mission companions—whether individuals, congregations, regional entities or entire denominations—resources for staying alert to new relational opportunities and for refraining from pressing companions beyond what the current tensions can sustain. Accompaniment begins with the pilgrimage of traveling into another's experience in order to listen deeply and learn about the companion's culture, challenges and experience of God, an ideal approach in today's polarized climate. It emphasizes not doing but being, not working but relating, not agreeing but understanding. Companionship grows through sharing bread together, discovering one another's life, developing friendship and offering solidarity to one another.

The bishop of a synod of the Evangelical Lutheran Church in America asked me shortly before that church's Churchwide Assembly decisions about sexuality in 2009 what they might learn from the Episcopal Church's experience in its relationship with the rest of the Anglican Communion. I suggested that they take initiative immediately to share their experience and explain their thinking with member churches of the Lutheran World Federation in other areas of the world. The economic and cultural power of the United States means that actions taken by USAmerican churches are often interpreted as an ecclesial expression of national privilege, presumption and dominance.

"Why have others not come to talk with us before now?" a bishop in Burundi asked a trio of Episcopalians in 2004 when we went to talk with church leaders in east Africa about the decisions the Episcopal Church had made about sexuality in 2003. It was a legitimate question. In the wake of those historic decisions, the church had not arranged for an immediate and intentional outreach to have conversation with other provinces about their rationale and possible impact. Instead, a global outcry set in motion a cyclical process of increasing polarization. Walking together in companionship calls us both to take the first step and to walk the extra mile.[9]

Antagonists in the conflict tend to feel they are the only ones concerned about mission, when mission is a concern on all sides. Further, we can say that the sexuality controversy is not a distraction from mission, but it is actually *about* mission. Progressives are zealous about the fullness of what they see as God's mission being extended to and through lesbians and gay men, and bisexual and transgender persons are increasingly included in this circle. Traditionalists are concerned that what they view as a repudiation of biblical morality will fatally compromise the integrity of God's mission. Dialogue and mutual understanding would be enhanced if, instead of excluding each other from the mission table, all sides could acknowledge that others have missional commitments in the controversy that are worthy of respect and discussion.

The Indaba Project of the Anglican Communion has formalized this missional dialogue. It is a listening process in which several dioceses known to disagree about human sexuality and located in different parts of the world visit each other to discover their mutual settings and perspectives. After listening attentively and growing in relationship they then, and only then, confer about the issues that divide them. The purpose is not argument, persuasion or agreement. Instead, they seek in conversation to understand where they agree and disagree and then explore how they can continue to collaborate in God's mission together. Sharing in God's mission is the criterion of whether the process is fulfilling its aim. Further, the process is designed to develop ways of addressing difference that will be helpful not only in the current conflict but in other now unanticipated conflicts.[10]

"Be Reconciled"

"We entreat you on behalf of Christ, be reconciled to God," Paul wrote to the Corinthians (2 Corinthians 5:20). We need to hear both that appeal and the appeal for reconciliation with neighbor that it entails. Broken relationships with the neighbor impair our ability to love God and to receive God's love. The relationships that have suffered in the current turmoil are wounds in the body of Christ that need healing. As we offer ourselves into God's reconciling mission in the world, we must be equally passionate to offer ourselves into God's reconciling mission in the common life of our churches.

Over the past half century churches in all parts of the world have struggled for the mutuality and interdependence in relationship that enhances collaboration around God's mission in the world. The fruit of that struggle has been rich. In the churches' current hour of need, that fruit must sustain us in our continued practice as companions in mission—listening, serving, learning, walking together, undertaking pilgrimage, bearing burdens.

From this perspective, the task of working through the current tensions in the churches should not be seen primarily as a political problem to be solved. Instead, it should be seen as a missional undertaking. The terrain of mission is difference, and certainly the current conflict involves major theological and ethical differences. Moreover, it is with one another that the churches generally undertake their mission work. As they struggle toward reconciliation with one another for the sake of God's work in the world, the churches are, by definition, seeking to be faithful to God's mission.

Notes

1. For book-length detail on the crisis, see Miranda K. Hassett, *Anglican Communion in Crisis: How Episcopal Dissidents and Their African Allies Are Reshaping Anglicanism* (Princeton, NJ: Princeton University Press, 2007).

2. http://www.anglicancommunion.org/commission/covenant/final/text.cfm.

3. Lambeth Commission on Communion, *Windsor Report* (London: Anglican Communion Office, 2004), para. 41. See also http://www.anglicancommunion.org/windsor 2004.

4. *Windsor Report*, para. 50.

5. Windsor Continuation Group, "Preliminary Observations, Part One: A Presentation at the Lambeth Conference," circulated sheet, Lambeth Conference, July 28, 2008. http://www.anglicancommunion.org/acns/news.cfm/2008/7/28/ACNS4480.

6. See news report of June 7, 2010, at http://www.ecusa.anglican.org/79425_ 122717_ENG_HTM.htm. Numerous other reports following developments can be found at Episcopal Life Online and at the Anglican Communion News Service.

7. News and analysis of the struggle over time can be found at http://titusonmission .wordpress.com.

8. For a more extensive and detailed account of developments up to 2009, see Titus Presler, "The Impact of the Sexuality Controversy on Mission: The Case of the Episcopal Church in the Anglican Communion," *International Bulletin of Missionary Research* 33, no. 1 (January 2009): 11–18.

9. Titus Presler, "Listening Toward Reconciliation: A Conversation Initiative amid Current Anglican Alienations," *Anglican Theological Review* 89 (Spring 2007): 247–66. See also the Walking to Emmaus Consultation at www.trinitywallstreet.org/welcome/ ?mission.

10. http://www.anglicancommunion.org/ministry/continuingindaba/whatis/ index.cfm.

CHAPTER ELEVEN

Meeting as Pilgrims:
A Challenge in Accompaniment

S hort-term mission at all levels of churches in Europe and North America has grown so much over the past twenty years that it has become a major component of the world mission scene. Many congregations and mid-level entities of the churches routinely send multiple teams of people each year on short-term mission, often abbreviated as STM. Teams typically include from ten to several dozen people, and they usually go to parts of the Two-Thirds World for periods of ten days to two weeks.

This phenomenon poses a significant challenge to accompaniment as the mode of mission in the twenty-first century. What depth of relationship can be cultivated when missioners visit for a week or two? What quality of listening can occur when they travel as sizable groups spilling out of vans to attend a church service, visit a clinic or build a school? Is true solidarity possible when the travelers' mission formation is inevitably limited, given the thousands of congregations and regional church bodies that sponsor STM teams?

Strengths and Vulnerabilities of Short-Term Mission

It is estimated that more than 1.5 million Christians from the United States go abroad on short-term mission trips each year, and that the money spent on short-term mission trips constitutes about 30 percent of all the funding devoted to world mission by USAmerican churches.[1] As we have seen, there is much to celebrate in how these engagements at the grassroots have broadened Christians' knowledge of each other in many parts of the world. Significant relationships of friendship and solidarity have been formed, and people on both sides of the encounter testify to how their faith has been deepened and their vision of the world church broadened. Some short-term mission participants feel their lives have been transformed by the experience, and this often bears fruit in later mission commitment or, at least, global involvement through channels other than the church. For instance, a high proportion of one-year young adult missioners in the various churches have previous experience of short-term mission.

At the same time, the newness of the phenomenon, the numbers of people involved, and the combination of brief time and considerable expense call mission activists and committees at all levels to careful discernment about the nature, purpose and stewardship of short-term mission.

Many short-term mission teams and trips are well prepared and implemented, but many others lack sufficient care and preparation. Mission understanding may be limited to zeal for fixing things for poor people. Preparation may include little about the religious life of those to be visited, or the social, economic and political complexities of their situation. Too often there is only minimal attention to the shared prayer and Bible study that would put the venture in gospel perspective and sustain the participants spiritually. Sometimes the project itself is not well conceived, as in painting a church or building a school where local people need employment and have the expertise to do the work better. In some cases, real time spent with people at the destination—the element that should be at the heart of any trip—is so minimal or artificial that teams return with little sense of the host communities and no lasting relationships. Group time upon arriving home is sometimes negligible, and individuals receive little help in reflecting on their experience and integrating it into their ongoing discipleship.

Such problems have been inevitable in the rapid growth of the STM movement as mission has been democratized and diversified in the churches. As STM's challenges have become clearer, many church bodies have developed guidelines for short-term mission teams, and now synods, dioceses, presbyteries, conferences and freestanding agencies frequently offer workshops about how to lead short-term mission trips. Numerous published handbooks are available, though they vary in the depth of missional understanding they offer. As leadership training has taken hold, the preparation of short-term mission teams has been strengthened, and overall the situation is improving.

For a congregation or mid-level church group, discerning whether, when and how to send a short-term mission team calls for engaging virtually all the issues explored in this book—sending, difference, poverty, reconciliation, companionship, networking—and it refocuses attention on the nature of mission. Through short-term mission trips, churches are sending people in the name of Christ into dimensions of difference—typically cultural, ethnic, linguistic, national and economic difference—so the movement participates in essential aspects of Christian mission. Endemic poverty is one major global expression of structural injustice and violence, so in focusing on countries of relative material constraint, short-term mission from any continent typically puts people into environments where there is opportunity to engage these dynamics in gospel perspective and to express solidarity with people who suffer because of them. While difference is exciting and inviting for some, it is frightening and repellant for many others, so the fact that so many people in Global North countries wish to encounter and explore formidable difference as Christians is cause for rejoicing.

Mutuality and Justice Issues in Short-Term Mission

Short-term mission calls us to address the often ambiguous balance between benefiting oneself and benefiting the other. Short-term mission advocates in the West emphasize how the encounter with difference challenges European and North American missioners' cultural assumptions and socioeconomic privilege and thereby assists global change. Along the lines of Jesus' words in Matthew 25:40—"As you did it to one of the least of these who are members of my family, you did it to me"—many participants testify that they have met Jesus in new and vivid ways on the trips. This is precisely the mutuality that mission should enact. At long last, North Atlantic Christians are not only acknowledging but celebrating that they have as much to receive as well as give in mission, as much to learn as to teach.

The question mark now hovers over the other side of the encounter. Are those who are visited in Two-Thirds World countries being embraced as equal companions? Are encounters being designed to facilitate a mutual exchange of gospel insight and life experience in personal vulnerability and candor? If the encounter is transforming one side, is it transforming the other side as well? Or, on the other hand, do those who are visited form a tableau from which the visitors take away a collection of exciting but superficial impressions? Are local people left feeling gazed at, photographed and questioned, but ultimately just as distant and objectified on the world scene as before? If so, then the short-term mission encounter is little more than missio-tourism.

Equally important for activists and mission committees to address is the justice that short-term mission, like all expressions of mission, is called to embody, especially in view of the usually unequal distribution of economic power between the European and North American teams that typically initiate visits and the communities they visit. Given the money expended on travel and accommodation, is there a comparable sharing of resources with the host community? Are such resources shared in ways that build capacity and leadership in the host community and avoid creating dependency?

Further, mutuality calls the Global North communities to receive visits from their companion communities as well as making visits to them. If that is unaffordable for the companion communities, the more affluent side of the relationship—whether a congregation, diocese, synod, presbytery or conference—must reallocate some of its resources from making visits to receiving visitors. In fact, church entities in the Global North often celebrate the large number of teams they send out, while the teams received from abroad are few and far between. This pattern erodes mutuality and threatens to relegate short-term mission to being simply another expression of Global North wealth and privilege.[2]

From Short-Term Mission to Pilgrimage

Pilgrimage is a fertile theme that shifts the rationale and spirituality of short-term visits in a more faithful and fruitful direction and protects them from the most common pitfalls. Pilgrimage offers an entirely different paradigm for the experience and provides a new starting point for conceiving and planning the initial brief interactions between groups of people in very different church settings.

"Religious people who walk" is how a Tibetan Buddhist defined pilgrims. More comprehensively, a pilgrim is a person who travels in order to discover God or deepen one's knowledge of God. The traveling motif of pilgrimage assumes the revelatory potential of experiences of difference, for travel takes one away from the habitual environment of home and into a different environment that offers the possibility of new perspectives and insights. Traveling to experience God anew is an element in many religions, especially Islam and Hinduism. Christians find biblical reference points for pilgrimage in the Hebrews' journey through the wilderness, Elijah's forty-day journey to Mount Horeb and Jesus' incarnational journey through the human story.

Pilgrimages to the Holy Land and other revered sites go back to Christianity's early days. The Protestant Reformation was skeptical of literal pilgrimages, especially as they had proliferated in the medieval period. Yet the King James Version's rendering of Hebrews 11:13—"they were strangers and pilgrims on the earth"—enshrined the concept of pilgrimage in English-speaking Christianity (more recent translations have "exiles" and "foreigners" in place of "pilgrims"). *Pilgrim's Progress* by John Bunyan, an Independent or Congregationalist, was one of the most popular books in history after its publication in 1678. It powerfully presented pilgrimage as constituting the Christian's journey of faith. The well-known hymn "He Who Would Valiant Be," each stanza ending with the phrase "to be a pilgrim," was based on Bunyan's work, and it is just one of many hymns that present Christian life as pilgrimage. Today Christians of many traditions go on literal, geographical pilgrimage not only to Israel and Rome but to Iona, Walsingham, Canterbury, Guadalupe, Compostelo and other sites. Sometimes a particular benefit such as healing is sought, but often the aim is more general spiritual renewal.

Recasting short-term mission as pilgrimage places God at the center of the experience, which has the purpose of spiritual growth and discovery. The journey is premised on travel, but the true destination is not a physical place but the companion community's experience of God in their setting. The sacred site is not where Jesus walked or where a saint was born or received a vision long ago. The holiness to be encountered is, instead, the companion community's life as they receive God, express God and live out God's mission in their context today.

Listening, conversing and forming relationships at a deep level are clearly the substance of this encounter, and it leads naturally into exploring the social, economic and political aspects of the companion's setting. The pilgrimage framework needs to be affirmed mutually, so that the host community is likewise focused on learning from the traveling community's experience of God. Pilgrims on both sides of the relationship are saying to one another, in effect, "We wish to grow in our relationship with God, and we are confident that we are being drawn more deeply into God through being with you." The visits of one's companion community to one's own setting should have a similar vision.

In this approach, work to be done *for* the companion community is not the initial agenda. Relating is the first step, and it is only out of such relating that further initiatives can be mutually discerned and engaged. Beginning this way honors the dimension of difference between the communities, and it invites exploration of deep companionship. It provides the firmest possible foundation for genuine networking in mission, for the multiple people involved on each side truly come to know each other in their settings. The network of relationships formed in such an encounter is the best basis for strategic planning.

Genuine mission trips follow later from such planning as the companions discern together what work they can undertake jointly in each other's settings. Relationship that begins with mutual pilgrimage should persist over time, and that in itself is an important commitment. The mission trips that follow should not be one-off ventures but part of a long-term plan of mutual engagement.

In the model I am suggesting, pilgrimage is both the concept and the term that would be used for the initial mutual encounters of groups between companion churches. For instance, a Minnesota Lutheran synod might organize a "pilgrimage" to a potential companion Lutheran church in the Czech Republic, from which a comparable "pilgrimage" might follow to Minnesota. Or a Presbyterian congregation might plan mutual "pilgrimages" with its companion congregation in South Korea. The agenda in each case would not be work of any kind, regardless how inviting or urgent, but rather listening, relating, accompanying, and discerning. As the companion churches then agree on further mutual engagement, subsequent short-term group visits might be called "missions" as the companions help one another fulfill God's mission in each other's setting. Later groups that are encountering the companion setting for the first time, however, would continue to be "pilgrimages" not "missions."

The point here is not to link the concept of mission with getting work done—an association that I dismantle elsewhere in this book—but to make a radical break in the conceptualization of initial group encounters between churches. As a phrase, "short-term mission" incorporates assumptions about doing things for other people that are presumptuous and disfiguring for future relationship. As a name, "pilgrimage" makes it clear that tinkering with the problems of short-term mission is insufficient. An entirely new starting point is in order.

Journeys called "pilgrimages" are naturally part of the "mission program" or "mission plan" of a church entity, but insisting on the term "pilgrimage" for initial exposure trips is integral to shaping the perspective of a congregation or regional grouping. This stance is important for mission planners as well as for team members. The concept of pilgrimage nurtures attention to spiritual depth in the formation of mission teams, mutuality in shared pilgrimage with counterparts in the companion church, and long-range planning beyond the current year.

Reconciliation is the ultimate test for mission pilgrimage and short-term mission, because that is the overall direction of God's mission in the world. Short-term visits that focus on dispensable tasks, shy away from deep relationship with the companions and rely on superficial impressions fail to fulfill reconciliation in any substantive or lasting way. Ventures that begin with deep pilgrimage into one another's experience of God bring to the surface the wounds and conflicts that need the healing that only reconciliation can bring. Such accompaniment in God's mission participates in God's work of reconciling the world in Christ.

Mission Pilgrimage in Practice

Bernard Mizeki Pilgrimage

Pilgrimage was the theme of a large-group journey to Zimbabwe from the United States in 1996 for the centenary festival of Bernard Mizeki, the first Anglican martyr in Central Africa. Focused on the several-day festival at the shrine of Mizeki's martyrdom, which draws the largest annual gathering of Anglicans in the world, it was easy to conceive the journey as a pilgrimage, for the USAmericans would be joining up to thirty thousand other pilgrims from the southern African region. In fact, it was the first known "pilgrimage" by USAmerican Christians to a Christian community in sub-Saharan Africa. The trip was a follow-up to an earlier missional relationship between the Episcopal Diocese of Massachusetts and several dioceses in Zimbabwe, so it could just as well have been organized according to work projects. Instead, because most of the pilgrims had not been to Africa before, attention was focused entirely on experiencing the vitality of African Christianity and forming relationships with Zimbabwean Christians.

The sixty pilgrims included a wide age range, nine to seventy-two, people both black and white, about ten teenagers, ten members of a monastic community and eighteen people from one parish. Affinity groups called "pods" were designated, each with its own coordinator. Orientation meetings started nine months before the trip with introductions to language, sociopolitical issues and Shona hymns in the context of shared worship. This served to prepare people thoroughly, and those not ready for such an intense experience dropped out. In Zimbabwe, the pilgrims divided up into small groups of five or so on each side of the festival for urban immersions and rural immersions in widely dispersed areas. They stayed in households, sharing family life and accompanying Zimbabwean pastors and lay folk in such ministries as parish visiting. Pilgrims and hosts alike testified that the pilgrimage had been transforming.

The Mizeki Pilgrimage, as it was called, was salutary. Its strengths were the lead-up and the relational aspects of the pilgrimage itself. Taking place within a longstanding missional relationship between Christians in the dioceses concerned, practical follow-up was not so much an issue. As leader of the venture, however, I can acknowledge that the enterprise was not perfect. It was expensive, and there was no provision for supporting a lasting ministry in Zimbabwe that would be a specific contribution from the pilgrimage. Many pilgrims stayed in touch with friends they made in Zimbabwe, but there was little relational follow-up with the group back in Massachusetts, beyond a couple of debriefing meetings and worship services. Today I would like to know more about how the pilgrimage affected the pilgrims beyond the immediate aftermath. How did it affect individuals' relationship with God? How were pilgrims drawn more deeply into God's mission over time? And what lasting effects did it have in the lives of our Zimbabwean counterparts?

Iowa and Swaziland

Pilgrimage is a primary experience in the companion relationship between the Anglican Diocese of Swaziland and the Episcopal Diocese of Iowa, according to Melody Rockwell, a nonstipendiary diocesan missioner for Iowa. "Through mission exchanges," she says, "Swazis and Iowans have developed close relationships in faith. The Holy Spirit is so alive and well in Swaziland. Time and again, we Iowans have received the gift of the Swazis' authentic witness to Christ and their deep and abiding faith in the midst of the highest incidence of HIV/AIDS in the world and severe hunger due to an extended drought."

"During my last time in Swaziland," Melody says, "Swazi people told me about extremely difficult situations they were in, yet often concluded, 'God is faithful, God is so faithful. I am blessed in my life.' To see that kind of witness is profoundly energizing. It has deepened my own faith, and others in Iowa have been touched in this way too. Once Iowans visit Swaziland, they return home just filled with the Spirit and wanting a continuing relationship." In fact, it was in Swaziland that Melody first felt God calling her to be a deacon, and she has since been ordained.

Iowa and Swaziland have been companion dioceses for more than twenty years, and short-term trips occur about every two years. Working with Swazis to assemble and distribute chlorinators to purify scarce water supplies has been a recent focus, first suggested by Paula Sanchini, a biology professor who is a member of the Iowa diocese. Thus practical projects have been important in the link, but developing friendships has been a major theme. "I have developed a love of the Iowans," said Mthunzi Ndlovu, a twenty-five-year-old Swazi who got to know the visitors while he trained to become a member of the Swazi chlorinator team.

Melody is grateful for the vision of Iowa Bishop Alan Scarfe and his support for bringing Swazis to visit in Iowa. An especially striking instance was the visit of Swazi Bishop Meshack Mabuza and his wife Lucy for a healing mission across the diocese with Scarfe and his wife Donna. "Sceptics warned that a healing tour would never work in Midwestern Episcopal parishes," says Melody, "but it had a huge, positive impact across our state. Services were scheduled for an hour, but they lasted three and four hours." This mutuality in spiritual gifts and in practical work has proved to be a growing feature of the interdiocesan relationship, which helps account for it lasting more than two decades. Now, instead of the relationship needing official renewal every three years, the two dioceses have a friendship covenant designed to continue in perpetuity.[3]

The short-term phenomenon is a different way of doing mission, and it makes accompaniment harder to fulfill. Setting it within the framework of pilgrimage helps keep it faithful to the breadth and depth of God's mission.

Notes

1. Robert Wuthnow, *Boundless Faith: The Global Outreach of American Churches* (Berkeley: University of California Press, 2009), 170–71, 180.

2. Karla Ann Koll stresses the importance of training for STM leadership in "Taking Wolves Among Lambs: Some Thoughts on Training for Short-Term Mission Facilitation"; see also the discussion of STM in Robert J. Priest, Douglas Wilson and Adelle Johnson, "U.S. Megachurches and New Patterns of Global Mission," both in *International Bulletin of Missionary Research* 33, no. 2 (April 2010): 93–96, 97–104.

3. Material on the Iowa-Swaziland companionship is derived from conversation and correspondence with Melody Rockwell and from the Diocese of Iowa website: http://www.iowaepiscopal.org/about_us/swaziland.php.

PART IV

What Is a Mission Companion Called to Be?

"I have become all things to all people, that I might by any means save some," Paul declared to the Corinthians. Defending his apostleship, his mission, he said he "became as" various groups of people of his day in order to "win" them to Christ—Jews, Gentiles, the weak (1 Corinthians 9:22). By this he meant identifying with the diverse groups of people who constituted his world of difference around the Mediterranean in the first century. He put himself in their sandals so that he could present the gospel in ways that would speak to them.

Ironically, management discourse today picks up on Paul's phrase—"become all things to all people"—to argue the contrary, that one *cannot* be all things to all people and still achieve one's objective. One needs to take a stand somewhere. We know from Paul's conflicted relationships that some in the churches felt his becoming all things to all people was an aspiration unfulfilled. While hard for any individual to fulfill, it continues to be an important aspiration for church communities. Trying to become all things to all people recognizes, honors and speaks to difference.

Paul did take stands: on God's reconciling work in Christ, on the sufficiency of the cross, on the free gift of grace, on God's vision for including all the world in the new covenant in Christ. Those stands continue to define the gospel that we share in Christian mission.

Yet "becoming as" the one who is different from oneself is the essence of accompaniment and companionship. In so becoming, one is letting the other's reality define one's own, not totally so as to neutralize the contribution of one's own reality, but enough for the other to experience compassion, solidarity and the sharing of burdens. Identity shifts and grows.

This identity of the mission companion is the subject of Chapter Twelve, and it sums up the book.

CHAPTER TWELVE

Seven Marks of the Mission Companion

How do the themes of democratization, sending, difference, reconciliation and accompaniment affect the tasks that those in mission carry out? What is an ethos for global mission that catalyzes reconciliation in a world of difference? As we learn from past mission, respond to the challenges of today and anticipate God's future in mission, what quality of presence and action are we called to cultivate and embody?

In the course of articulating a vision for world mission in the twenty-first century, the Episcopal Church laid out seven characteristics of the mission companion—whether the companion is an individual missionary or a mission team, a congregation or a mission agency, a mission committee or a mid-level regional grouping, a denomination or a communion.[1] The roles reflect ecumenical mission thinking and are relevant to a wide range of churches. They continue to be helpful, especially as refracted through the themes of difference and reconciliation.

While "the mission companion" can be a group or an institution, describing the marks in personal terms stresses the incarnational urgency of mission companionship: it lives through people being with people, not primarily through programs and financial transfers. It also reminds us of the unique value of the long-term residential missionary in the global mission of the churches.

The Seven Marks of the Mission Companion express practically the themes of this book. If a missionary, a mission team or any leadership group in world mission keeps these marks in view, it is more likely to respond faithfully to God's call in mission.

1. The mission companion is a *Witness*

"You will be my witnesses," Jesus said to his disciples before the ascension. In journalistic and legal settings, a witness is someone who has seen something that others may not have seen and whose testimony is therefore vitally important. Indeed, courts regard testimony as an obligation and failure to testify as an offense. On a more positive note, sharing good news is one of the most natural human instincts, whether people are announcing a wedding, a birth, a healing or any great event in their lives. What Jesus' disciples had seen was not a theology or doctrine, but a person and a series of events that disclosed a compelling story, good news, the evangel of God at work in their story, journeying with them to reconcile them with God and their fellow human beings. It was to this story that Jesus asked them to bear witness. So they told the story of what they believed God was doing through the stories of their own lives.

"Evangelism," a word that means simply good-news-ism, is at its best simply an act of companionship. Venturing into difference, Christians express companionship through walking in solidarity with others in their journeys. They listen to the hurt, fear and anger others may be experiencing and let those stories resonate with what they have experienced in their own lives. They listen to the other religious paths people may be following and allow those spiritualities to speak to their own. As they feel moved, Christians share in vulnerability their own stories, which include weakness, fear and alienation, and how God in Christ has met them in their journeys. They enter into dialogue with other religious viewpoints, eager to learn and understand how others have felt led. Argument is not the method, nor is conversion the aim, for it is the Holy Spirit who brings people to Christ. The aim is simply to tell the story as part of God's movement to reconcile people to themselves, to God and to one another. This view of evangelism differs markedly from common stereotypes, but there is no reason to surrender evangelism to false stereotypes and misguided practitioners.

For mission companions, the mandate of witness means being frank and open about the centrality of the Jesus story in our identity, work and vision as Christians—something companions from the Two-Thirds World are typically eloquent about when they visit in the Global North. When mission committees plan short-term mission trips, participants should be encouraged to share why they do what they do in mission. In fact, their hosts will likely be surprised if the missioners do *not* give "an accounting for the hope that is in you" (1 Peter 3:15). The contemporary tendency to stress deeds rather than words in mission lops off half of the ministry of Jesus himself, who ministered extensively in word as well as in deed. Synods,

dioceses, presbyteries, conferences—all should share the gospel foundation of their outreach. Regardless of their particular assignments, missionaries need encouragement to understand their work in gospel terms and to
share that grounding with others.

2. The mission companion is a *Pilgrim*

"My thirty-five years in Malawi have brought me much joy and love, lots of
adventure and not a little fear, taught me more and enriched me in more
ways than I can express," said Stewart Lane, an Episcopal missionary. "It's
been a good life and I am so thankful that we took the totally mad step of
coming here. To add to that the hope, however faint, that I may actually
have given something in return, is sweet." My wife Jane and I, together with
our four young children, spent two weeks of orientation with Stewart and his
wife, Leslie, when we first went to Africa. They shared their struggles with us,
their doubts, joys and hopes. Some years later Leslie died suddenly of cere-
bral malaria, underlining the depth to which she gave her life to the people
of Malawi. Stewart wrote these words long after that, when he himself retired
as a missionary and continued living in Africa.

What Stewart Lane expressed with particular eloquence is what most missionaries say today—they receive more than they give, learn more than they
teach, and feel like children at feet of the very different cultures and religions in which they work. Many participants in briefer visits say the same, and
I have suggested that initial "short-term mission trips" be reconceived,
planned and named as pilgrimages. Pilgrimage presupposes not only difference, but the reality that there is much to be learned in environments of
difference. So the first tasks are seeing deeply, not analyzing, listening deeply,
not speaking. Most important, we need to go asking, "What is God saying to
me in this world of difference? What can I learn about God through the religious experience of our companions?"

The implications of pilgrimage for both sides of many mission encounters are radical. For Westerners, it means relinquishing the fix-it mentality
with which many are tempted to go, as well as the condescending question,
"What do you need us to do for you?" For companions from the Global
South, it means relinquishing agendas to network for funding, scholarships
and program assistance as they go North. A good way to begin is for the two
sides to agree on a very different plan: "We're meeting in order to experience each other's lives. We'll tell each other our stories. We'll pray together.
From there, we'll join in discerning how God is leading us together." It is in
such receptivity that companions can come to know one another's historic
wounds and help each other toward the healing of reconciliation.

As all of life is a pilgrimage into God, so also the longer pilgrimages in mission are often especially revelatory. Learning local languages and becoming expert in indigenous culture, longer-term missionaries have insights that can illuminate the way for short-term pilgrims and the sending church. The cumulative effect of the Five Crises of Mission Awareness (see Chapter Eight) led mainline churches to reduce missionary appointments radically in the twentieth century, and subsequent declines in membership and financial support have not enabled them to support the renewed interest in mission service at the grassroots. Longer-term missionaries should be regarded as going on pilgrimage on behalf of the entire church, with an increase in their numbers offering to the church the enhanced benefits of discovery, insight and relationship that the mission pilgrimage brings.[2]

3. The mission companion is a *Servant*

Difference and domination—the two are related in the genesis of human sin. What is unfamiliar triggers a need to find our bearings. As much by reflex as by intention, we do that by reverting to the bearings that are familiar to us, thus imposing these older patterns on the new situation. Long before we actually begin pushing anyone around, simply analyzing a situation only in terms of one's own cultural, organizational and professional categories is an effort, even if unconscious, to dominate the situation. When undertaken only with a view to what habitually makes us feel comfortable, our emotional adjustment to a new setting can likewise be a process of seeking domination.

"The Son of Man came not to be served but to serve," said Jesus (Mark 10:45). Mission organizations today rightly take it for granted that mission companions work according to the host church's priorities and that missionaries do not take charge of institutions in one another's settings. Instead, we work alongside one another, taking our cues from the host church's leadership, with Jesus' servanthood as our model. Nevertheless a mission committee or a companion synod can dominate a relationship simply through the categories it insists on using in correspondence and consultation. Even while serving meals to disaster victims, a mission team can dominate by not listening to their stories or by setting up its super-efficient, culturally alien logistics. A missionary can dominate from a secretary's office as well as from a principal's office.

Servanthood begins as we open our eyes and ears to new signals in the different setting—different cultural signals that mean different things for family, community, work, spirituality, play, economics, politics. Some patterns may immediately seem life-affirming in revelatory ways that are easy to celebrate. Other patterns may disturb us as life-denying. Immediate analysis is inevitable in our disturbance, but we need to bracket our conclusions as provisional while we give provisional authority to the criteria of the different culture so that we can explore the nuances and seek deeper understanding. Being willing to sit at the feet of our companions' culture, letting their worldview challenge our own, letting their urgencies pervade our own—that is the discipline of servanthood in mission.

4. The mission companion is a *Prophet*

Prophecy in the Jewish and Christian tradition is often associated with foretelling, but that is one part of the larger task of *forthtelling*: proclaiming forthrightly and courageously the truth of what God is up to, even when that truth challenges those with religious and civil authority. Amos, Jeremiah, John the Baptizer, Jesus the Messiah—they all proclaimed truth to power and suffered for it. When a mission companion has truly traveled as a pilgrim and worked as a servant in the dimension of difference, prophecy can be a vitally important ministry—sometimes to the host setting, sometimes to the home setting, sometimes to both.

The pilgrim who has gone in search of God and the servant who has listened deeply to the host culture may find there are abuses that need to be named and confronted. Being an outsider, a foreigner, is not just a disqualifying disability, as is often thought. It is also a source of insight as the outsider's informed but different perspective exposes truth not so accessible to those inside a setting. Sometimes it is appropriate to offer quiet support to those in the host setting who are in the best position to speak truth to power. Sometimes it is the mission companion from outside who is called to name the truth. Christians in the Global North have often been challenged by the observations of Global South companions about how much money western churches spend on administration and architecture while membership declines and evangelism is neglected. Christians in the Two-Thirds World have sometimes been challenged by Global North companions about unjust uses of money and power. Occasionally the service of residential missionaries has ended as a result of such truth-telling. However uncomfortable, prophecy should be received as a vital expression of companionship, not as its abrogation.

The other direction of missional prophecy is to the home setting. Missionaries and mission teams from the Global North today often use the term "conversion" to describe how experience in the Two-Thirds World transforms their worldview and hence their evaluation of their home church and society. Challenging questions emerge from intersections of affluence and poverty, power and subservience, individualism and communalism, other religions and Christianity. Watching catastrophe unfold while in New York City on September 11, 2001, I was struck by e-mailed comments from Episcopal missionaries around the world on that very day. They expressed great concern for people in the United States. They also were not surprised by the attack in light of what they had experienced as the U.S.A.'s impact in the wider world. From the anguish of difference, they were prophesying to the church that had sent them.

5. The mission companion is an *Ambassador*

"So we are ambassadors of Christ, since God is making his appeal through us," Paul wrote to the Corinthians. "We entreat you on behalf of Christ, be reconciled to God" (2 Corinthians 5:20). Prophecy seeks to trace the outline of what the reign of God should look like in the world, so it advocates for justice in the knowledge that there is no peace without justice. Yet truth-telling and confrontation must have in view not simply defeat for one side and vindication and restitution for another, important as those outcomes are. Rather, in both tone and aim, mission companions must join with God's overall purpose, which is the healing of relationships that only reconciliation can bring. Mission companions must always be asking, "Is this a reconciled community? If not, how might God be working to bring reconciliation? How can I join in God's reconciling mission here?"

The appeal on behalf of Christ is also an appeal on behalf of the company of Christ's people, the church, which is sacramentally the body of Christ in the world. Any individual or group involved in mission represents not only oneself or one's committee or one's conference, but also the entire church from which one comes. So those going out in mission—whether individually or as teams or even in correspondence—must network as widely as possible within their own churches so that what they say and do has a coherent relationship with the mission outreach of their church as a whole. A group may feel called to "push the envelope" in some way, but they should at least be aware of the potential impact of their innovation and be in dialogue with those whose approach may differ.

"Bringing greetings" from others sometimes sounds artificial in church meetings, whether public or private. However, it is a good practice in mission companionship to set oneself the task of taking greetings from colleagues and leaders as one prepares to go out. If we realize we have no particular and explicit greetings to convey, that should alert us that we have not networked sufficiently with others in our church community. By contrast, Paul the missionary was at pains to send the greetings of colleagues to his readers and to ask them to pass greetings on to others. As we confer with colleagues, we will genuinely be ambassadors, and the greetings will be genuine.

Personal habits and style are sometimes sensitive issues for an ambassador of the church in another setting. These can include the question of whether one is direct or indirect in communication, whether one smokes or drinks, whether one uses first or last names in addressing someone, how and with whom one expresses affection. Visitors sometimes want to express themselves just as they would at home and regard conforming to other standards as insincere and oppressive. Until one has lived in solidarity with one's hosts, pilgrimage and servanthood call for behaving in ways that do not distract from the mission that God has underway. As with many aspects of mission engagement, long-term missionaries who have worked within the local culture are key advisers for short-term visitors.

6. The mission companion is a *Host*

Mission companionship means that each party is traveling to the other, not just one side doing the visiting and the other being visited. The historical predominance of the West going to the East, or the North going to the South, nevertheless continues in many interchurch links between different parts of the world, largely as a result of financial inequality. This perpetuates patterns of privilege, power and beneficence that need challenge and modification even if they are hard to overcome entirely. A helpful approach is for South-to-South and North-to-North companionships to be established, as well as South-North relationships. This enables a congregation or a mid-level regional grouping to compare and contrast relationships in order to bring them as much as possible into parity with each other.

"Do not neglect to show hospitality to strangers, for by doing that some have entertained angels without knowing it," we read in the Letter to the Hebrews (13:2), a reference to the three visitors to Abraham and Sarah (Genesis 18:1–15). Hosting is a vital dimension of mission. Just as our going out in mission depends on others being willing to receive us, so the mission from others that we need depends on our receiving them. Attentiveness to logistical needs of travel, rest, lodging, diet and so on is basic to hospitality. At a deeper level, hospitality in mission companionship means exploring and being vulnerable about the ways in which we need the other—for prayer, counsel, perspective, encouragement. It means being open to differences, which sometimes can be as startling as those we encounter abroad. Hospitality calls us to share our lives with the guest and enable the guest to gain traction with the dynamics of our own social, organizational and cultural setting. It means giving the visitor the widest possible exposure to the life of our community and church. If in hosting we mirror the pilgrim and servant journey we seek to live abroad, we will be opening the encounter to God's movement to reconcile the historic and personal wounds that need healing. In such a spirit, we may indeed find that we have been entertaining angels.

A consistent challenge for USAmerican denominations has been fulfilling their aspirations for receiving longer-term missionaries for assignment in the United States, whether through churchwide mission offices or the efforts of synods, dioceses, presbyteries and conferences. The United Methodist Church has a number of such assignments, but the achievement of most churches is well short of goals. Naturally the major obstacle is finance, especially in view of declining churchwide budgets and continued needs abroad, where missionaries can be funded at much lower cost. However, this priority needs continuing attention by mission planners at all levels.

7. The mission companion is a *Sacrament of Reconciliation*

"Whoever welcomes you welcomes me, and whoever welcomes me welcomes the one who sent me," Jesus told his disciples (Matthew 10:40). "As you did it to one of the least of these who are members of my family, you did it to me," he declared in the parable of the sheep and the goats (Matthew 25:40). Then there were the eucharistic words: "Take, eat; this is my body" (Matthew 26:26). "You are the body of Christ and individually members of it," Paul wrote in extending the body image to the community (1 Corinthians 12:27).

Such scriptures suggest that Christian identity is more than affiliation, and that joining God's mission movement is more than function. Identity does not consist only in our being affiliated with Jesus through loyalty and belief. Mission does not consist only in the function of getting certain kinds of work done. Both identity and mission are freighted with the very presence of Christ. In receiving a missioner, the host receives Christ present in the missioner. In ministering, the missioner ministers to Christ present in those across a boundary of difference. The Christian community is the very body of Christ extended, distributed and at work in the world.

Clearly we are on sacramental ground. Classically, a sacrament is an outward and visible sign of an inward and spiritual grace. We are used to ritual washing as the sacrament of new birth in Christ through baptism, and ritual bread and wine as the sacrament of the body and blood of Christ in Eucharist. These sacraments take their place within the communal sacrament of the church itself being the sacrament of the continuing presence of

Christ in the world. Every minister—and therefore every Christian—is a sacrament of Christ at work in the world.

Since reconciliation is the overall direction of God's mission in the world, it follows that every sacramental grace participates in that healing passion of God. We see this in the sacramental grace of Eucharist, when Christ offers his body and his "blood of the covenant, which is poured out for many for the forgiveness of sins" (Matthew 26:28). A Christian on mission, then, is a sacramental sign of God on mission to reconcile the world, that is, to reconcile people to God and to one another in Christ. A sacramental approach to mission encourages a spirituality that sees the mission encounter as occurring on holy ground. The burning bush of God's presence blazes as each side in the meeting recognizes God living and speaking in the other.

A sacramental approach to mission may startle a mission committee concerned to get teams out to dig wells or triage medical care after a disaster. It may feel uncomfortable to a denominational office concerned to maximize a shrinking budget for mission personnel. It may feel novel to an individual wondering whether to "go out with the church" or sign up with a secular initiative like the Peace Corps or Volunteer Service Overseas. Yet sacramentality is real and essential to our missional call as Christians. Moreover, the sacramental dimension of the mission of reconciliation keeps the church and its missioners focused on the incarnational urgency of people being with people to heal relationship, rather than focused on the important but ancillary dimensions of money and program.

All these seven marks of the mission companion involve encounter with difference, and all bear on reconciliation. They represent different facets of how mission activists, whether individuals or communities, can develop healthy and fruitful mission relationships as companions with others. They intersect significantly with qualities or approaches to mission as advocated by entire churches. Presbyterian World Mission, for instance, cites dignity, empowerment and partnership among its six core values. Lutheran Global Mission stresses transparency in communication and finance, shared decision-making and diversity of gifts among twelve criteria for accompaniment. The Anglicans' Ten Principles of Partnership include mutuality, interdependence, transparency, solidarity and meeting together. Convergence is a keynote in mission vision today.

God has accompanied us in Christ for the sake of reconciling the world. As we go global with God, the call in mission is to accompany others so that they may know the companionship of God—and so that we ourselves may know it with them.

Notes

1. Standing Commission on World Mission of the Episcopal Church, *Companions in Transformation: The Episcopal Church's World Mission in a New Century* (Harrisburg: Morehouse, 2003), 5–10. In the vision statement, each mark is simply one key word, followed by commentary. Here each mark is placed in a sentence beginning "The mission companion is . . ." and the last mark is expanded from "sacrament" to "sacrament of reconciliation." The commentary here is my fresh reflection and interpretation in connection with a set of marks that I had a role in developing.

2. The number of USAmerican missionaries serving abroad was about 130,000 in 2010, more than a quarter of the 443,000 missionaries serving around the world from all branches of Christianity on all continents. The proportion of them from the mainline denominations was small. Todd M. Johnson and Kenneth R. Ross, eds., *Atlas of Global Christianity*, 1910–2010 (Edinburgh: Edinburgh University Press, 2009), 259–261.

A Longer View

The journey of Christian mission takes us beyond the dilemmas and crises of our own day or any day. The destination is beyond us, in the vision God has of a reconciled human community, a consummated universe. Such vision draws us forward with resolve and joy. That is the revelation offered to St. John the Divine, where the company of God's people stand radiant, not with their differences effaced but with their differences obvious:

> I looked, and there was a great multitude that no one could count, from every nation, from all tribes and peoples and languages, standing before the throne and before the Lamb, robed in white, with palm branches in their hands. (Revelation 7:9)

The human community in all its created difference stands as one company in companionship with one another. I dare to imagine that the differences will be as interesting and revelatory there as they are here, and maybe more so.

In the vision of ultimate fulfillment, the drama of God's own venture into difference through the Lamb reconciles all to God, and all now stand reconciled with one another. No wonder the heavenly company breaks into one continuous song of glory on their own behalf and ours:

> Amen! Blessing and glory and wisdom
> and thanksgiving and honor
> and power and might
> be to our God forever and ever!
> Amen! (Revelation 7:12)

STUDY GUIDE

Going Global with God highlights mission shifts in the churches, explores strategic and theological issues that they raise, and suggests ways to respond to challenges in world mission today. Whether you are reading alone or with a group, questions for reflection and discussion can help focus your thinking and facilitate your learning. In addition to the study and discussion questions offered below, a more complete study guide for the book is available at www.churchpublishing.org/goingglobalwithgod.

Introduction

As you read about the mission work of Susan's congregation in western New York, think about your own congregation. How do you reach out, both locally and globally? How has that work affected you? How has it affected the congregation?

What interests you most in the upcoming chapters as they are outlined? Why?

What surprises, challenges or puzzles you about the discussion of terms? What do you think of terms like Two-Thirds World, Global North, development, denominations and USAmerican?

How do you respond to the closing reflections about mission—being taken to the edge, discovering difference, making mistakes, thinking about mission?

Chapter One — A Movement Underway:
Global Ferment in Local Churches

Where do you see world mission initiative coming from in your church situation? Is it mostly from the congregation, or the mid-level beyond the congregation, or the churchwide headquarters?

Do you know young adults who have gone out in mission to other parts of the world? If so, what is your understanding of their motivation and work? Read their blogs on the church websites and discuss the stories that interest you especially. You might also consult the following blogs:

- Edward Johnson: jamesedwardjohnson.blogspot.com/2008/07/am-i-my-brothers-keeper.html
- Melanie Jianakoplos: melaniespineapplediaries.blogspot.com/2010/02/grace-kirkwood-youth-group.html
- Ciona Rouse: www.umc.org/site/apps/nlnet/content3.aspx?c=lwL4KnN1LtH&b=5138783&ct=8044245

Discuss your own congregation's mission. What are its strengths and weaknesses? What strikes you about the congregations described in this chapter?

What is the world mission outreach of your presbytery, diocese, synod, conference or other mid-level church unit? How does your own congregation relate to it?

Chapter Two — From the Ground Up:
Mission Democratized

Consider the poles presented in mission organization: centralization vs. localization, professionalization vs. deprofessionalization, concentrated authority vs. democratization, uniformity vs. diversification. What has been your experience with the way the church organizes for mission in your context?

Compare the horizontal networking of the worldwide web with other aspects of your life, like work and neighborhood organizations. Are you more comfortable with horizontal or vertical structures of communication and authority? What works best in your church life and why?

What do you think about the political aspects of mobilizing for mission as presented from the New Testament? Are political realities good, bad or neutral in the church's life?

How, in your own mission experience, have you seen the church being "one, holy, catholic and apostolic," as stated in the Nicene Creed?

Chapter Three — Sent by God:
The Nature of Mission

Among the jostling views of mission, which one do you identify with most? Which one bothers you? Have you been part of a discussion where people were arguing about what mission is?

Does the notion of God being on mission make sense to you? Does discerning what God is up to in the world clarify or confuse the task of mission for you?

Discuss the comprehensive definition of the nature of Christian mission: "Christian mission is the activity of sending and being sent, by God and by communities, across significant boundaries of human social experience to bear witness in word and deed to God's action in Jesus Christ in the power of the Holy Spirit."

Think about the history and evolution of the word "mission." Do you feel sent in your Christian life? If so, by whom and to do what? If not, think about why that might be.

If your congregation has a mission, purpose or vision statement, analyze it in terms of the distinction between ministry and mission.

Chapter Four — Ministry in the Dimension of Difference:
Mission's Terrain

Two missionaries in the opening stories mentioned a need to "get out of my comfort zone." What does that phrase mean to you? Do you find it helpful in understanding motivation for mission?

A key contention in this chapter is that "mission is ministry in the dimension of difference." How does this understanding help you think about mission? If it doesn't help, what alternative understanding would you suggest?

Consider the role difference played in mission thinking during the Century of Self-Criticism, and then compare that with the role of difference in earlier periods of mission.

Analyze the work of your congregation and regional church unit. How much of this activity reaches out to encounter and form community with those who are different from and outside your church fellowship?

Reflect on the concept of difference as a category of human experience. How do you define your own social group and your place in it? How are you and your group different from other groups? Try to identify what may be helpful about wrestling with such questions.

In what ways does your congregation want to become more diverse, and why? How has embracing difference helped your congregation? How have you found the experience problematic?

Identify what is new for you in the biblical discussion of difference. What other biblical stories of sending into difference occur to you?

In what ways do people in your church or wider community engage difference? In what ways do you see difference making people in your context uncomfortable?

Chapter Five — Reconciliation: The Direction of God's Mission

Discuss the various examples of reconciliation work in church and society. Where in the life of your community, your church and your mission work do you see needs for reconciliation most clearly?

Discuss the biblical and theological exploration of reconciliation. Do you find it helpful to read scripture through the lens of reconciliation?

Do you agree or disagree with the assertion that various kinds of mission all work toward reconciliation?

Discuss the claim that all human oppression is built on exploiting human difference. How is that borne out, or not, in your context?

Discuss the claim that a focus on reconciliation radicalizes mission. How would your mission work change if you always asked whether reconciliation is occurring?

Chapter Six — Accompaniment and Companionship: The Mode of Mission Today

How would you describe mission relationships you have had with people in other parts of the world—or locally, if you have not been engaged with global mission? What were the joys, and what were the challenges?

Discuss the three accompaniment stories by missionaries: Frances Wilson, Ben and Bobbie Chase and Justin Mutter. In what ways do their reflections connect with your hopes around mission?

What do you think of the distinction between partnership and companionship? Which term do you prefer?

Discuss the Anglican and Lutheran reflections on accompaniment and companionship. How could they help as you approach mission work?

Discuss the story of the companion synod relationship between Colorado and Madagascar. Do you have an experience where simply telling stories built relationship?

Chapter Seven — Networking for Mission:
A Challenge in Democratization

Have you and your church experienced mission difficulties that you trace to the decentralization of mission today?

How might you consider organizing a community of mission practice around an initiative that your church is undertaking in world mission?

Have you had experience of a denominational or ecumenical mission network? If so, how has that been fruitful? If not, discuss possibilities that could be helpful to you.

Chapter Eight — Missionary Calling and Identity:
A Challenge in Being Sent

Discuss the Five Crises of Mission Awareness as you and your church experienced them historically and in your current thinking.

What do you think about the words "mission" and "missionary"? Are you comfortable with them, or do you believe they need rehabilitation? What alternative words do you suggest?

Discuss the similarities and differences among the mission priorities of the various churches. Do you find the lists helpful for your work?

How do you respond to the biblical and theological point that God needs our companionship in mission at the same time that God is our companion in mission?

Chapter Nine — Poverty and Wholistic Mission:
A Challenge in Difference

Think about your own experiences of being poor. What stands out for you about being poor? What outreach did you experience from other people? From your own experience of poverty, what did you learn about ministry with poor people?

Think about your experiences with people who are poor. What stood out for you about the poverty of others? In what ways did you feel moved to reach out to poverty?

How does your church community talk about mission in relation to poverty? Do you undertake forms of mission—ministry in the dimension of difference—that are *not* related to poverty?

In what ways do the two biblical discussions of mission and poverty help you to understand the argument that mission is broader than the problem of poverty?

Is your church's mission wholistic (that is, addressing people's physical, emotional, economic, social, and spiritual needs)? If it is not, which way does it tip, and what could restore a balance among different emphases in mission?

Chapter Ten — Churches in Turmoil:
A Challenge in Reconciliation

Think about conflicts of whatever kind within your congregation, mid-level church grouping and denomination. How have they affected the church's mission work, whether in the short term or longer term?

What has been your experience of discussion about sexuality in your church setting, either local or regional? How has it affected mission? Does your experience resonate with some of the effects narrated in this chapter?

Discuss how the concepts of accompaniment and ministry in the dimension of difference could serve as approaches in the current turmoil. Does it help to consider reaching out to others in the discord as a kind of mission rather than a distraction from mission?

Chapter Eleven — Meeting as Pilgrims:
A Challenge in Accompaniment

Discuss your community's experience of short-term mission. What were the strong points? Where has it fallen short of expectations?

Discuss the importance of mutuality and justice in short-term mission. Have companions visited you as well as you going to them? How do you feel about how funding and other resources have been shared?

How do you respond to pilgrimage as a new starting place for conceiving and planning short-term visits with your companion churches?

Chapter Twelve — Seven Marks of the Mission Companion

Discuss each of the Seven Marks of the Mission Companion. Which ones confirm your sense of mission identity? Which ones are most challenging to you?

How can each of the marks be lived out by church communities as well as by individuals? Consider your congregation, your regional grouping and your denomination.

Reflecting on the book as a whole, what has been helpful to you in thinking about your participation in God's mission in the world?

Epilogue: A Longer View

This meditation sees the themes of difference, reconciliation and companionship in the framework of God's consummation of all things beyond the end of time. Do you find this perspective helpful? Why or why not?

FURTHER EXPLORATION

The literature of mission is vast, and it ranges over many areas of interest. Here is a selection of current resources that may be helpful for further exploration.

Bosch, David J. *Transforming Mission: Paradigm Shifts in Theology of Mission*. Maryknoll, NY: Orbis Books, 1991. A theological discussion of mission, with considerable biblical and historical material.

Butterfield, Jane, ed. *The Scripture of Their Lives: Stories of Mission Companions Today*. Harrisburg, PA: Morehouse Publishing, 2006. Reflections by twenty contemporary missionaries about their life and work.

Carr, Philip, director, and Jane Butterfield, producer. *Windows on Mission*. New York: Episcopal Church Center, 2006. Twelve short films on two DVDs about eleven contemporary missionaries in Africa, Asia and Latin America.

Corbett, Steve, and Brian Fikkert. *When Helping Hurts: How to Alleviate Poverty without Hurting the Poor . . . and Yourself*. Chicago: Moody Publishers, 2009. A practical guide for mission work in the encounter with poverty.

Douglas, Ian T., ed. *Waging Reconciliation: God's Mission in a Time of Globalization and Crisis*. New York: Church Publishing, 2002. Essays on missional challenges, especially in view of 9/11.

Elmer, Duane. *Cross-Cultural Servanthood: Serving the World in Christlike Humility*. Downers Grove, IL: InterVarsity Press, 2006. An anecdotal and cultural discussion of servanthood with biblical and theological grounding.

Gittins, Anthony J. *Reading the Clouds: Mission Spirituality for New Times*. Liguori, MI: Liguori Publications, 1999. A discussion of mission spirituality based in biblical and theological perspectives.

Groves, Phil. *Global Partnerships for Local Mission*. Cambridge, UK: Grove Books, 2006. A practical booklet on developing relationships between churches, supported by biblical and theological discussion.

Johnson, Todd M., and Kenneth R. Ross. *Atlas of Global Christianity, 1910–2010*. Edinburgh: Edinburgh University Press, 2009. A compendium of statistical data on world Christianity accompanied by historical analyses.

Little, David, and Tanenbaum Center for Interreligious Understanding, eds. *Peacemakers in Action: Profiles of Religion in Conflict Resolution.* New York: Cambridge University Press, 2007. Case studies from around the world, each with background and discussion.

Mattam, Joseph, and Joseph Valiamangalam, eds. *Building Solidarity: Challenge to Christian Mission.* Delhi: Indian Society for Promoting Christian Knowledge, 2008. Essays on mission's relation to reconciliation and solidarity.

Muck, Terry, and Frances S. Adeney. *Christianity Encountering World Religions: The Practice of Mission in the Twenty-first Century.* Grand Rapids: Baker Academic, 2009. A theological and practical treatment of interreligious encounter in mission.

Oborji, Francis Anekwe. *Concepts of Mission: The Evolution of Contemporary Missiology.* Maryknoll, NY: Orbis Books, 2006. A survey of the range of emphases in ecumenical mission reflection today.

Presler, Titus. *Horizons of Mission.* Boston: Cowley Publication, 2001. An overview of mission history, theology and practice from an Anglican standpoint.

Richter, Don. C. *Mission Trips That Matter: Embodied Faith for the Sake of the World.* Nashville: Upper Room Books, 2008. A discussion of the spirituality, theology, strategy and logistics of short-term mission trips.

Robert, Dana L. *Christian Mission: How Christianity Became a World Religion.* Malden, MA: Wiley-Blackwell, 2009. A mission overview in relation to themes of vernacularization, conversion, cultural encounter and political imperialism.

Sanneh, Lamin. *Disciples of All Nations: Pillars of World Christianity.* New York: Oxford Univeristy Press, 2008. A study of the growth of Christianity as a movement that takes root in human cultures.

Schreiter, Robert J. *The Ministry of Reconciliation: Spirituality and Strategies.* Maryknoll, NY: Orbis Books, 1998. A series of meditations on reconciliation, each one arising from reflection on a biblical story.

Stanley, Brian. *The World Missionary Conference, Edinburgh 1910.* Grand Rapids: William B. Eerdmans Publishing, 2009. A definitive treatment of a pivotal event for the Western mission movement.

Stone, Bryan. *Evangelism after Christendom: The Theology and Practice of Christian Witness.* Grand Rapids: Brazos Press, 2007. A comprehensive biblical, historical and theological discussion of evangelism.

Thomas, Norman, ed. *Classic Texts in Mission and World Christianity.* Maryknoll, NY: Orbis, 1995. A reader's companion to David Bosch's classic volume *Transforming Mission* (above).

Walls, Andrew. *The Cross-Cultural Process in Christian History: Studies in the Transmission and Appropriation of Faith.* Maryknoll, NY: Orbis; and Edinburgh: T & T Clark, 2002. Essays that offer breadth and depth in understanding Christianity as a world movement.

Walls, Andrew, and Cathy Ross, eds. *Mission in the 21st Century: Exploring the Five Marks of Global Mission.* Maryknoll, NY: Orbis, 2008. A collection of essays by mission practitioners and scholars from around the world.

Wuthnow, Robert. *Boundless Faith: The Global Outreach of American Churches.* Berkeley: University of California Press, 2009. A sociological study set in the context of globalization.

Yates, Timothy. *Christian Mission in the Twentieth Century.* Cambridge, UK: Cambridge University Press, 1994. An overview of the theological currents that guided mission in the twentieth century.

INDEX

BIBLICAL REFERENCES

References in brackets provide citations that do not appear in the book.

Location	Citation	Page	Subject
Part I — What's Happening Today in Global Mission?	Matthew 16:3	1	Jesus' answer to those asking for a sign
Chapter One — A Movement Underway			
Young Adults Abroad	Proverbs 3:27–28	5	Help the needy
Mission Giants in Congregations	John 21:15–19	8	Jesus tells Peter, "Feed my sheep" and "Follow me."
Chapter Two — From the Ground Up			
Mission Politics in the New Testament	Luke 10:1–9	28–29	Jesus sends out seventy disciples
	Luke 10:17–20	29	Seventy return from mission
	Luke 9:49–50	29	Jesus rebukes disciples for disapproving stranger exorcizing in his name
	Numbers 11:29	29	Moses rebukes Joshua for disapproving prophets outside of seventy commissioned
	Matthew 16:13–20	29	Jesus gives Peter keys to the kingdom
	John 20:21–23	29	Jesus commissions disciples after resurrection
	John 17:20	29	Those who believe through disciples have responsibility for mission
	Acts 2:42–47	29–30	Holy Spirit at Pentecost empowers with gifts
	Acts 7	30	Stephen preaches and is killed
	Acts 8:26–40	30	Philip bears witness to Ethiopian
	[Acts 9:1–31; 13–14]	30	Paul's conversion, preaching to Gentiles, and conflict with Jerusalem church leadership
	Acts 15:1–21	30	Jerusalem council endorses mission to Gentiles
	1 Thessalonians 1:8	30	Young church grows rapidly
	[Galatians]	30	Paul rebukes Galatians for backsliding into Jewish law

189

[1 Corinthians 4:21]	30	Paul threatens Corinthians "to come to you with a stick"
[Philippians 4:2–3]	30	Paul asks Philippians to help reconcile two church leaders
Revelation 2–3	31	John exhorts seven churches
Acts 2:42	33	Church is devoted to teaching, fellowship, breaking bread, prayers
Part II — What Does It Mean to Go Global with God?		
Matthew 13:51–52	35	Jesus highlights scribe trained for God's kingdom
Chapter Three — Sent by God		
What Is God Up To?		
No specific citations	40	Old Testament: Creation, Flood, God talking with people, Exodus, Jericho, captivity and deliverance. New Testament: Jesus, miracles, cross and resurrection, Pentecost, Cornelius and Peter, Paul's conversion
Genesis 18–19	41	Abraham is visited at oaks of Mamre
Genesis 32:24–30	41	Jacob wrestles with nocturnal visitor
Luke 24:47–49	41	Jesus anticipates sending of Holy Spirit
John 20:21–22	42	Jesus breathes on disciples
Luke 9:1–2, 10	42	Twelve on mission are "apostles"
Sent across Boundaries to Witness		
Chapter Four — Ministry in the Dimension of Difference		
Biblical Resonance for Grounding Mission in Difference		
Genesis 12:1–3	61	God sends Abram to a new land
Jonah 1:1–3; 3:6–9	61–62	Jonah is reluctant to go to Ninevah
John 1:14	62	"Word became flesh"
John 12:46	62	Jesus declares himself light in the world
John 11:27	62	Martha acknowledges Jesus as Messiah
John 17:18	62	Jesus sends disciples as he was sent by God
John 1:1	62	"Word was with God and was God"
No specific citations	62	Jesus' encounters with difference: Gerasene demoniac, Roman centurion, sinful woman, Samaritan woman, woman in adultery, Zaccheus, lepers and others

No specific citations	63	Parables about outsiders
Matthew 15:21–28	63	Jesus and Canaanite woman
Mark 7:26	63	Jesus and Syrophoenician woman
Matthew 25:31–46	63	All nations to be judged
Luke 13:29	63	Vision of messianic banquet
Luke 9:2	63	Jesus sends twelve disciples
Matthew 10:1–6	63	Disciples sent to "lost sheep" of Israel
Matthew 10:18	63	Disciples will be dragged before secular authorities
Matthew 28:19	63	Jesus sends disciples to all nations
Luke 24:47	63	Jesus sends disciples to all nations
Acts 1:8	63	Jesus sends disciples to "ends of the earth"
Acts 2:11	63	Diverse peoples hear of God's "deeds of power" at Pentecost
Acts 8:1–4	63	Stoning of Stephen is followed by persecution
Acts 8:14, 26, 29	63–64	Peter, John, Philip are sent into difference
Acts 10:5–8, 17–22	64	Peter is sent to Cornelius the centurion
Acts 9:15	64	Paul is sent to Gentiles
Galatians 2:8	64	Apostolates of Peter and Paul
Romans 15:19–20	64	Paul summarizes his mission

Chapter Five — Reconciliation

Reconciliation in Scripture and Theology

Genesis 3:9	72	God calls out to Adam in Eden
Genesis 33:10	73	Jacob celebrates reconciliation with Esau
Hosea 2:14; 3:1	73	God's love is expressed through Hosea's call
2 Corinthians 5:13–15	73	Reconciliation central in God's purpose
2 Corinthians 5:16–21	73	Implications of Christ dying for humanity
Mark 15:34	74	Jesus' cry of abandonment from cross
Matthew 26:27b–28	75	Jesus' words at Last Supper
Romans 3:23	75	"All have sinned and fall short"
2 Corinthians 5:20	75	Plea to Corinthians to be reconciled to God
2 Corinthians 5:18	76	Ministry of reconciliation